Translation Notes:

1. German is left in the text (with English glosses) for concepts that the English world recognizes and borrows, such as *Heimat* (homeland or home) and other words that are not commonly in German dictionaries and can be partially understood by dissecting the original German, such as *Oberstadt* (uptown).

2. Old spellings from quotations of medieval texts have been standardized, such as "brisach" translated to "Breisach."

3. Sometime inconsistent spellings—usually in surnames—I have left as they are. Perhaps the inconsistency reflects that of the primary sources.

4. All footnotes in the original text are designated in the translation, but sometimes I have abbreviated them, translating only when there is extra information beyond mention of the source.

–Claire Insel

Hans David Blum

Jews in Breisach: From the Beginnings to the Shoah, 12th–19th Century. Volume 1

Edited by Erhard Roy Wiehn

Hartung-Gorre Publishing, Konstanz

Cover photograph: Rheintorstraße (Judengasse) ca. 1935 (in the middle, Hans David Blum with parents and sister); back cover: view from the former Synagogengässle of the *mikvah* and the west façade of the synagogue before 1936 (photographs: Hans David Blum, Hauptstaatsarchiv Stuttgart [Central State Archive, Stuttgart]). Jacket: Heide Fehringer, printing: Lokay Printing, Reinheim/Odenwald

1898-1938-1948-1998	
50	years State of Israel
60	years November pogrom
100	years Meeting of Theodor Herzl with Grand Duke Friedrich I of Baden on Mainau Island

Contents

Title page of Calendar Calculations by the Breisach Rabbi Simon Blum (ca. 1640-1707, Jewish National Library, Jerusalem)

Breisach in the 17th Century: Far left, houses of Judengasse (copper engraving by Matthäus Merian, 1638, Stadtarchiv Breisach [Breisach City Archive], above); Breisach City and Fort with the New City "Saint-Louis" to the northwest, 1697 (copper engraving by G. Bodenehr, 1720, Stadtarchiv Breisach).

[Upper engraving titled: "True Reproduction of the Fortress City and Border Crossing Breisach"]

[Lower engraving titled: "Breisach As It Stood at the Conclusion of the Peace of Ryswyck, Anno 1697"]

Community Leader Lipmann Guenzberger (1803-1879) with wife Hindel née Geismar (1806-1883), photo ca. 1860 (published in Ludwig Kahn, *Die Nachkommen des Nathan Günzburger* [*The Descendants of Nathan Günzburger*], Basel 1971)

Caption: Judengasse (today Rheintorstraße) before 1899: detail of a postcard from the Breisach publisher Jacob Rosenberg (original: Helmut Kiefer, Breisach, above); View from Judengasse (Rheintorstraße), ca. 1935, of the synagogue destroyed in 1938 (photo: David Hans Blum, Hauptstaatsarchiv Stuttgart)

Top postcard: "Greetings from Breisach"

Hans David Blum

Acknowledgement

It has been an enormous task these past years locating and putting together the puzzle pieces for the historical work that now lies before us. It is hard to thank the many people who contributed to this book. Unfortunately it is not possible to name all of them here, but I am obliged to express my sincerest gratitude for their friendly assistance and their diverse and valuable contributions.

I would like to express special thanks to my friend Mr. Martin Bier (from Müllheim). It was he who selflessly stood by me these years past, with encouragement, good counsel and much of his time. Without his true support this book could not have appeared in its current form.

Mr. Uwe Fahrer, the untiring Breisach city archivist, deserves the same praise and heartfelt thanks. He devoted countless hours and days of his free time to the creation of this work. Thanks also to Mayor Vonarb (Breisach) for his great interest and sponsorship of this publication. My gratitude extends as well to Mrs. Manuela Stein (Breisach) for her wonderfully efficient production of a clean copy of the manuscript, a difficult task that she accomplished with professionalism and great personal effort.

Last but not least, I thank my wife Lottie for the many years she helped me and for her endless patience.

October 1998

Dedicated to the memory of my dear parents

Ludwig Blum
born April 30, 1871 in Breisach
died January 8, 1951 in Manhattan, New York

Mathilde Blum
née Weil
born March 31, 1877 in Emmendingen
died December 22, 1960 in Bronx, New York

Author's Foreword

The one-time Jewish life of the picturesque mountain town of Breisach am Rhein is remembered today, sadly, by only a few eyewitnesses now living scattered across the world. There was their cradle, their ancestral home (*Heimat*), where everyone knew everyone and all lived their lives in peace.

Many recall visits and vacations at the homes of relatives and friends who lived there. They came from neighboring towns or further afield and have preserved lovely memories of the Jewish milieu. They all knew the familiar houses, cottages and corners of the former Judengasse, renamed Rheintorstraße in 1933, the middle of which was adorned by the well-built synagogue with adjoining ritual bath and, behind it, the old cemetery. In memory remain the little benches, the quaint steps of the long corridors, their walls furnished with niches for candles, the cobbled courtyards, stables, barns and gardens, the sukkahs (foliage huts) installed beneath the tiled roofs. Nor to be forgotten are the former Jewish hostelries, where people came to socialize and whose rooms were used for different community events. The picturesque cathedral, the old city gates, the wheel well, like the sparse remains of the fort and castle walls, still bear witness to the time of the earliest documented arrival of Jews in Breisach.

Breisach occupied a reputable position among the sister cities of the Upper Rhine centuries ago. It was in a position to form alliances; at the time of the first Jewish settlement it had its own mint; and it was a strong fortress. Its dominion extended over a half dozen communities right and left of the Rhine. It enjoyed virtually unlimited self-governance, with its own jurisdiction, even during the long period of attachment to the House of Austria. As merchants, noble and moneyed patrician families possessed their family seats in the *Oberstadt* (upper city). The rest of the population had to settle below at the foot of the mountain, where the so-called *Vorderstadt* (front town) developed, likewise the *Hinterstadt* (back town), where eventually most of the Jews lived. With the razing of the fortress under Empress Maria Theresia in 1741, as well as the withdrawal of the garrison and various authorities, the city suffered a harsh blow. It met almost total demise in 1793, when French revolutionary troops reduced it to rubble and ash; Judengasse also burnt almost entirely to the ground.

Valuable documents and archive material on the significant Jewish community in Breisach fell victim to the great fire. It is regrettable that no later attempt was made to report extensively on the changing fortunes of the Jews in this Rhine city. After the forced dissolution and deportation of the remaining community on October 22, 1940, its rich community archive also disappeared.

It is not unusual that the history of a Jewish community should be written only after its downfall. The venerable and large rural community of Breisach am Rhein was never an object of rigorous research. After the deportation of the last inhabitants and the destruction of the community archives, documents had to be assessed and numerous other sources investigated for the purpose of discovering historical pieces of the puzzle. This happened out of love for the former *Heimat* community and its haunting milieu. It happened as a reminder of our ancestors to whom this little piece of earth had been native soil for generations. It is intended as a remembrance for the emigrants who escaped hell just in time and, scattering themselves across the Earth, were able to seek out a new *Heimat*. Above all, this is meant to be a lasting memorial to the unforgettable victims of woeful persecution, those who never found a grave.

Jackson Heights, New York, August 1998

Martin Bier: Preface

With this publication by Hans David Blum, Breisach and its surroundings enjoy the unusual good fortune of receiving, at this late date, an excellent and very personal contribution to its local and regional history. This contribution to the history of Breisach Jews and their community, both as an independent community and as one sharing the destiny of the city of Breisach and its dominion, demonstrates meticulous scholarly research and a thorough use of sources. So are clearly conveyed both the spirit and the reality of living and working together in one of the larger Jewish communities of its time, along with "its" city and surroundings.

This city and its region, with their many familial connections, was their permanent residence—until "next year in Jerusalem," a very old, traditional wish in Judaism, a dream surviving uninterrupted for centuries, to be able to return to one's old, own *Heimat* and free independence in Israel, with Jerusalem as its religious center since the time of King David, for 3000 years. But Breisach was without doubt the place where one lived under known, trusted or unchangeable but accepted conditions, where one probably was born and grew up, perhaps after generations of one's own people. The "Breisach Surrounding" was a city that, in that time, stood under various, at times frequently changing commands. The changes were driven by the significance of this city on the cliffs over the Rhine, by its key position in the power struggle for economic authority and strategic impact, through destruction, reconstruction and restoration of the former political and economic significance of the city until its complete destruction in 1793.

A definitive end to its earlier significance followed with the changing of inner-European power relations, which collapsed beneath Napoleon's new order and its complete break with the past. The change of authorities in and above Breisach impacted the rules of intercourse among ranks and other social groups in the city, with results by turns relieving and aggravating. That applied especially to the minority of Jewish inhabitants and their partial inner autonomy, even when they were declared "Protected Jews" of the Emperor, required to pay corresponding protection money and special taxes.

Drawing upon these developments, researched from period sources and portrayed objectively, with restraint and without embellishment, this book makes accessible to the reader the many bitter events to which earlier generations of Breisach Jews were subjected. Thus, despite many terrible catastrophes, an illuminating image emerges of Breisach's Jewish history. The thoroughness of the work and its reserved portrayal make clear: a Breisacher with roots in the city has written a local history motivated by a dominating love of and devotion to Breisach and its Jewish community. This community, however—after the hopeful 1862 decision for the equal rights of Jewish citizens, and their own cultural, scientific, and humane enrichment of society—fell complete victim to the criminal vandalism and barbarism of Nazi anti-Semitism, unimaginable today, and thereafter also the city itself as consequence of the Second World War unleashed by the Nazi state.

Only a few Jewish survivors from Breisach and their descendants are still living, scattered around the globe yet tied to Breisach despite the horrible events of the past. Thus the city figures not as a political community of today but as a bond of human history and culture encompassing the people of Breisach past and present. The people of Breisach themselves were and are the elements of this bond. Remarkably, the sources of this local history reveal at how many places near Breisach and further afield Jews were already living at that time, at least intermittently.

Hans David Blum, the author of this work, was born November 6, 1919 in Breisach and registered as the son of Breisach citizen and merchant Ludwig Blum and his wife Mathilde (née Weil from Emmendingen, Breisgau). The father's ancestors came from Alsace and North Switzerland, from Bavaria, and, further in the past, from other German lands. The name Blum appears quite early in the history of Breisach and its surrounding region. Genealogical records indicate that his mother's ancestors lived in Weil der Stadt in the 14th century, residing in the interim in Stühling or Switzerland, and that they came to Emmendingen in 1716. They were residents and citizens of this city until the annihilation of the German Jews by the Nazi state.

Hans David Blum first spent the usual four years in primary school in Breisach, and thereafter attended the local *Realschule* (secondary school) until 1936. Here his interest in the history of the Jewish community as part of the (political) *Heimat* community of Breisach was awakened and he studied the subject for the first time. This interest was developed and especially encouraged by Professor Max Weber (of the Breisach *Realschule*), whom Hans David Blum greatly esteemed. The roots were thus put down for a lifelong, if sometimes interrupted by necessity, dedication to, even a passionate for Breisach Jewish local history. Not least, there emerged as well his interest in the history of the Jewish community of Breisach and its manifold connections throughout the region, including Southern Germany, Alsace and Northern Switzerland.

The cantor and teacher Michael Eisemann contributed significantly to this engagement. A beloved teacher of the Bible and Hebrew (from the first grade and later in *Realschule*), Eisemann taught the student Hans David Blum the Hebrew script and language so well that he could copy the often illegible and uninterpretable Hebrew epitaphs from the approximately 250 grave stones then standing in the old cemetery. Additionally, he was in due time in a position to take down in writing around 240 still legible *mappot* preserved in the *mikvah* (ritual bath), which documented the initiation of eight-day-old boys into the Jewish community and found an honorable and lasting use as Torah binders. Such *mappot* were often artfully embroidered with Psalms and other texts or wishes for the boy's life, written or painted, and often adorned with Jewish symbols or political signs that made visible the bond of the boy's parents with the city and its dominion. This large and interesting Breisach *mappot* collection, historically enlightening in its symbolic imagery, fell victim to the pogrom of November 10, 1938. It is survived only by the transcriptions that Hans David Blum produced in his youth.

The hurtful alienation of Jewish citizens and neighbors by longtime alleged friends and "good acquaintances," the consequence of anti-Semitic persecution through the Nazi system since the seizure of power in January, 1933, also touched Hans David Blum personally and very painfully. The Nazi-decreed exclusion of Jewish children from all higher and postgraduate education was bitter. Hans David Blum therefore emigrated in 1936 to Basel, living with relatives under restrictive right of stay. There he resolved to finish his education with a technical specialization.

After European liberation from illegitimate Nazi rule, he and his parents went to the U.S. His parents had been deported on October 22, 1940, in the so-called Bürkel campaign, with all the Jews from Baden and the Palatinate. They were taken to the French internment camp Gûrs at the foot of the Pyrenees. Fortunately, they received asylum in Switzerland before those Jews staying in Gûrs were sent to the Nazi death camps of the East. Only after difficult integration and the establishment of financial security in the new *Heimat* could the author again turn to that subject so important to him: his research into the history of the Breisach Jewish community and its now more important documentation, before the last knowledge and remaining private documents could disappear along with the last witnesses.

This book is devoted to those former and still living members of the old Breisach Jewish community and their descendants, to the victims of the Shoah, but also to the citizens of Breisach. Many irreplaceable documents fell victim to the destructive rage of the Nazi command and the war; so, too, Hans David Blum's notes and copies left behind in Breisach. Whatever collection and research was still possible, was accomplished with extraordinary industry. This work has made Hans David Blum a widely recognized expert on Jewish history in our region and beyond. The present volume concerns is concerned primarily with events from the late Middle Ages through the supposed equality of all citizens of the state of Baden, finally achieved in 1862. Only a short overview is provided of the period that follows, to the destruction of German Judaism and 1945. We can look forward to the second volume, concerning this last period in history of the Breisach Jewish community. At the end of this preface, there remains only to wish that this remarkable and very unique work of local history should arouse the interest it deserves.

Müllheim, September 1998

Erhard Roy Wiehn

Preliminary Note from the Editor

I first dealt with the history of Breisach Jews while working on my anthology *Oktoberdeportation 1940 – Die Sogennante "Abschiebung" der Badischen und Saarpfälzischen Juden in das Französische Internierungslager Gurs und Andere Vorstationen von Auschwitz 50 Jahre danach zum Gedenken"* [*The October 1940 Deportation—The So-Called "Deportation" of the Baden and Saar Palatine Jews to the French Internment Camp Gurs and Other Preliminary Stations of Auschwitz, 50 Years Later in Commemoration*, Konstanz, 1990]. It includes respective text excerpts from both Louis Dreyfuss and Günther Haselier (pp. 223-34 and 944-46).

In August 1990 we visited the now late Louis Dreyfuss in Breisach to discuss the publication of his survivor's account, titled *Emigration nur ein Wort? – Ein jüdisches Überlebensschicksal in Frankreich 1933-1945* [*Emigration Only a Word? A Jewish Story of Survival in France, 1933-1945*, Konstanz, 1991], which debuted at the University of Constance already on March 5, 1991, and on March 24 in the author's presence at the Öffentliche Bücherei in Breisach. Louis Dreyfuss was one of the first Jews to leave Breisach in 1933, visiting his destroyed hometown again right at the end of the Third Reich, and he remained the only one to resume residence in his hometown. As I wrote in the foreword to my anthology, *Emigration nur ein Wort?* is and will remain "an unusual story of life and home, an episode in contemporary history worthy of record, and thought-provoking reading today on the events of that time" (p. 12). My conversations with the then 90-year-old Louis Dreyfuss have remained unforgettable until today.

I have all the more appreciated Hans David Blum's intended book project, which I first learned of in summer 1992 in Breisach. Surprisingly, I obtained the first draft of the text *Juden in Breisach* from Dipl. Archivist Uwe Fahrer (Breisach) at the beginning of August 1998, and the finished text by the beginning of October 1998. Thanks to the unusual dedication of Hartung-Gorre Publishing (Konstanz) and Lokay Printing (Reinheim/Odenwals), the present volume came into being with astonishing speed for the 60th anniversary of the November pogrom. The book will in future be recognized as valuable reading on German Jewry. The author's vita and sources for the work will be provided in the anticipated second volume. What is written and published will not be quickly forgotten.

Before Sukkot 5759 – October 1998

In Memoriam

The Deaths in the Breisach Jewish Community through Racist Persecution, 1935–1945

Last name, First name	Born	Died
Baehr, Hermann	3/9/1878	1/16/1941, Gûrs
Baehr, Margot	3/23/1911	7/18/1942, Auschwitz
Bergheimer, David	2/28/1877	12/31/1942, Auschwitz
Bergheimer, née Levi, Jenny	5/21/1879	Assumed dead (8/10/1942)
Bergheimer, Emilie	6/28/1880	12/31/1940, Gûrs
Bergheimer, Jakob	?	Nov. 1938, Dachau
Blozheimer, Ludwig	10/5/1895	1943, Trzebinia (Poland)
Breisacher, Benjamin	5/6/1872	12/11/1940, Gûrs
Breisacher, Korina	9/19/1885	12/17/1940, Grafeneck (euthanasia)
Breisacher, Luise	11/10/1879	Assumed dead, Auschwitz
Breisacher, née Model, Mathilde	4/14/1872	11/14/1940, Gûrs
Breisacher, née Blozheimer, Melanie	10/14/1881	Assumed dead, Auschwitz
Breisacher, Melanie	10/12/1903	Assumed dead, Eastern Europe
Dreifuss, Else	12/30/1908	8/1/1941, Gûrs
Eisemann, Michael	6/4/1894	2/1/1939, Freiburg (suicide)
Felsenstein, Hedwig	6/20/1884	1942, disappeared, Eastern Europe
Geismar, Edmund	1/1/1889	Assumed dead, Auschwitz
Geismar, Emmy	9/6/1900	1942, disappeared, Eastern Europe
Geismar, née Joseph, Lina	9/14/1889	Assumed dead, Auschwitz
Geismar, Ludwig	1/19/1896	Assumed dead
Geismar, née Uffenheimer, Rosa	8/31/1879	Disappeared in Auschwitz

Geismar, Theodor	6/29/1869	9/7/1941, disappeared
Geismar, Wilhelm	12/26/1873	1942, Gûrs
Greilsamer, née Breisacher, Camilla	1/1/1880	9/16/1943, Pau (Southern France)
Greilsamer, Fanny	6/9/1885	5/1/1935, Breisach (suicide)
Greilsamer, Hermann	6/14/1876	1939 (?), Grafeneck (euthanasia)
Greilsamer, Julius	5/25/1905	1942, disappeared, Eastern Europe
Grumbach, Emil	7/3/1868	11/21/1938, Dachau
Grumbach, Fanny	?	Dec. 1940, Gûrs
Grumbach, Flora	8/17/1903	Disappeared in Auschwitz
Guenzburger, née Kleefeld, Rosa	9/13/1876	8/21/1943, Villeneuve (Southern France)
Kaufmann, Hermann	11/7/1874	12/27/1941, Récébédou (France)
Kaufmann, née Levy, Jenny	7/31/1887	Assumed dead, 10/22/1940, Gûrs
Kindermann, née Kahn, Babette	9/3/1885	9/8/1942, Theresienstadt
Kindermann, Siegfried	5/26/1879	6/9/1943, Theresienstadt
Kleefeld, Johanna	7/3/1904	Disappeared in Auschwitz
Levi, née Kahn, Julia	7/4/1883	3/30/1944, Theresienstadt
Levy, née Eppstein, Julie	4/19/1877	1/24/1942, Rivesaltes
Levy, Rosa	8/30/1905	Disappeared
Levy, Marie	12/22/1875	Disappeared, Eastern Europe
Mock, Abraham	3/10/1870	2/17/1942, Noé (France)
Mock, née Karlebach, Jenny	?	12/8/1940, Gûrs
Mock, Max	10/9/1872	1/7/1942, Aix-en-Provence
Model, Lydia	8/28/1889	Assumed dead (Aug. 1942, Eastern Europe)
Mueller, Moses	10/9/1856	11/12/1940, Gûrs
Rosenberg, née Rosenberger, Johanna	12/3/1870	10/27/1941, France

Rosenberg, Julius	10/11/1900	12/31/1944, Auschwitz
Roth, née Wurmser, Sophie	10/3/1882	2/20/1944, Noé (France)
Strauss, Hilda	1/18/1889	Disappeared, Eastern Europe
Strauss, née Mock, Josefine	10/8/1861	9/7/1941, Récébédou (France)
Strauss, Julius	10/13/1892	Disappeared, Eastern Europe
Uffenheimer, Adolf	9/17/1864	Assumed dead, 10/22/1940, Gûrs
Uffenheimer, née Roos, Anna	3/3/1873	1/1/1941, Gûrs
Uffenheimer, Flora	7/17/1899	Assumed dead, 10/22/1940, Gûrs
Uffenheimer, née Kaufmann, Sitta	7/23/1893	Assumed dead (11/15/1941, Riga)
Weil, Alfred	12/1/1923	Disappeared
Weil, née Uffenheimer, Bertha	6/29/1870	Disappeared (10/22/1940, Gûrs)
Weil, née Friedberg, Betty	5/8/1888	Disappeared, Eastern Europe
Weil, née Greilsheimer, Luise	8/1/1880	Assumed dead (Belzec or Majdanek)
Weil, Melanie	12/24/1885	Disappeared, Eastern Europe
Weil, Moritz	5/29/1879	Disappeared, Eastern Europe
Weil, Siegfried	9/2/1883	Assumed dead (Belzec or Majdanek)
Weinberg, née Model, Fanny	9/15/1897	Disappeared in Auschwitz
Weinberg, Max	3/25/1884	Assumed dead (1942, Auschwitz)
Wertheimer, née Kohlmann, Helene	4/15/1888	Assumed dead (1942, Auschwitz)
Wurmser, née Levi, Balbine	2/2/1897	Assumed dead (1942, Auschwitz)
Wurmser, Salomon	9/9/1885	Assumed dead (1942, Auschwitz)

The First Reports of Jews in Breisach: 12th–14th Centuries

The time of the first two crusades at the end of the 11th century initiated a migration among the Jews who had come to Germany with the Romans. One assumption is that many sought refuge in areas on the Upper Rhein, settling primarily in the larger and smaller cities protected by walls, where they practiced commercial and financial businesses.[1]

Breisach could already have been considered an attractive place for settlement for just such reasons. Situated on the shore of a large waterway, it possessed its own mint and a protective fortress. In his chronicle for the year 1793 the Breisach prebend Protas Gsell claims, on the basis of "old writings or city archives," that Jews were received 100 years earlier in Breisach. Originally numbering twelve families, they were said to have multiplied later and built a synagogue.[2] A large part of the local archives (city, cathedral, religious houses, Jewish community) fell victim to fire during the destruction by French revolutionary troops in September 1793. Thus, it is possible that the chronicler could have referred to a document that once available document that no longer exists.

"The Jews appeared as natives in Breisach for the first time in the year 1156, settled in a ghetto of twelve households," writes another local historian, Deacon Pantaleon Rosmann.[3] A source citation is missing.[4]

Accordingly, settlement would have occurred when the mountain city church and mint belonged to the Bishop of Basel (1006-1185)—at the end of the 12th century when, under the Staufer and Zähringer dynasties, civil and commercial life developed. The strong fortress tower on the castle hill overlooking Judengasse, destroyed in 1793, the enormous enclosing walls, and Kapf Gate date to this time, as well as the wheel well on the mountain plateau. Water was drawn manually from the Rhine water table through its 42-meter-deep shaft.

After an 1185 treaty between King Heinrich VI and Bishop Heinrich of Basel, only merchants were allowed to settle on the mountain.[5] As servants of the Imperial House, the Jews received direct protection by the Kaiser, who issued them protection letters for payment.

---

[1] In the 12th century there were an estimated 20000 Ashkenazi Jews in today's French and West German regions (personal communication from Professor Hanns Reissner, who died in New York in 1977).

[2] Protas Gsell, *Ursprung der Stadt Altbreisach, geweester alter- und Beschreibung jetziger Lage* [The Origins of the City of Old Breisach: A Description of the Former and Current State]. A copy of the missing original can be found in the Breisach city archive. Report by Gsell in Zwi Avneri, *Germania Judaica*, Volume II (1968), p. 125.

[3] P. Rosmann and Faustin Ens, *Geschichte der Stadt Breisach* [History of the City of Breisach], Freiburg, 1851, p. 153, thereafter Josef Schmidlin, *Breisacher Zeitung* [Breisach Newspaper] 1/11/1936, p. 24, report in *Germania Judaica*, Volume II (1968), p. 124.

[4] Haselier found nothing in his thorough research that could support Rosmann's claim (personal communication).

[5] Haselier I, 80, 86, 90.

A document dated August 13, 1230 records that King Heinrich, son of Friedrich II, stayed in Breisach along with various counts and dignitaries. On that day he pardoned Count Egeno of Freiburg, who had been accused of capturing Jews "near Freiburg" who had the King's protection (*judeos nostros*).[6] According to local historians, the affair concerned Breisach Jews. Josef Bader[7] assumes this entirely from the fact that Jews had already been present much earlier in the adjacent Staufer city Breisach, then an imperial possession.[8] Haselier additionally points out that the expression "judeos nostros" used by the king, as the place of their capture, apply primarily to Breisach Jews. Likewise the circumstance that the matter was handled in Breisach, seems to indicate that the Jews imprisoned by Count Egeno were at home there.[9]

That the imperial tax register of 1241 does not mention tax from the Breisach Jews, does not prove that none lived in the city in these years. One may conclude only that in this year they paid no money to the King's chamber, whereas there are explicit citations for the Jews of Oppenheim (Rheinhessen), Wetzlar, Boppard, Sinzig, Worms, Speyer, Kaiserslautern, Strassburg, Basel, Hagenau, Schwäbisch Hall, Schwäbisch Gmünd, Augsburg, Esslingen, Ulm, Konstanz, Überlingen, and Lindau .

The first reliable report of the presence of Jews in Breisach comes from the time of imperial cities (1273-1330): a city document issued on December 27, 1302, naming the Jew Smariant, resident of Breisach.[10] The document concerns a complicated financial matter involving the deceased Hildebrand Spenlin as guarantor and debtor, as well as the city of Konstanz and one Heinrich Schuler of Freiburg. This Schuler gives Smariant a receipt for a sum of unknown amount.[11]

One of the two imperial stewards in Upper and Lower Alsace, Count Ulrich of Pfirt, had been appointed custodian of the city of Breisach during an interregnum. Among other promises, he vowed to the city council and citizens of Breisach on September 30, 1313 to leave the Jews alone, or in other words: not to drive them from the city.[12] Jews are believed to have immigrated from Strassburg to Breisach in the first quarter of the 14th century, around the time that Breisach received the staple right and reached greater economic significance as the only loading point between Basel and Strassburg.[13]

---

[6]Document from 1230 VIII 13, Breisach (GLA D54; Printer: Hefele, FUB I, p. 35).

[7]Bader, *Die ehemaligen Breisgauer Stände* [The Former Estates of Breisgau].

[8]Freiburger Stadthefte [Freiburg City Brochure] 1963, 6, p. 2

[9]Haselier, *Hist*. I, p. 102

[10]Stadtarchiv Konstanz / doc. no. 8053; printer: Fr. Hefele, *Freiburger Urkunden Buch* [Freiburg Documents Book] III, p. 12f. *Germania Judaica* 1968, p. 124, offers the previously accepted year 1301 as the date of the document. Rosmann, p. 203, incorrectly names a Moses as financier and the sons of Hesse of Üsenberg as guarantors.

[11]Haselier I, p. 135 ff.

[12]Document from 1313 IX30, Breisach (GLA 65 1312 fol. 52v-53-r).

[13]*Die Jüdischen Gemeinden in Baden*, p. 49.

The aforementioned Breisach Jew Smariant is named again in a document from May 29, 1316, in which Burkart of Üsenberg attests to having assumed the debts his son-in-law, Margrave Heinrich of Hachberg, had incurred with Smariant.[14] One can estimate the amount that Smariant had lent the margrave from the fact that Heinrich mortgaged to his father-in-law, as security in return for his surety, the fortress and city of Burkheim, his margravial rights and possessions in the valley of Oberrotweil and Oberbergen, as well as the village of Jechtingen.[15] This suggests that Smariant was a prominent financier. He is named in the register of farm taxes for Breisach for the year 1319: he also owned a farm, as well as two neighboring houses in Vicus Leonis (in the northeastern *Oberstadt*). His neighbor was the Jew Salmann from Bern, who paid two *soldi* in farm taxes.

The Jews were in no way concentrated in a ghetto then as they were in later periods; rather, they lived among the Christian population scattered about the city. In Vicus Leonis, Smariant and Salmann from Bern were almost the only Jews—on the other side of the street only the Jew Maiger was resident. Above the Phlegeler Gate (Hagenbach Tower) lived the Jews Löwe and Gutela as neighbors of Siegfried Schultheiss and Eberlin Smied, respectively. Isack and Meiger[16], sons of Smariant, as well as a certain Jacob of Breisach are also named as creditors to the city of Freiburg in the years 1326-1328.[17]

The Breisach Jews were originally placed under the immediate authority of the King.[18] For this reason it was possible for Karl IV of France, pretender to the throne, to promise them to Duke Leopold of Austria in 1324[19], as an assurance that Leopold, in accordance with his promise, would advocate for the election of the Frenchman to the German kingship.[20]

On June 11, 1330, the city of Breisach allied itself with Duke Otto of Austria, who had inherited the Austrian forelands, with the end of protecting them from Ludwig of Bavaria and the imperial stewards he appointed to Alsace and Breisgau. A demand from the city—"he should also leave us the Jews"—was also contractually honored and the Jews thereby made subject to the city.[21] King Ludwig was, however, at first not in agreement with this step. But when he

---

[14]GLA Karlsruhe 21/202; printing: Richard Fester, *Regesta of the Margrave of Baden and Hachberg* I, Innsbruck 1900, hl 57.

[15]Haselier, *Gesch.* I. p. 135 ff.

[16]Adolf Lewin, *Juden in Freiburg i. Br.* [Jews in Freiburg im Breisgau] reports verbatim: "Isaac 'Smeriandes son' and his brother Meiger" and translates Smeriand with the Hebrew name Schmarjahu.

[17]Schreiber 263, no. 132, 270 no. 134, 280 no. 142; thereafter *Germania Judaica*, Vol. II, p. 124-45.

[18]*Germania Judaica* II, p. 124.

[19]*Germania Judaica* note: MG Const V 794, no. 952.

[20]Doc. of 1324 V II 27 (MGH, LL IV, Volume 5, p. 792f).

[21]Document from 1330 VI 11. According to Haselier I, p. 146, two copies of the document were issued: to the city, in GLA Karlsruhe 21/53, and to the duke, in the Staatarchiv Breisach (Doc. 13). Document according to *Germ. Ind.* II, p. 124; A.a.O.VI 672, no. 294f.

reconciled with the dukes of Austria the following year, he pledged them, among others things, the city of Breisach and its Jews[22], and Karl IV repeated this pledge on May 26, 1348.[23] A pledge of June 16, 1331, brought the Jewish residents of Breisach under Austrian protection. Although the Jews paid their taxes to the King, or rather to his magistrates, the city must also have had some advantage from them. Subsequently, the city council had to take steps to ensure their safety, as Jewish persecutions raged from 1336 to 1338 in Alsace, Franconia and Swabia. Their leader, a certain Armleder, explained his alleged murder among other things as a desire to revenge Christ's death.[24]

In consequence of the upheavals, Breisach united in 1338 with a large number of towns and lords to suppress Armleder's bands and his supporters in the cities.[25] In 1345, it joined the "*Landesrettung*" to fight the "crowd" persecuting clerics, laypeople, and Jews.[26] A gentlemen's bar by the name of "Zum Juden," located in the *Oberstadt*, is mentioned several times in records of this period. The sheriff's ordinance of 1330 often refers to patricians as the ones "vom Juden" ("from the Jew"), as the bar (possibly at the southeastern entry to Radbrunnenallee) was designated as their meeting place. It remains unknown whether the structure had previously belonged to a Jewish resident or been a Jewish place of prayer.[27]

A report from 1348 states that a large earthquake cost many people of Breisach their lives.[28] The Black Death soon followed, a horrible plague epidemic that spread from Southern France and caused widespread death among the population.[29] In ignorance of the true circumstances and in superstitious fear, people blamed the Jews for causing the plague by poisoning the wells and springs.[30] The Armleder movement and its religious hatred of the Jews produced a fury that led to Jewish massacres, beginning in Swabia and Bavaria in winter 1348 and continuing on the *Oberrhein* (Upper Rhine) at the beginning of 1349, whereas the plague did not break out until summer 1349. Some magistrates of the old imperial cities united in the "*Landesrettung*" to uphold order, because they knew that the killing would not stop at the gates

---

[22]Document (see Haselier I, p. 148) from 1331 VII 16; see *Germ. Judaica*, p. 125: Oberrhein. Stadtrechte II 3, 21 no. 13.

[23]See Germ. Jud. p. 125: MG Const VIII 600, no. 594. Wiener 223, no. 47.

[24]B. Rosenthal, Heimatgesch. d. badischen Juden [Local Hist. of Baden Jews], p. 17

[25]Germ. Judaica, p. 124. Oberrhein. Stadtrechte III 3, 99, no. 83. Wiener 50, no. 178, Haselier I, p. 146, p. 209

[26]Germ. Judaica, p. 124: Oberrhein. Stadtrechte III 3, 102, No. 87, Wiener 50, no. 179

[27]Haselier I, p. 153

[28]Rosmann, p. 212, gives 1/27/1348 as the date of the earthquake

[29]Haselier I, p. 159 writes that in Breisach no supporting documents about the plague itself are available. A letter of the Breisach Jewish community from 1755, concerning the selection of a cemetery plot, recalls that the *Oberstadt* was spared the plague. Haselier I, p. 159 reports: During the digging of a construction site for the Breisach kindergarten, to the east of Muggensturmgasse and north of St. Joseph Chapel, in 1939/40, approximately 20–30 skeletons were found only 20 cm below the top soil. The site was interpreted as a medieval plague cemetery.

[30]B. Rosenthal, Heimatgeschichte (Local History) p. 18

of the Judengasse.[31] Strassburg mayors and aldermen took pains to bring about normal court proceedings. A street crowd's demand that the Jews be driven away was met with resistance, as was the pressure of the guilds in Basel.

At a meeting of the cities and barons with the bishop of Strassburg, the city achieved nothing despite its energetic advocacy for the Jews: it was decided that all Jews were to be expelled from the Upper Rhine region, and a campaign against them began immediately.[32] A missive from the city of Breisach in late 1348 to the Strassburg mayor and council reports on testimony from a baptized Breisach Jew about supposed well poisonings by former fellow believers.[33] Hundreds of Jews were burned without trial on January 9, 1349, on the Rhine Island near Basel.

Eight days later charges were brought against the Jews in Breisgau. According to reports of the Freiburg city council, first "all Jews were arrested."[34] After gruesome punishment some confessed under compulsion, apparently also accusing fellow Jews from other towns. In this way, Meiger Nase "confessed" to having laid a little sack, one span long, in a Freiburg well chamber[35] and to have returned to its place a keystone that had been previously removed. Four Breisach Jews supposedly discussed with him how they could poison the wells of Breisach and other places: Uele Smeriandes, Juedeli, Schoebeli and Vivelmann.[36]

Freiburg communicated this confession, forced from Meiger Nase under torture, to Breisach, likewise ordered an examination of the four accused people and thus managed to get the same "confessions" from them. Under torture, the Breisach Jew Salman declared that for 20 guilder he bought poison in Villingen in the Black Forest (*Schwarzwald*) and poisoned the wells with it. Schoebeli gave him the money.[37] Schoebeli and three other Jews (Uele, Smariant's son; Juedeli; and Vifelman [sic]) "confessed" to having consulted with Meiger Nase in Freiburg about the well poisoning; Meiger was also said to have been present when they put the poison in the wells. Also, all other Jews from Strassburg, Basel, Breisach, and Freiburg knew about the poisoning attempts. The Breisach Jews were accused of creating an opportunity for themselves to relocate to the *Oberstadt* through eradication of the Christians.[38] The Breisach Council hurried to

---

[31]Ismar Elbogen, Hist. der Juden in Deutschland, Berlin 1935, p. 70

[32]Elbogen, p. 70

[33]A. Glaser, Metz, Gesch. der Juden in Strassburg, 1924, p. 74

[34]H. Schreiber, Urkundenbuch d. Stadt Frbg. 1, Freiburg 1828, p. 378, no. 193; thereafter Dr. Adolf Lewin, Gesch. d. Juden in Freiburg, p. 144 ff

[35]Haselier, Gesch. 1, p. 160; Rosenthal, p. 18

[36]Lewin translates the names as Uri Schmeril (schmarjahu), Judel (Jehuda), Schabse (Scheftel) and Feibelmann (Fribel)

[37]Mainfraenk. Yearbook V 99, Nr. 2

[38]Haselier I, p. 160: Meiger Nase in Freiburg "confessed": "that the Jews in Breisach had said that they wanted to have the Berg themselves, and that he personally was there when the wells were poisoned."

send these statements to Freiburg.[39] Likewise, Breisach communicated the results of the investigation to the Würzburg Council upon the latter's request.

According to the reports produced in Freiburg, an accused man by the name of Jeckli Joliep claimed that rather than the aforementioned Meiger Nase, a Strassburg Jew by the name of Swendewin planted the poison, which he had gotten for 20 guilder.[40]

Two Jews from Basel, Koeppeli and Anscheli, supposedly sent it with directions to poison the wells "ultimately everywhere" in the land, which supposedly was done wherever possible between September 8 and October 16—"everywhere" between Freiburg, Breisach, and Endingen.[41]

Court reports in Freiburg name additional accused people such as Gotliep in Waldkirch, said to have obtained poison from an Anselm of Vehringen (Ihringen?) and also a certain Liepkind, who under torture admitted to also knowing about it. After many other "confessions" were extorted, the burning of Freiburg Jews was carried out on June 30, 1349. Only the 12 richest Jews, pregnant women, and children were spared.[42] In Waldkirch, Breisach, Neuenburg, and Endingen they met the same fate. The Breisach Jews were burned on the basis of "confessions."[43] The burning took place after January 23, 1349, the date of the letter to Würzburg, in which the death of the accused men is not yet mentioned.[44] The sources reveal the presence of Jews in Breisach again in 1376[45], but the way they are mentioned clearly demonstrates that no strong anti-Jewish resentment remained in the city.

No less than the Cistercian Monastery Pairis, situated in the Vosges, sold in this year a house to "the wise, modest Jew, Vivil Kint, resident in Breisach," and to his heirs[46]—not on the city

---

[39]Schreiber 376 ff, Nr. 193

[40]B Rosenthal

[41]Ad. Lewin, p.44

[42]H Schreiber

[43]Germania Judaica II, p. 125. Source: Dr. Siegmund Salfeld, *Das Martyrologium des Nürnberger Memorbuches*, Berlin 1898 (Source z. Gesch. d. Juden in Deutschland, Vol. III).
Inside: Martyr sites at the time of the Black Death, newly edited from the old Deutzer memory book. In the Hebrew section appears . . . on p. 83, in German on p. 284 the listing is given for Breisach after that for the Alsatian places Enheim and Kaysersberg and outside Sennheim and Rosheim.
The anti-Semitic pogroms destroyed almost all Jewish communities in Central Europe, whose names and martyrs were eternalized in so-called memory books.
Dr. Adolf Kohut, *Gesch. der deutschen Juden*, Berlin, also cites the old Deutzer memory book and names Breisach as a martyr site of the time of the Black Death between Ehnheim and Basel.
Groups of Ashkenazi Jews fled at that time to Bohemia, Moravia, Schlesia, and Poland, where they took their German language with them and created Eastern Judaism. From this came about the Yiddish language, a mix of Middle High German, Hebrew, and other languages of their various stays. The return flow to the West began again with the persecution by the Chmielnicki in the 17th century and lasted into the 20th century.

[44]Germania Judaica II, p. 125, note 18.

[45]In Freiburg there was documentation of Jews again in 1360.

[46]Haselier

margins or on Judengasse, but on the mountain, as free property subject only to the bishops' tax. This Vivil Kint may well be a descendant of the man of the same name listed in the 1319 farm tax register.[47]

In early October 1383, the city of Strassburg, which had already readmitted individual Jews in 1368 and 1375, allowed an additional nine families residence for six years, among them Et Mathis from Breisach; in 1387 he was taxed 25 florins and his brother Salmon of Breisach, 20 florins.[48]

In Konstanz around this time, Jews declared themselves ready to have a tower built for the city, as compensation for their acceptance.[49] It is possible that the Breisach *Judenturm* (Jew's Tower), mentioned in a document in 1390, came into being the same way.[50] It lay near the residence of the family "zum Rine," thus in the area where the *Judenstadt* (Jews' City) or Judengasse later appears. At that time the tower, along with the Augustinenberg and Sternhofgasse, formed a type of ghetto, which developed at the north edge of the foothills to the mountain.

At the same time that the Jews were expelled from France in 1395, plague-like outbreaks were occurring repeatedly, and history again reports of the accusation of a Breisach resident. The city of Freiburg received, in response to an inquiry of June 13, 1397, a report from Colmar that Count Bruno von Rappolstein had imprisoned Jews in his castle in Rappoltsweiler, tortured and killed them for confessing, like a certain Jew David in Thueringheim,[51] that that they had poisoned wells with powder.[52] A Schaffhaus "teacher" (rabbi) was said to have given the poison to an Aschaffenburg beggar, the Jew Meiger. David of Thueringheim tried to save his life by promising to hand over other complicit Jews. He "confessed" that the Jew Jacob in Breisach had slipped him the poison there secretly, "since next the Jews of Breisach had a wedding and the same Jacob told him to take the poison to Thueringheim and throw the poison into the wells."[53] This event took place while the Jews of Breisach were celebrating a wedding, continued David, and Jacob had also given him money for the purpose of mixing poison, some of this money coming from a certain "Schekahn" who had traveled from Basel for the festivities.[54]

---

[47]Haselier

[48]Strassburg State Archive

[49]Rosenthal

[50]Document from 1300 VII 24 (Münster Archive)

[51]Today Tuerkheim in Alsace

[52]Schreiber

[53]Haselier

[54]Theodor Nordemann reports that countless Jews left in 1397 from Basel, presumably out of fear of new persecutions on the basis of rumors of well poisonings in Alsace. The refugees put themselves under the protection of the Duke Leopold of Austria.

Between Persecution and Tolerance: 1424–1600

A new blow befell the Breisach Jews when Kaiser Sigmund, who governed the lands of Archduke Friedrich while he was outlawed from 1415 to 1425, approved the expulsion of Jews from the old Further Austrian cities Breisach, Freiburg, and Neuenburg on February 24, 1424. He also agreed that from then on, no more Jews could come in, although he also imposed the condition that no damage be inflicted to the body or property of the expellees.[55] There is no documentary proof that they were still tolerated in the Breisach "Jewish city," despite previous assumption to the contrary. Nor is there record of a general expulsion or prohibition of settlement, unlike the case of Freiburg, which in 1424 had banned Jewish residence "for all time."[56]

When Duke Friedrich IV of Austria reacquired his lands on January 29, 1429, he reassured the citizens of Breisach that he would permit them their old privileges and, among other things, "the favor that he would not require them to have Jews."[57]

By 1446 the presence of Jews can again be verified in Breisach, as well as Krozingen, Gottenheim, and Neuershausen.[58] They could apparently survive in individual cases on Austrian territory and establish small settlements. A privilege issued by Duke Albrecht of Austria,[59] in Breisach in 1446, read favorably for the Jews of Alsace, Sundgau, Breisgau, Thurgau, and Swabia: whoever slays or injures a Jew should be executed at once; the Jews should also enjoy all the rights due to Christians; [...]

[...] they may buy or lease property anywhere, where they may also bury their dead undisturbed, etc. However, this privilege was not always observed.[60]

Whether Jews continued to live in Breisach after this time is doubtful, as sources give no evidence of their presence until the Thirty Years War.[61] The tavern "zum Juden" is again mentioned in 1473, when the Burgundian governor Peter von Hagenbach was causing havoc in

---

[55]The Jewish community in Baden reports: At the same time, those in Waldkirch were also banished. They settled in the neighboring places of Krozingen, Gottenheim, and Neuershausen, and maintained their relationship to Freiburg until 1543, when the city prohibited all its inhabitants from doing business with Jews. Expelled individuals could also be found in villages of the Upper Baden margravate, and in the Basel diocese (Sulzberg, Schliengen, and Weil). From then on Jews could enter only in the accompaniment of a Freiburg city worker and had to wait at the gates until the council sent one out to them.

[56]Haselier

[57]Source from 1429 I 19, Innsbruck (City Archive Breisach, Nr. 92). The record is fairly damaged from the big fire in 1793.

[58]Freiburg notebooks 1963 (also shown in correspondence with author Dr. Schwineköper 1978).

[59]Rosenthal, without indication of source

[60]In the era of 1400-1450 there were at most some hundred Jewish families in Middle Europe.
(Dr. Lewin Rabbiner, Hoppstätten, in a letter from 8/13/1938 to Teacher Berthold Rosenthal, Mannheim. In B. Rosenthal, Archive of Leo Baeck Institute, NY – Correspondences.)

[61]Haselier

Breisach. A tax register from 1537 mentions a house "across from the Jewish shul,"[62] yet it is not proven that the synagogue was functioning at that time. It is possible that "shul" is merely the old term for this building, which might even be identical to the gentlemen's tavern "zum Juden."

While Austrian Freiburg refused to accept Jews in 1446 and later, some obtained residence in a nearby town. This is attested by a horrible event that occurred in Endingen am Kaiserstuhl, near Breisach. There, in 1462, a beggar family with two small children supposedly sought quarters for the night,[63] and the wife of Rabbi Elias offered them the barn as shelter. Local and foreign Jews were celebrating Sukkot with them in their house. By the following morning, the beggar family had disappeared without a trace. Neighbors claimed to have heard a terrible cry in the night. Eight years later (1470), the undecayed bodies of two children and two adults were found among the bones when the ossuary was dismantled.[64] They were immediately assumed to be the beggar family that had disappeared so mysteriously years earlier.

Elias (Helya), as well as his brothers Eberlin and Merklin, "confessed without torture or grief" that they had murdered the Christians with the assistance of a Jew from Pforzheim. The blood of the children was to be used as chrism for circumcisions. A large tribunal, to which all neighboring towns sent representatives, condemned the three accused men to death on the basis of their extorted confessions.[65] They were dragged on cowhides through the village and then outside to the "Judenbuck" ("Jew Mountain"), where they were burned; the remaining Jews were expelled.[66] Emperor Friedrich III condemned the actions of the people of Endingen. He commanded that the Jews still imprisoned be freed and no one be further accosted about the matter.

The eventual Emperor Ferdinand I enacted restrictive ordinances[67] against the Jews in 1526, while he was Archduke of Austria. Because they remained ineffective, these ordinances were sharpened in 1547.[68]

In 1535, the increase in the number of Jews already led to complaint and the promise of redress. The Jews were supposedly "disadvantageous" because of their usury. In fact, as of August 20, 1540, only 70 Jewish families still lived in the Ensisheim region (including

---

[62]GLA 66

[63]Rosenthal

[64]Freiburg Notebooks, page 3

[65]Rosenthal

[66]A tablet with depictions in the house of Rabbi Elias portrayed the events still into the 19th century, one a Jewish play originating in the 17th century dramatizing the incident and frequently performed. The mummies of the four victims were preserved in the Endingen Church until 1970, and those of the children were carried in parades still in the 20th century. Only after intensive research and enlightenment was this tragic case in Jewish history rectified, and a "Rehabilitation after 500 Years" was attained especially because Dr. Toni Oelsner and Karl Kurrus in Freiburg succeeded in these efforts. (Composition, New York, December 16, 1966 and July 31, 1970.)

[67]Rosenthal

[68]In the Austrian foreland Upper Alsace in 1547, the right to settle was restricted to one family per locale; the Ensisheim Synagogue was closed for worship; and the Jews had to wear particular clothing and a yellow mark.

Breisach), predominantly in small communities.[69] In this year, after the death of the provincial governor, the government of old Further Austria in Ensisheim summoned all Jews residing in its domain on both sides of the Rhine, to submit their letters of protection for renewal.[70] Names are included in the summons.[71] That Breisach is not named in the list of places is evidence that in 1540 no Jews lived there. Additionally, it is clear that the Emperor had expelled them from "some districts along the Upper Rhine"—evidence for this is found in records pertaining to a case against the city of Colmar, which was brought before the superior court in 1549 by R. Josel of Rosheim, in his capacity as "commandant of the Jews" and community leader of Tuerkheim, Winzenheim, Ammerswiller, Tankelsheim (Dangolsheim), Surbourg and Hagenau.[72] Despite the expulsion, they did have the right to go through Sundgau, Breisgau and Alsace, and to visit the markets.

The Jews could not be blamed for usury. The Emperor could have accorded them this right, because they were not permitted to pursue skilled crafts and trades. One could just as soon implicate the wholesale merchants for driving up the price of foodstuffs. That the Emperor expelled the Jews from districts along the Upper Rhine[73]—Jews who doubtless had earned this castigation ("qui ont sansdoute mérité leur Chatiment")—does not justify a decree against the Jews of the Colmar region, because they did nothing to deserve punishment. Despite the efforts of the lawyers, Josel von Rosenheim's [sic] attempt to intervene with the Emperor was unsuccessful.[74] In 1555 admission to Colmar was prohibited[75] and the trial lasted until 1572.

In 1573 Ferdinand issued a so-called "usury mandate pertaining to Christians as well as Jews" with the provision that by June 1, 1574, all Jews were to be removed and no more tolerated thereafter.[76] After the Austrian government in Ensisheim had expelled them, some settled on the Swiss border and founded communities in the diocese of Basel.[77]

---

[69]Dr. med. Achilles Nordmann, The Israeli Cemetery in Hegenheim, Basel 1910

[70]Rosenthal, p. 37: in Sulzburg there were at this time three Jewish families; in Krozingen, Wolfenweiler, and Neuershausen, two per unit. In 1534 the speech of the *Hintersassen* (resident without citizenship) Liebermann Jew von Malterdingen occurs; in 1543 there is a complaint from Chaim von Neuershausen; and in 1544 Freiburg city complains that Jews live in Krozingen (Josslin von Krozingen) and Gottenheim.

[71]Colmar City Archive AA 173 No. 26; E. Scheid, *Gesch. d. Juden im Elsass*, outlines the lists, although imprecisely. For the places with names, the place Turkehiem/ Alsace is missing. In Rixheim there were two families, in Habsheim three families. Lazarus lived in Ensisheim (a dossier exists about him in the Colmar city archive with regard to a trial, in which Josel von Rosheim also interferes. In another place, maybe in Alsace, live Mussig, Seligmann, and Gerser (from Picard Letter, Colmar 7/3/74). To the right of the Rhine the following are named in 1540: Krozingen: Joslin and Abraham (two families); Sulzburg: Jesajas, Ysaac. Libmann (three families); Wolfenweiler: Marx, Lemar (two families); Brutback: Hayim (already named there in 1524); Tiengen ob Waldshut; Simon, Simon Abraham, Mathis, Schmahel; Neuershausen: Chaim and N.N. (two families).

[72]Revue des Etudes Juives

[73]Guggenheim, Schweiz p. 65

[74]Bernh. Blumenkranz

[75]ibid, p. 146

[76]Rosenthal

New settlers came to Muelhausen,[78] Istein, Schliengen, Steinenstadt, Haltingen, Mauchen (near Müllheim) and Huttingen.[79] In the name of the Jewry of old Further Austria, Ule, a Jew from Schliengen, addressed an appeal to the government to pay for permission to attend the free market and trading day in Freiburg. The petition was refused.[80]

From Tolerance to Settlement Politics: 1618–1700

Neither the Breisach council reports, which began again in 1601, nor other sources give evidence as to whether Jews lived in the city or carried on commerce there around this time. The first accounts of a settlement originate in the time of the Thirty Years War, when contemporary Jewish communities also arose in neighboring Sundgau. After gradual migration from East to West and emigration from the war-ravaged lands of the Rhine-Main area, refugees searching for new settlement possibilities might also have reached the Upper Rhine.[81] Period surnames like Hess, Schwab, and Frank, point clearly to their bearers' Southern German origins.

Those first appearing with surnames in the fortress city of Breisach—Wormser, Geismar, Schnaitticher (Schnatticher), Ulmer, and Guentzburger—named themselves after places where they, or their fathers, were born and from where they had moved away. The origins of these immigrants can be partially traced to the Austrian margravate Burgau, where there had already long been Jewish communities, for example in Günzburg, Ulm, Schnaittach, and Pferrsee.[82]

In 1617 came the command for immediate deportation from communities directly subordinate to the margravial government: Günzburg, Burgau, Haldenwang and Scheppach.[83] The expulsion ultimately took place in the year 1623. Refugees moved to more tolerant Austrian locales in Bavarian Swabia.[84] "We must attribute to this fact the spread of the Günzberg people in Southern Germany and in Alsace," reckons the historian Rabbi M. Ginsburger, basing his

---

[77]E. Scheid, p. 107
Ibid., p. 134: Among the villages on the Swiss border that took refugees after the expulsion from Ensisheim were Hegenheim, Oberdorf, Duermenach, Bouschwiller, Blotzheim, Ober-Hagenthal, Nieder-Hagenthal; further north we find them in Soultz, Wintzenheim, Hattstadt, Brisach, Biesheim, Bergheim, and Reguisheim, etc.
In Lower Alsace: Rosheim and surroundings, Rosenweiler, Dachstein, Bischheim, Saverne, Dinsheim, Dambach, Schveinheim etc., as well as other districts. By 1689 there were 587 families.

[78]Dr. med. Achilles Nordmann, The Israeli Cemetery in Hegenheim

[79]Rosenthal

[80]Dr. Ad Lewin

[81]Fl. Guggenheim-Gruenberg

[82]Cf. Louis Lamm

[83]L. Löwenstein

[84]E. Ganzmüller: In 1618 the Jews obtained a letter of protection for their right to live in Neuburg, Thannhausen, Hürben, Binswangen, Pferrsee, and Ichenhausen in Bavaria.

claims on research by Rabbis A. Taenzer and L. Löwenstein.[85] Thus, it is no accident that, 20 years after the above-mentioned expulsion, people calling themselves Günzburger, Ulmer and Schnaittacher surfaced in Breisach, conventionally naming themselves after their places of origin. The Wachenheimer, Ries, Hiltenfinger and Olesheimer appearing later in the region were of the same origin.

In his memoirs, the contemporary Ascher Halevy of Reichshoffen[86] portrays the situation of immigrants of that time on the upper reaches of the Rhine. 1628 was a year of inflation in the lowlands and uplands, as far as Basel. "And impoverished Jews came by the hundreds this year, more than in the previous ten years. And they became numerous and multiplied truly to six in a vineyard."

Although local documents of Jewish history in Breisach are missing for the time of the Thirty Years War, this obscurity is illuminated by the scant entries in the revenue rolls of nearby Alsace. "Poor Elias from Breisach" appears on March 12, 1629, in Bergheim in Alsace, where he is registered for paying a toll.[87] In 1639, shortly after the capture and occupation of the starving stronghold of Breisach by the French, "the Jew from Breisach" is named for purporting to be exempt from duty upon entering Ottmarsheim because he must buy horses for provision.[88] Likewise in Ottmarsheim, "Natton from Breisach" paid a toll on January 11, 1641, on a cart carrying nine hundredweight of brass, five hundredweight of pewter, and six hundredweight of copper.

In the Alsatian areas neighboring Breisach, e.g., in Strassburg-Episcopal Markolsheim, but also in many baronetical locales, the Jews were not expelled as in old Further Austria.[89]

---

[85]M. Ginsburger, *Die Günzburger im Elsass*, p. 5 ff. The author reckons that holders of the name Guenzburger in Müttersholz are identical to those of the family Ollendorf. With that exists the possibility that the origin in Ollendorf (Aulendorf) be searched in a place between Ulm and the Bodensee. According to Ginsburger (p. 26), the name Ulmer and Guenzburger also alternate in the same family.

[86]M. Ginsburger, *The Memoirs of Ascher Levy in Reichshoffen (Alsace), 1598-1635* (Published 1913). A typical example of a stage-by-stage migration from East to West comes from the valuable notes of the narrator about his father Elieser Haveli, who came from the Bavarian Olesheim in the Altmühl area. He then lived in Esdorf and moved in 1603 to Bizingen "near Wiblingen" in the Kurpfalz, west of Heidelberg. Ascher himself settled in the Alsatian Reichshofen.

[87]M. Ginsburger, *Wandernde Juden zur Zeit des Dreißigjährigen Krieges, Jahrbuch der Gesellschaft für die Geschichte der Israeliten in Elsaß-Lothringen*, 1917, pp. 11-27. Salo Wittmayer Baron reports on it in *A Social and Religious History of the Jews,* Vol. XIV. Notes, p. 401 [in English]:
These date, based on the revenue rolls of 1620-51 recording payments of the Jewish personal tolls collected from each entrant, and preserved in the Colmar district archives, are quite informative about the places of origin of the migrants. This is basically true despite the frequent negligence of collectors omitting small tolls or none received from beggars and occasional practical jokes by the wanderers when they listed such nonexistant localities as Hanwna, Schickershausen, or Schodten weisich (consisting of corrupted Hebrew words to connote Flattery, House of Drunkards, and I know a stupid one) as their prior residences.

[88]Ottmarsheim, not far from the left bank of Rhine, lies 15 km east of Ensisheim.

[89]Included in the Austrian Forelands:
1.   Foreland Austria: Sundgau, Alsatian territory, Black Forest, Württemberg, and the Breisgau.
2.   Swabian Austria: Swabia, Nellenburg, Hohenberg, Upper Danube, and Margravate Burgau.
3.   Named Countship vor dem Arl. Vorarlberg
(from Friedrich Metz, *Vorderösterreich*, 1967)

Therefore, it is possible that from this point on, Jews primarily from Alsatian places settled in Breisach, which had now almost attained the status of a capital city of the French occupied territory.[90] Surely this owes to the favorable disposition of the Governor General of Erlach, appointed in 1639, who, along with the French occupational authorities, endorsed the re-admission of Jews.

From this point on, details of their resettlement can be gleaned from the reports of the Breisach city magistrate. The first reference in the council report, dated September 15, 1642, is to a *Judengarten* (Jewish cemetery).[91]

A revealing document describes the first Jew to settle in Breisach after its conquest by Duke Bernhard of Weimar (December 17, 1638), who was in the pay of the French: he was one of the retainers of the duke, who died seven months later, on July 18, 1639, in Neuenburg (Neuchâtel). The dossier with the document carries the title: "The Jewry of Old Breisach and the Jurisdiction of Its Magistrate Concerning Said Jewry, 1753-1767."[92]

The writing itself is a 1681 request, recopied in 1753 and certified by the Breisach Chancery, in which the four Breisach guildmasters, Jean Jacques Freitag, Laurent Lamprecht, Jacques Remes, and Jean Georges Murer complained about the Breisach Jewry to the *intendant* of Alsace, Jacques de la Grange, and requested their expulsion from the city that then belonged to France. The writing, dictated with odious intolerance, contains the following excerpted declaration[93]:

> Among our most observed customs and privileges have always been the ministration and observance of the (Catholic) religion, which over time have obstructed the insinuation of straying members of the so-called reformed religion, and especially of the Jewish people, which we have detested. The city of Breisach City, which before its subjection to Swedish rule never suffered infestation by Lutherans, Protestants, or Jews, received its first bloody wound through the settlement of a single Jew belonging to the retinue of the Duke of Weimar. Others crept in during the ensuing confusion, who have since cast deep roots in the Breisach mountain, a population that has grown greater in number, richer in goods and—through their public idolatry in the recently erected Breisach synagogue, with the assent of some weak Catholics—(ever) prouder.

In the Breisach Council reports preserved since 1601, we find the first indications of the presence of Jews in the city in 1643:

> April 14:   Marx the Jew should report to Andres Müller, secretary of the court martial, concerning protection money.

---

[90]Haselier

[91]Haselier

[92]GLA

[93]Translation from the French

May 16:   The (house) sale between Nathan Ulmo the Jew and Adam Willhelm is confirmed; but said Jew is to assume responsibility for existing debts on the house. The other request regarding the closing of the street is denied.

On April 26, 1643, the Jewish doctor Paul Jacob, son of Isaac from Metz, was baptized in Breisach Cathedral in an elaborate civil ceremony. He may have had a particularly close relationship to the Royal Lieutenant d'Oysonville, who is registered as the first godfather of the elite of the French occupation.

The Latin entry in the baptism registry of the Catholic parish of Breisach (Vol. I, p. 373) reads, in German translation:

On April 26, *anno* 1643, a Jew and mature man, doctor of medicine, of French nationality, from Metz, was baptized: Paul Jacob, here in Saint Stephen's Church in the city by me, Johann Georg Hanselmann, unworthy pastor and deacon, with great ceremony and in the presence of many illustrious men, in particular the Count de Guébriant, Commander of the French-Weimar army, and with great participation of the people.

Godparents were the noble Baron Paul d'Oysonville, General Lieutenant of the Most Christian Imperial Majesty in France, and the illustrious Lady N., Countess de Guébriant, wife of the aforementioned commander. Other godparents were Lord de Pessillière, Royal Governor of Alsace in Zabern, Lord du Clausier, Captain and Royal Commandant in Colmar, Baroness Maria Cleopha von Kageneck, née Reinach, Baroness Maria Katharina von Roggenback, née Äscherin von Binningen.

Around the same time, the records refer to another Jewish home buyer besides Nathan Ulmo. On August 8, 1643, a citizen complained to the Breisach Council because the French occupation had sold the rear house of the hostelry "zum Salmen," on which a claim of the citizen's was insured for over 600 guilder. The council determined that there was also a municipal mortgage in the amount of 400 guilder on this structure and submitted objections to the various occupying authorities against selling the pledge.[94]

In the council meeting of February 18, 1645, it became known that the General Auditor and City Major (*Stadtmajor*) had sold the above-mentioned rear house to Max Schnatticher the Jew. It was ruled that the buyer should pay the sales price to the owners of the mortgage or relinquish the pledged property to them. The chief sheriff (*Oberschultheiss*) stated that the Governor "wanted to know nothing either of the supposed donation of the Lord General Director or the sales contract." After that, the council could decide how this corresponded with the interests of the citizen's petition and its own interests.[95] We can read between the lines that the liberal mindset of the French occupational powers under the leadership of the Governor of Erlach and the Governor d'Oysonville not only helped the new Jewish settlers plant roots but also

---

[94]City report from August 8, 1643

[95]City report from February 18, 1645

29

benefited them in other ways.[96] By decision of the city council on November 7, 1643, "Davidt the Jew" had to pay a punitory 10 crowns because he was said to have made a sale against commercial rules; but the Major General waived the fine, as the council report further indicates.[97] Councilman Engler was advised, according to a report from June 18, 1644, to settle within three weeks a debt of 28 doubloons owed to "Nathan the Jew," whom he had promised to pay on behalf of his brother.[98] This Nathan surely was the same as Nathan Ulmer (Ulmo), who had bought a house a year earlier in Breisach.

On August 27, 1644, a fight occurred in the hostelry "zum Löwen" between the house servant and "the Jew Nathan's boy." The boy had just been carrying a bowl of water and a (room) key in his hands, thus he was an overnight guest.[99] That Jews were resident in Breisach is certain from a decree of the Governor of Erlach, which was discussed in the council meeting of August 16, 1646. The "New Market," an illegal market event at the so-called fire mortar near Biesheim, was wholly forbidden; furthermore, von Erlach issued a ruling on the bridge toll: publicans at said place, as also the Jews here should pay the toll exactly as others, likewise the Jews and citizens of Markolsheim."[100]

If the French authorities had initially favored the resettlement of Jews in the fortress of Breisach, it appears that they later wanted to stop the influx. As the council report of August 16, 1646, indicates, Governor von Erlach ordered that one should "henceforth not let any more Jews in and the locals should refrain from all troublesome sales."[101] According to the report from September 19, 1646, he had the General Auditor explain to the council that "he is not against taking in new citizens, as many as one can have; yet those under protection in Breisach (without rights of citizenship) and without sufficient justification, particularly regarding religion: they are all to cease attempting (to acquire rights of citizenship), so that we can better proceed with our command and with the city."[102]

In the Winter of 1646/47 there were quarrels about ritual slaughter of livestock, and the council had to pass the following ordinance: "When the Jews want to slaughter, the butchers

---

[96]Johann Ludwig von Erlach, born in Bern October 30, 1595 and died in Breisach January 26, 1650, was appointed French Governor on October 6, 1639 and resided in Breisach Castle. Shortly before this, the victorious Captain Bernhard von Weimar, who had retained the wish to make the conquered Breisach a capital city of its own sovereign territory, had died.

[97]City report from November 7, 1643

[98]City report from June 18, 1644

[99]Haselier

[100]City report from August 16, 1646

[101]Haselier I, p. 388
In general, one took Jews who applied for admission as residents (without citizenship) because of the decrease of the population (city report 8/27/1646 and 3/24/1646 with lists of the accepted residents). As of January 1647, a foreigner could buy citizenship rights for just an additional 10 guilder in guild money dues.

[102]Haselier I, p. 388

should let the blood run dry, whether advisable or not; the Jews are to pay them an *Orthsthaler*, and as much to the city."[103]

In the same year, a female Jew was baptized.[104] A council report entry from July 16, 1648 says that the cattle of a Jewish owner were driven to pasture with the Breisach herd. The toll gate to Thann in the Upper Alsace gives not only one more hint that Jews were again resident in Breisach, but also evidence that they were partially earning a living in the area. "A Jew" from Breisach "on foot" paid a toll on July 1, 1647 in this Upper Alsatian village, and on December 12, 1647, Meyer Gintzburger from Breisach passed through the same toll.[105] A petition to become a protected citizen was defeated in 1648. The report from September 11, 1648, states: "Mame Ebstein the Jew requested protection. However, because Lord General Lieutenant von Erlach had long ago decreed that from that point on none more would be admitted, he and his wish were denied."[106]

Another picture from the final years of the war: In the last year of the war (1648), the commandant of the fortress at Breisach assigned the Jew, Mathias in Markolsheim, Alsace, the duty of buying cattle for the provisioning of French troops.[107] Mathias went on his way with the intention of purchasing cattle in the area of Waldstädte (Waldshut). "Arriving at the *Feuermörsel* (the fire mortar) of the city of Breisach" (in the area of Biesheim), he met a salesman traveling to his hometown Basel, with whom Mathias rode a stretch and to whom, as a precaution, he entrusted his money upon separating. Further on, the noble young Lady Masquin from the area of Weissenburg met him and told him, upon learning the purpose of his trip, that there were cattle with farmers in Hertingen (near Müllheim), which were, however, poorly tended and thus of negotiable price.

Mathias drove then over the Rhine and reported immediately to the chief bailiff in Rheinweiler, whom he did not find at home, however. Thereupon he bought the cattle in Hertingen under the condition that the animals be brought to him in the next Alsatian village. The priest, the bailiff, and other citizens were present at the transaction. The priest even posed the trustee of the cow.

On another day, Mathias traveled with the priest to Basel to pay him off the purchase price. After receiving the money, he assured "by priestly honor" to keep his word. When Mathias arrived at the appointed place, however, the cattle had not arrived. The saleswoman sent word to him that she had the cattle driven to Rheinweiler, but there the margravial governor seized them

---

[103]City report from January 26, 1647

[104]Zosa Szajkowski, *Franco-Judaica*; *Convertiten*, p 123 No. 1454: Daniel Rueker, *Christliche Judenpredigten* "Bey der Tauff einer geborenen Jüdin . . . stattgefunden am 30.5.1647 zu Brysach." (Christian Jewish prayer "At the Baptism of a Jewish-born female. . . took place on May 30, 1647 in Breisach.") Strassburg, 1647

[105]M. Ginsburger, *Wandernde Juden zur Zeit des Dreissigjährigen Krieges* (Wandering Jews at the time of the Thirty Years' War)

[106]Haselier I, p. 388 reports: The decree of Erlach was not against the admission of Jews particularly, but was mainly directed at protected relatives, whose number relative to the citizens had gotten large.

[107]Compare city report from February 16, 1648

because the buyer had invaded Baden without an escort and even stayed overnight. The governor reported the incident to the margravial government, which at that time was located in Basel. It ordered that the cattle be brought to Oetlingen (near Lörrach) and the governor should not have let the Jew walk but "taken him by the head, which is to be done in the future." Mathias reported the incident to his employer and stated that he did not do anything disorderly, much less commit an act of lèse majesté, of which he was accused, nor breach the escort rule, "which would never be held and accepted in this time of war, since one cannot protect the Jews with it, as in times of peace." He declared that he had relied upon the royal (French) protection that he had, with which he up to now had acted with safety in all places of the margravate for many years, and never has the same been expected of or desired by any Jew."

Mathias finally requested help from the commandant, either with the cattle or money, which would otherwise be impossible to acquire, or otherwise that he be compensated for damages.[108] He expressed the opinion that the margrave "should have no preference in the matter so that he might know the true nature of the affair."

The commandant then demanded the release of the cattle from the bailiff in Rheinweiler. The latter responded that he obstructed delivery to protect the interests of his farmers: they had kept the animals at great cost throughout the winter, only now to find them unjustifiably taken away when they, the farmers, hoped to benefit from them. "In order to acquire cattle, their lack of financial means aside," they had believed, "people knew that said cattle would stay and be left with them for the price at which the Jew purchased them. Incidentally, it was supposedly not the bailiff who ordered the seizure but the margrave, to whom the commandant might turn, which is what happened.

The margravial chancellery answered the commandant from Breisach: One does not want to assume that he desires to contest the right of the government to take away the cattle. However, one does not want to deprive him of the cattle, provided that he send the Jew to the chancellery so that one might compensate him. The documentary account ends with this. How the thing ended is not apparent.[109]

The best description of the cultural conditions of that time, Grimmelshausen's *Simplicissimus*, gives a true reflection of the physical and spiritual desperation of the long war as it came to an end, devastation that the author as a soldier saw with his own eyes. He also has Jews appear at several places in his novel and thereby elicits, with both poetry and truth, a gruesome image from the Breisach landscape: "As I looked around a little, I saw not far from us [in the Breisach area] a boy standing stock-still by a tree; I pointed this out to Olivier [the narrator's escort] and thought to tread carefully. "Ha, fool!" he answered. "It's a Jew who I've tied up; but the rascal however froze before long and croaked." And with that he went to him, knocked him under the chin, and said, "Ha, you dog, you also brought me many lovely ducats." And as he moved his chin in a particular way, some doubloons rolled out of his mouth, which the

---

[108]B. Rosenthal, *Heimatgesch.*, p. 88

[109]B. Rosenthal, *Heimatgesch.*, p. 88

poor rascal had carried away even into his death. Olivier grabbed him by the mouth and got out twelve doubloons and a precious ruby."[110]

In 1648, at the end of the Thirty Years' War, Breisach "finally" went to France. Governor Erlach, who had again accepted Jews during his twelve years in office, died on January 26, 1650. Thereafter, on 6 September 1650 the royal French government renewed the protection letters of Jewish fathers, specifically the following names: Gaiszmer (Geismar), Marc Schnattich (Schnaitach), David Gindzburger (Günzburger), Nathan Benedict, and Heium Wormbser (Wormser).[111]

Identical documents within the text convey that the occupants in Breisach could live there and act as other citizens. The toll officials were prohibited from demanding higher taxes than from other citizens; and thus was confirmed the permission to settle previously issued by the late General Erlach:[112] "After the production/presentation, it was authorized and confirmed to Gaiszmer the Jew, on the occasion of his humble application and confirmed: that, just as in times of the late Lord General Lieutenant von Erlach he remained in this city, within and outside it, free and unencumbered to move and act the same as other citizens, residents, and subjects;

therefore, from here on every man is made to know of such information, but especially all and those, as much in this city and fortress as other places in those lands belonging to our government where decreed tolls are commanded to hold said Jews and other citizens and subjects to the same toll and not to burden them with higher tolls. Breisach, 6 September 1650."

The Marquis de Tilladet, Erlach's successor in office since May, signed the writ of protection.

Beginning in 1650, multiple royal edicts were issued to expel the Jews.[113] This was also the case on 26 February 1651, when Ludwig XIV gave the following order: "Not wishing to suffer Jews to live in Breisach, no more than in other places of my kingdom, at present, as this city is united with my crown, I send you this letter to inform you. . . that I would consider it well for you to make those who are found there leave Breisach."[114]

The provincial governor was therefore supposed to drive all the Jews out of the city and its regions within a certain time to be determined by him. This terrible news surely moved the Breisach Jewry to look around for a new place to live. A passport originating from that time, issued on 3 March 1651 by the Royal Breisach Governor Marquis de Tilladet, authorized the Jew David N. (Guentzburger) the safe escort he had requested, and passage to Jechtingen for the period of one year for himself, his wife, and children.[115] In the margin of the same document, a

---

[110]Haselier I, p. 370, assumes that Grimmelshausen knew the events of that day from the third volume of "Theatrum Europaeum" and with poetic fantasy and license, wrote up the wartime experience.

[111]His son Alexander Doterle was born in Breisach, according to later sources, around 1644 and became a French army contractor.

[112]According to a notice in the District Archive Colmar (C 1082), the original was delivered to the Karlsruhe General Land Archive (Rep. Ensisheim, Convolut 25, Fasc. 345 Nr. 2).

[113]Rosmann-Ens, p. 425; B. Blumenkranz, *L'Histoire des Juifs en France*

[114]André Neher, *Principes et Applications de la politique de Louis XIV.*

[115]GLA Karlsruhe (Jechtingen lies 12 km north of Breisach)

postscript added by the Royal Lieutenant Charlevoix on 3 August 1651 confirms the passport's validity until its expiration.[116]

Ludwig XIV's command to expel the Jewish population from the city and province was not fully executed. A note of debt in favor of Jacques Geismar of Breisach, issued in 1652, demonstrates continued residence.[117] It concerns a horse transaction, in which the buyer died shortly afterward.

The city reports also testify to the presence of Jews in the years 1654–56 and royal writs of protection for Alsatian and Breisach Jews had piled up since 1657.[118] Reports from the city council indicate that Duke Mazarin had again pressed, by means of personal negotiations on 1 October 1671, for the expulsion of Jews, Lutherans, and Calvinists in the interests of maintaining purity of religion.[119]

As "Gouverneur d'Alsace," he commanded all Jews in Alsace to leave the province within three months. Again nothing drastic happened. The Breisach municipal authorities deployed, as it also happened in wider France, a delaying tactic and decided "unanimously" on the expulsion within two months, "but without prejudice of privilege, if it would serve Your Majesty's interests or the city's convenience to accept the same and to eject them as desired."[120]

A royal edict of 4 October 1671 finally countermanded the pursuit of expulsion for the whole province.[121]

The decision to tolerate Jews further likely had various origins. Payments of protection money provided a desired revenue source that one did not want to relinquish; and the Jews were needed as brokers for provisioning the army.[122]

By 1652 the French authorities had re-introduced the head tax (*peage corporel*). Two years later, Jews who had been subject to the crown of old Further Austria prior to 1648 were treated as "foreign" Jews who were permitted to pay this head tax over the course of three years.[123]

---

[116]Charlevoix had held office since 1645. Tilladet was driven out and replaced by Count d'Harcourt in August 1652. The latter was dismissed along with Charlevoix in 1654.

[117]District Archive Colmar, Records of the Conseil Souverain, Serie 1B

[118]Haselier I, p. 449 (Nach E. Scheid, *Histoire des Juifs de Haguenau*, REJ Vol. 8, p. 24 B. Some refugees from Poland came to Hagenau and settled in 1657 in surrounding places, e.g., in Batzendorf, Dauerndorf, and Wittenheim.)

[119]City Archive Breisach

[120]Haselier I, p. 450

[121]R. Reuss, L'Alsace zu XVII

[122]B. Blumenkranz, *L'histoire des Juifs en France,* p. 149

[123][French] "one treated as strangers the Jews of lands previously controlled, who left the province to do business. They had the capacity to pay the péage for three years." (Blumenkranz, p 149)

In 1672, the Breisach *intendant* Poncet de la Rivière introduced a protection payment of 6 ½ florins per family in all of Alsace, in addition to the 6 florins for the previous head tax and soccage tax that Jews had to turn over to local rulers.

The Breisach magistrate commanded on 20 August 1673 that "all the local Jews [contribute] two franks monthly for supplying" the French military: specifically, a contribution of wood and lights for the guard service, which was also demanded of newly settled French citizens.[124] The six family fathers residing in Breisach are named:[125] David Guenzburger, Alexander,[126] Lazarus, Salomon,[127] Marx,[128] and Alexander Doterle. Due to an ordinance of *intendant* La Grange, they had received in 1674—as in all of Alsace—the same privileges as the Jews in Metz.[129]

Various notaried documents and reports in Alsace provide further insight into the activities of individual Breisach Jews. David Guentzburger lived in Ensisheim in 1664[130], but some time prior to 1673 he moved back to his earlier place of residence, Breisach. In the course of resettlement policy of the time, the "populating" of the weakly settled city, even the seat of the "Conseil Provincial d'Alsace," the governing body since 1651 and the replacement for the one-time seat of government of old Further Austria, was moved from Ensisheim to Breisach in April 1674.[131]

The Council report of Sulz (Upper Alsace) of 9 January 1676 details that a Johannes Mueller, known by the name Johannes Aule, confessed to owing 300 *livres* for different articles to David Guenzburger of Ensisheim, now in Breisach, and his heirs.[132]

David Guenzburger was still living on 24 February 1688, as is attested by the Hebrew signature of his son Simon "Gintzbourgeois, Juif de La haute de Brisach," who together with Salomon Geismar signed a certificate of debt on this day in the Sulz notary office. He signed as "Schimon bar Jakob Ruben David. . . ," in other words, that his "father may live happy days." The aforementioned Johannes Aule and also Anna Maria Hoffek are again recorded by David Guenzburger as debtors in the 1676 document.[133]

---

[124]The fortress was besieged by the emperor for a time in 1673.

[125]Haselier I, p. 450

[126]Later the family with the surname Rieser appears.

[127]Salomon may have belonged to the Spirer or Geismar family

[128]Marx, and also Alexander Doterle, belong to the Wurmser family

[129]B. Blumenkranz, *Histoire d. Juifs,* p. 456

[130]District Archive Colmar, Kempf von Angreth Notary

[131]Haselier I

[132]M. Ginsburger, *Die Guenzburger im Elsass*

[133]Ginsburger, p. 7

Another debt certificate from 2 May 1688 was signed by Salomon Geismar with the Hebrew signature "Schlomo ben Pinchas" and Isaac "Quintzburger," both living in Breisach.[134] The latter is also named on 14 January 1688 in the records of the Milly notary and could be the same as a Geinsberg (Guenzberg) registered as the owner of a house in Breisach, according to a certificate of 31 January 1688 in the city archive.[135] The same Isak "Kuensbourger" signed a mortgage with Mathis Hanauer in the Ville Neuve de Brisac (New Village of Breisach) on 25 June 25 1688 and another with Jakob Foulhaber on 29 February 1694.

A dangerous rumor affecting the Jews in Breisach came about through the city commandant of Offenburg in 1676. He reported to the council there that the Offenburg Jews had conspired with those of French Breisach and would plan some act of treason with that city. He requested that the Offenburg council deport the Jews. A few days later, the "protected" Jews Salomon von Grafenhausen, Samuel von Rust, Hirsch-Levi von Kippenheim, and Jakob von Orschweier were subjected to interrogation. They affirmed that they did not associate with the Breisach Jews, indeed that they could not because the Breisach Jews allegedly ate pork and kept neither the Sabbath nor the laws....[136]

Margravial records mention another, previously undocumented Jewish merchant from Breisach: He was registered on 28 February 1680 as "Abraham, the Jew of Breisach," paying for safe conduct in Sulzburg.[137] Maybe he is the same as the "Jew of Breisach" registered again on 6 February 1681 in Sulzburg, who paid 6 crowns for body tax.[138]

Slowly the families multiplied. According to the reports of someone traveling through, there already existed in 1681 "a small, Jewish synagogue, where they could keep their rituals, thanks to a tribute that each family paid."[139] Alsatian memory books (*Memorbücher*) show that French Breisach was already the home of some rabbis of Upper Alsace by 1681.[140]

The Hagenau memory book names Rabbi Eisik Werd, son of Jakob Juda, as rabbi of Upper and Lower Alsace, and as having died on Monday, 29 Cheshvan 1675. According to an entry in the Niederehnheim memory book, he was "Aw Beth Din" in the holy communities of Breisach and Hochrhein. He was pious, modest, and always occupied with the Torah.[141]

---

[134]Personal communication v.S. Picard, Colmar from 9/1/1976

[135]Poisignon, Records of the Breisach City Archive

[136]Otto Kaehni, *Gesch. der Offenburger Judengemeinde* [Hist. of the Offenburg Jewish Community], p. 9, Sonderdruck from "Die Ortenau"

[137]Ludwig Kahn, "Über Wanderungen der Juden in Früheren Jahrhunderten" [About migrations of Jews in earlier centuries]. In *Jüd. Taschenkalendar* [Jew. Pocket Calendar] Basel 1959/60

[138]Ludwig Kahn. *Gesch. der Juden in Sulzburg* [Hist. of the Jews in Sulzburg]

[139]Haselier

[140]M. Ginzburger, *Les Memoriaux Alsaciens*, in REJ. Without indication of sources, Theodor K. Weiss (*Die Juden im Bistum Strassburg, in Alemania* [The Jews in Strassburg tower], Zeitschrift für Sprache, Kunst und Altertum, Bonn 1895, p. 108) writes: "The French King always had appointed a rabbi for all of Alsace since 1657."

[141]REJ. Vol. 41, 123

He is the same as R. Isaak Bisik ben Jehuda, who also held office in Metz as rabbi and mohel.[142] R. Jirmija ben Juda also held office as rabbi, with a seat in Vieux Breisach (Old Breisach) before 1681, but he was eternalized only in the Niederehnheim memory book.[143]

His simple grave in the Mackenheim old cemetery carries the following inscription: "Here was buried Gaon, the Aw bet Din, our teacher and rabbi Jeremia, son of R. Jehuda of blessed memory, on 14 Ellul 445 (Thursday, 13 September 1685)."[144]

The Niederehnheim (Niedernai) and Hagenau memory books record R. Simon Blum as rabbi in Breisach and Hochrhein.[145] We learn of his doings and his sphere of influence as mohel (circumciser) and rabbi in Upper Rhenish places from his little book written in Hebrew, which is now preserved in the Jewish National Library, Jerusalem. Rabbi Simon may have been born around 1640. He was still living in 1707. The picturesquely designed title page of his calendar calculations, as well as his drawings of the zodiac, show an artistic aptitude.

His 144 entries of circumcision of Upper Alsace, northwest Switzerland and French Breisach come from the years 1668 to 1690, the 14 marriage entries from the period 1672 to 1679. He calls himself Schimon, son of my lord father, Gaon Naftali Hirtz Blum, may he live to old age (1668). Gaon Blum died before 1683—a grandson, Naftali Hirtz, son of R. Simon, was named after him in this year.[146]

He is also named as a Breisach rabbi in an undated entry in the memory book from Endingen, Switzerland. Furthermore, R. Jirmija ben Juda, who had his seat in Breisach before 1681, also held office as a rabbi, but he was eternalized only in the Niederehnheim memory book.[147] At a request of the Jews of the provinces, Sr. De La Grange, intendant of Alsace, published a decree on 30 April 1685 to the effect that differences of whatever nature between Alsatian Jews should be settled by their rabbi.[148]

Did this perhaps refer to Rabbi Juda Loeb, son of R. Isack Mosche Neuburg from Worms? According to the Worms memory book he died on 9 Tamus 5451 (1691) in Breisach and

---

[142]His son R. Jakob ben Isaak Werth died 11 Siwan 1688, a daughter Sprinz 1712 and another daughter Lea on 15 Ellul 1721 (*Revue*, Vol. 41, 124)

[143]REJ, Vol. 41, 136

[144]Frdl. Personal communication from Günter Boll, Müllheim-Feldberg

[145]It is noteworthy that Simon Blum is already written in before the entry about R. Eisik Werd, who died in 1675, but in the Hagenau commemorative book Blum appears only after Werd. It concerns R. Simon Blum, whose son Naftali Hirsch Blum was rabbi in Uffholz and whose grandson Marx got married in Uffheim in 1753 (marriage contract in Colmar district archives).

[146]Naftali Hirtz Blum, son of the Rabbi Simon, later also became a rabbi and mohel, who further used his father Simon's little book for his numerous entries. Family names are missing still in these times. Naming of the places of residences and individual information about the entrants in connection with later documents, however, allow for the individual family names to be recognized.

[147]REJ. Vol 41

[148]M. Ginsburger, Samuel Levy, Rabbiner Financier, in REJ Vol. 67 (1914)

was also buried there.[149] The memory book from Aub dedicates the following entry to him: "Yehuda ben Isaak Neuburg from Worms; he occupied himself his whole life with Torah and good deeds, buried in Breisach."[150]

According to this foreign report, there was a very old grave site in Breisach, the location of which is no longer verifiable through documents.[151] However, it could have been a matter of a gravesite supposedly existing earlier on the northern slope of the lower Augustinerberg. In the garden that extends behind or between houses today, parallel to the much more deeply laid Judengasse (Rheintor), a few grave stones still stood at the time of the First World War as silent witnesses of previous centuries.

The reminiscences of different Breisach Jews point to "Rosenberger's Garden," with entrance left (west) of the residence at Augustinerberg 13 (according to statements from Erika Levi-Kleefeld, Theo Guenzburger, Bertold Blum, and Ludwig Dreyfus). According to Dreyfus, there were still a few stones, leaning against the terminal north wall that separated the Rosenbergers' garden from the strip of garden approximately two meters lower, belonging to the house of Rosel Geismar-Uffenheimer. According to statements of the former teacher and researcher Otto Geismar from Breisach, who died in London, a stretch of land would not have been planted in Rosel Geismar's garden, which extended east and had an "upper entrance" at the lower Augustinerberg (bigger gate with half-round arches), because it had previously been a cemetery. Willi Greilsamer, living today in Florida, claims that there was a way up to this gravesite laid on the hillside of Sternhof Alley, from the middle of Judengasse out through Bloch Rosel's deep garden on the steep south end.

Lothar Blum believes that the cemetery was laid behind the houses on the upper Sternhof Alley, consequently about 20 meters west of Rosenberger's Garden.

The "Ville Neuve de Brisach" (Strohstadt)

Rabbi Aaron Worms was the first officially recognized chief rabbi of Upper and Lower Alsace and was confirmed by the French government on 21 May 1681.[152] It emerges from the sources that this rabbi, born in Metz, was supposed to make his seat of office in the "Ville Neuve de

---

[149]Worms memory book, Berlin edition, p. 26

[150]Aub memory book, entry 101

[151]B. Rosenthal, *Heimatgeschichte der badischen Juden*, p. 186, and after that F. Hundsnurscher and Gerhard Taddey, *Die jüd. Gemeinden in Baden,* p. 51, report without sources a "cemetary laid out around 1550." Around this time no Jewish community in Breisach is documented. Only in the Thirty Years' War did the need arise for a burial place situated nearby. The report is in any case false when it says that it concerns the old cemetery lying directly behind the former synagogue, because this was originally established only after a 1755 treaty.

[152] *Encyclopedia Judaica*: "Das Judentum in Geschichte und Gegenwart" [Judaism in the Past and Present]. After that he was also named Rabbi Isak Aaron Worms, son of R. Joseph Israel from Worms, who in the Metzer memory book becomes known as scholar and good-deed-doer. R. Joseph Israel, son of pious R. Abraham Aberle Meir from Worms and relative of R. Chaim Bacharach in Coblenz was first rabbinate-assessor in Metz, then rabbi in Trier and Bingen am Rhine, where he died on 9 September 1684 (Roshashana).

Brisach" (Strohstadt), where the "Conseil Souverain d'Alsace" (Sovereign Council of Alsace) from Breisach had also moved in the same year.[153]

R. Aaron Worms was directed to take residence in the same quarter that was approved for new Jewish settlers in the newly built city.[154] Here in "Neuf Brisach en Alsace" (often confused with Neuf-Brisach, built only in 1700, which lies several kilometers to the southwest), the rabbi signed on Thursday, 11 Chestovan [5]442 (November 1681), an approbation for printing the book . . . (Mikur Chaim) by his relative R. Jair Chaim Bacharach (1638-1702)[155] and was called by this latter "Rabbi Aaron of Breisach." The words "Neuf-Brisach en Alsace" demonstrate that after his official appointment, R. Worms stayed some time there, where he practiced as chief rabbi of Upper Alsace.[156] The only surviving documentation of his activities in the Ville Neuve consists of a short, undated writing, according to which he was summoned before the court because he had "opposed" a woman.[157]

The still small Jewish community at that time combined with the lack of a synagogue (documented in the *Altstadt* only as early as 1681) may have moved the rabbi to transfer his seat of office there. According to the entry in the Niederehnheim memory book, he was "Aw Bet Din in the holy community of Breisach and Hochrhein. He was devout, modest, and always occupied with Tora."[158] His office in the mountain city did not last long, however; from 1685 to 1693 he was already active in Mannheim, where he issued another letter of approbation on 22 Adar II 5453.[159] When Mannheim was destroyed by fire, he found employment in his birthplace Metz and died there on 25 July 1722 (11 Aw 5482).[160]

According to the Metz memory book, he presided over different communities and provinces for over fifty years.[161] Thus, his first year in office was 1672. What then was the origin of the aforementioned Ville Neuve de Brisach, which became the new headquarters of the "Conseil Souverain d'Alsace" instead of Breisach; as well as the seat of administrative office for

---

[153]Haselier

[154]Contents of the sources in REJ VIII

[155]Chavoth Jair, p. 236

[156]Abr. Cahen, *Le Rabbinat de Metz 1567-1811*, p. 48-49

[157]Pers. communication from S. Picard, Departmental archives, Colmar, from 9/13/1973

[158]M. Ginsburger, *Les Memoriaux Alsaciens*

[159]Leopold Loewenstein, *Geschichte der Juden in der Kurpfalz* [History of the Jews in Kurpfalz], according to whose remarks, R. Aaron Worms would have also previously been a rabbi in Trier, from where he directed a ritual inquiry to R. Gerson Ashkenazi. (See *Legal Opinion* "Awodat Hagerschoni" Nr. 18.)

[160]According to David Kaufmann, *Le communeauté de Metz 1699-1702* in *REJ,* Vol. 19, p. 117-119, R. Aaron Worms was the most desirable candidate in a re-election for rabbi. When Rabbi Broda left Metz in 1712, the rabbi office stayed occupied four years and was in the meantime filled by two assessors, R.A. Worms and Benjamin Smigrod, until 1716.

[161]The Metz memory book names two sons of Aaron Worms (REJ). One daughter, Merle, who died on 10/4/1772 in Schwabbach, was the wife of Landesrabbiner Josua Heschel (1693-1771) in Schwabbach and Ausbach.

the Jews of Upper and Lower Alsace, assigned to R. Aaron Worms, first rabbi appointed by the French government? The village Biesheim on the left bank of the Rhine, which belonged to the city Breisach, had lain in ruins since 1638. The city itself situated on the right bank of the Rhine as well as its fortress, which was severely damaged in the Thirty Years' War, needed to be completely rebuilt. In order to complete the extensive "Vauban" fortress, straw-covered barracks were erected in the 70s outside the city, on a large island existing then between two arms of the Rhine, to house the countless functionaries, troops, and workers.[162] So originated the name "Ville de Paille" or "Strohstadt" (Straw Town).[163]

In the year 1680 various Jewish families were already living among the new population: a document conveys that in this year eight Jews were each in arrears in the protection payment of 10 florins.[164] Beyond this fine they still had to pay head tax in the amount of 2 to 10 livres, as well as other taxes, in order to go about their business. Around this time it was decided to reconstruct the barracks city as a modern residential city. Streets were built that led to a center with public buildings. In the court building next to the new mayor's office, the "Conseil Superieur et Souverain d'Alsace" moved its office from the *Altstadt* (18 June 1681). Only later was a synagogue built next to the Catholic Church.[165] Strohstadt, also known as Ville de Paille, assumed the new name "Ville-Neuve de Brisach."[166] There was a general concern to attract new settlers, who in 1683 had to promise to build a house within six months. The intendant requested that landowners build within four months, otherwise their land would be taken away as a rate of "15 sols la toise carree" or 15 sols per 1,949 meters square (1 toise = 1,949 meters). Jews dealt particularly in cattle and horses or worked as butchers. They enjoyed certain privileges: they were free of the obligations to quarter soldiers and help fortify the city, but they had to supply horses for royal service.[167]

When a cattle epidemic broke out in 1682, they had to slaughter their cattle under the supervision of the meat inspector in Jakob Levy's slaughterhouse. Of the 207 houses and barracks existing in 1685 there were fourteen Jewish property owners with about twenty households.

---

[162]The island lying on the left Rhine bank stretched a bit south across from the Rhine Gate, toward the Rhine to the "green Gießen" at that time, south of Biesheim. The St. Jakob entrenchment (Fort St. Jacques) lay on the left Rhine bank. The decorative Rhine Gate, laid on the old branch of the Rhine "Schwanen," was built already around 1670 as entrance to the Rhine bridge made of oak planks.

[163]At the highest point of Strohstadt as of 1680 the Breisach mayor and council were subordinate to the provost (Haselier). In 1685 the new town became independent.

[164]Document in Colmar District Archive (Personal communication Mr. S. Picard, Colmar)

[165]In his travel report of 1681, Louis de L'Hermine does not yet tell of this synagogue, just of a small synagogue that he saw in this year in the *Altstadt* (Haselier I, p. 449) (Louis de L'Hermine, *Memoirs de deux voyage et séjours en Alsace 1674-1776, 1684*...published by E. Meininger (1868) reports of a village of barracks in 1674/75, in 1681 of a solidly built city; Haselier)

[166]The original name "Ville de Paille" is specified as a birthplace of some Jews later living in Wintzenheim.

[167]Personal communication of S. Picard, Colmar

The records also report on dissensions in the Breisach suburbs.[168] The priest brought a charge against the proprietor of the inn "Zum goldenen Löwen" (Golden Lion) in 1685 because he had allowed the Jews to dance during Lent. Another complaint was lodged against a butcher who slaughtered cattle and sold meat during the first weeks of fasting without permission. In the same year, a punishment was inflicted on the four Jewish butchers Wolf Bloch, Jacob Levy, Witwe Mathis, and Jacob Wormser[169] by the "controleur des poids" (weight inspector), a punishment that occurred less frequently in the case of Christian butchers who committed the same delinquencies. In 1688 Jewish butchers no longer undertook to slaughter animals themselves; according to a Breisach enactment, it was arranged that two Christian butchers were to deliver good meat for six rappen per pound, which was then sold for eight rappen.

By 1687, twenty-four Jewish families lived in the Ville Neuve de Breisach. Cattle and horse traders were at that time accused by farmers, originally from neighboring Biesheim, of allowing their herds to graze in larger numbers in the "Ried" communal pasture. The judgment determined that the meadow could forthwith be used for cows but not for horses. An undated list (ca. 1690) detailing "what each should give to the royal service in terms of horses," it is stipulates that the twenty-seven Jewish households of that time were required to give thirty-eight horses.[170] The countless Jewish inhabitants of the Ville Neuve now harbored the wish to build an independent community. On 30 June 1692, twenty-three heads of families chose three representatives: Wolf Block, Isaac Netter, and Meyer Raby. They had a yearly sum of 50 livres to dispose of at their discretion. This amount, raised by contributions of community members in accordance with their abilities, could be exceeded only consent of four additional members, specifically: Jakob Heymann (Wormser), Jakob Levy (Markolsheimer), Salomon Spirer (from Speyer) and Samuel Metz. The three "Chefs de la communeauté" (bosses of the community) were also authorized to excommunicate a member if need be; the excommunicant, however could, be appeal to the rabbi in Breisach.[171] The document concerning this vote on 30 June 1692, written in German as well as in French, bears the following twenty-three signatures:

Isaac Netter, Jacob Levy, Jakob Heymann, Borrach, Salomon Spirer, Meyer Moutzig,[172] Samuel Werth, Wolf Bloch le vieu, Abraham Raphael, Abraham Bloch, Salomon Guelb, Aaron Gueismar,

---

[168]Wolf Blochalt and Jacob Levy came from Markolsheim. Mathis lived in House No. 193 of Ville Neuve. Jacob Wormser came from the Breisach *Altstadt*, where his brother Alexander Doterle was still living at the time and as horse handlers supplied the royal army.

[169]M. Ginsburger [in French]: We undersigned confess and make known that we have chosen and elected as our superiors, Wolf Bloch, Isaak Nettre, and Meyer Raby, to whom we gave power to dispose annually of the sum of 50 livres tournois to that sum each of the community will have to contribute following and in proportion with their capacity. And the three aforementioned elected will not be obliged to account for . . .
Completed at the UN de Brisac 30 June 8012. Signed . . ."

[170]In 1689 not more than 522 Jewish families lived in all of Alsace (M. Ginsburger).

[171]The report written below in German expressly names the "Rabi of Breisach;" the one in French the "Rabis" only as an instance of appeal.

[172]The one who signed only as Meyer Moutzig is identical to Meyer Raby, the new representation of the Ville Neuve Community, who is observed as a rabbi only this one time during this election. For this reason, M. Ginsburger ventured to report in *Monatsschrift f. die Gesch. u. Wissenschaft des Judentums*: "Only on 30 June 1693 (!) did the

Susmenlé, Adam Levy, Judas Bloch, Wolf Levy, David Bloch, Wolf Bloch le jeune, Meyer Senné, Marx Wormser, Hirtz Jud, Hirtz Levy, and Goetschel Levy.

In an appeal from 8 July 1692, Wolf Bloch, Isaac Nettr, and Meyerlé explained to Bailiff Scherer of the Ville Neuve that the Jewish inhabitants in this same place would have proliferated and carried on commerce in a short time.[173] They had to sometimes deliver horses and other things for the King's service but had not yet had any authorities to advocate for them in the court if necessary, to enforce regulations, or to provide judgment according to their laws in cases of possible discord within the community. Wolf Bloch, Isaac Nettr and Meyerlé, all three of whom lived in the Ville Neuve, now claimed to have been elected "chefs et superieurs" (bosses and superiors) by majority decision. At the end of the petition, the undersigned Meyer requests of the bailiff that he confirm him as community leader. On the same day (8 July 1692) Bailiff Scherer of the Ville Neuve recognized all three of the elected officials as community leaders.[174] There is no indication, however, that Meyerlé Moutzig was appointed rabbi.

1693 saw the composition of a text titled "Specification deren Juden so wie unter Ihre aller christlichen Königlichen Majestät Schirm in der Newstadt Breysach sich auf halten tundt" (Specifications for those Jews residing in the Ville Neuve de Brisach under the protection of Your Most Christian Royal Majesty).[175] Among the thirty-three names included, one can often

---

Alsatian Jewry elect a new rabbi in the person of Meyer Moutzig, who lived in Ville Neuve" (Ginsburger also writes: "After R. Ahron Worms, appointed in 1681, was working already in 1684 in Mannheim, a rabbi for Alsace appears in this time period who was not appointed by the government, maybe because Ahron Worms had not filed his resignation.")
M. Ginsburger, in the article "Samuel Levy, Rabbin et Financier," REJ Vol. 65, p. 275, reports again in French that Meyer Moutzig on 30 June 1693 was elected and indeed by the Jews of Upper Alsace, but in no way confirmed in this office by the government (Meyer Moutzig is the ancestor of the Carmoly family, which should derive its name from Colmar).

[173]REJ, Vol. 66, p. 124 [in French]: "To the Royal Bailiff of the ville neuve de Brisach. Humbly beseeching Wolf Bloch, Isaak Nettr and Meyerlé humbly beseech you, all three Jews living in this Ville Neuve, saying that their nation has recently grown after little time to a large number of families. Those aspiring and trading one like the next as best one can and like their community, which is sometimes charged with supplying horses and other things for the service of His Majesty, but there hasn't again been one boss or superior among them to regulate all that which could be imposed upon them by the justices and to have executed the ordinances as well as to render a decision regarding the differences that could occur within their said community by reason of their law; to this end, the said community.
. .
With regard to the gentleman in question and the information given above, may it please you to receive this suppliant for the boss and superior of the Jewish community concerning the things said here and without prejudice of all authority. From 8 July 1692 Meyer."

[174]REJ, 124 (Archive Dep. Colmar, Neuf Brisach Office of Notary [in French]: "Regarding the request presented by Wolf Bloch, Isaac Netter and Meyer Moutzig, all three Jews of Ville Neuve, report that, by the act of last June 30, they were chosen by the plurality of Jews of that village for their chief to receive and for the service of the king and for the good of the public and also to lead in the synagogue for the ceremonial festivals of their laws concluding . . . to the reason the said request signed by Meyer the said act of June 30 signed Isaac Netter, Jacob Levy, Jacob Heymann Borach, Salomon Spirer, etc. . ., we have accepted the aforementioned Bloch, Isaac Netter and Meyer Moutzig as chiefs of the aforementioned Jews to preside in the synagogue over the ordinary ceremonies of their laws. . .
Ville Neuve de Brisach 8 July 1692 – Scherer"

[175]It is self-evident that in the period 1670-1700, a back and forth of Jews between the new city and the old Breisach city was occurring due to familial but also business reasons.

clearly recognize places of ancestry like Altstadt Breisach, Markolsheim (Bloch), Bergheim, Riedwihr, Sennheim, Kippenheim, Öttingen, and Ettenheim.

By 1695, when the whole island city had become independent, the Jewish community numbered forty-four heads of household, including two "maitres d'ecole" (elementary schoolteachers) and two people who gave lessons in their house in addition to other income. Keeping domestic servants ("domestiques") required another particular tax: a livre for each female employee or servant ("Valet").[176]

Salomon Levy	30	Wolf Bloch	6
Wolf Bloch	30	Porack	5
Marx Wormzer	30	Samson Levy	5
Scheyele Wesch	30	Judas Bloch	10
Hirtz Levy	20	Marx le jeune	3
Samuel Edinger	10	Hirtz de Riedwihr	5
Guetz Levy	15	Isaak Katz	8
Heymand Bloch	15	Isaak le jeune	5
Komprere Mausse	12	Heymand Wormzer	5
Joseph Kleinsamer	12	Lanzemandel?	1
Jaquelet Spirer	10	Hirtz de Kepenheim[177]	2
Wolf Levy	10	Salomon le jeune	-
David Bloch	10	Samuel Vert	6
Jacquelet Levy	10	Abraham Rafflei	2
Isack son of Alexandre	10	Feiss de Heiteren	5
Abraham Levy	10	Isaack Mayerlet	2
Emanuel Levy	10	Abraham Bloch	6
Meyerlet de Heiteren	10	Samuel Schwobbe	1
Jocholle	10	Abraham Kann ("the big	6

---

[176]For 32 Jews in 1695 the head tax came to a higher amount than for the Christian residents. Thus 4 Jews each paid an amount of 30 livres, 5 others 20 livres, 23 each 6 livres. In comparison, the tax collectors or the "fondeur" were exacted only 30 livres each, the artisans in fact only 6 livres. Bakers, business owners, small tradesmen and artisans were taxed with one or two livre respectively.

[177]Hirtz ben Schlomo Kippenheim was according to a circumcision entry by R. Simon Blum on 21 Ellul 1671 of Sandig bei Abraham, little son of Ischay in Bollwiller (Ischay = brother-in-law of Hirtz)

		Jew")	
Widow de Salomon Spirer	5	David Isaack the doctor	6
Samuel Rizer	5	Abraham Katz	6
Meyerlet	5	Aaron Levy	6
Jacquelet Kainn	8	Aaron Keismar	6

In 1695, the Breisach *Altstad* was named in documents as the seat of the *Landrabbiner* [or *Landesrabbiner*, Ger. or Yidd.; *rav medinah, av bet din*, Heb. This is a locally elected rabbinical official mainly in charge of facilitating tax collection], Arie Juda Loeb Teomim, also called Loeb Schnapper. The community leader of that vicinity and the Ab Beth Din (*Landrabbiner*) Arie Juda Loeb Teomim met each other in Cheshvan 1695 at a meeting in Blozheim regarding the Hegenheimer cemetery, which was established in 1673: Teomim was the descendant of R. Aron Worms, the first to be entrusted with this office by the French government.[178] Both had their seats of office in Breisach. Teomim both wrote the report of that meeting—which makes it particularly valuable—and also certified the three written decisions with his signature. He signed (in translation): "Thus spoke the little A.J.L. Th. Rabbi with his seat in the holy Breisach community and vicinity at the present time" (L'eth ato)[179] . . . .

It may be assumed without further consideration, writes Nordmann, that Teomim was touring as *Landesrabbi* and thus, as with others occupying this position, attended the meeting and wrote the report. For his troubles, the "Raf" was paid a royal thaler, two trente-sous, and a dinar.

Loeb Teomim was a kind of itinerant rabbi, who also went to Endingen and Lengnau in the Surbtal and therefore assumed the title of Swiss rabbi.[180] On 23 June 1697 "the mayor and the magistrates of the old, fortified city of Breisach" gave the rabbi (his name is not mentioned) an attestation in French.[181] According to this document, Jews had been living in the city "since inconceivable times," having their rabbi with royal permission, for themselves as well as for all fellow believers in the province. The last one approved had already lived over three years there. He had constantly mediated quarrels among Jews, especially in regard to synagogue and religion, in the rest of Alsace as well, and such matters are handled in the city of Metz. The Breisach magistrate had until that time foresworn to intervene in their privileges. They paid for the right of protection from the king and the lords of the region where they lived. This document bearing the city seal was signed by the court clerk Brunk on 23 June 1697. Only a copy of the original manuscript, certified by him two days later on 25 June and further endorsed by the Breisach Commandant Chetardaé, has been preserved; its text is as follows:

---

[178]Dr. med. Achilles Nordmann, Der israelitische Friedhof in Hegenheim [The Israeli Cemetery in Hegenheim], Basel 1910

[179]M. Liber in REJ (1914) p. 282 reviews the book of Dr. A. Nordmann and observes of this expression L'eth ato, p. 105: Arie Juda Loeb Teomim signs apparently as a provisional rabbi.

[180]M. Ginsburger, Memoriaux

[181]Breisach City Archive

"We the mayors and magistrates of the ancient and fortified city of Breisach certify that since time immemorial Jews have been established in this city; that they have their rabbi by permission of the king as much for themselves as for all the Jews of the province; that the most recent rabbi was received in this city three years ago; that the said rabbi has at all times settled the differences among the Jews particularly concerning the ceremonies and the discipline of their religion as is observed in the city of Metz and likewise in all the rest of the province of Alsace of those affairs. The said magistrate of Breisach has never claimed to acknowledge any prejudice of their privileges, which they have maintained until the present by paying for the right of protection that they owe to His Majesty, and by payment to the particular lords of their places of residence. In fidelity to this, we have had the ordinary seal of this city affixed to the present documents and had them signed by our usual court clerk. Done in Breisach this 23 June 1697. Signed Brunck and to the side is written "ceque dessus contient voite la Chetardac, Commander of Breisach."

Sealed with the arms of the said city, collation on the original subsigned by me, royal notary established in the city of Breisach, subsigned and here found to be in order, done in the said Breisach this 25 June 1697, initialed by Brunk"

The magistrate's attestation proves that the last appointed rabbi had lived in the Breisach *Altstadt* since early 1694, thus not in the Ville Neuve; and that, according to the Blozheimer reports of 1695, this was the well-known Rabbi Arieh Loew Teomim.

His jurisdiction extended to Breisach and the Alsatian province.

According to an edict from intendant de la Grange, dated 17 June 1694, all Jews living in Lower Alsace were prohibited from requesting the services of any rabbi other than the one appointed by the Upper Alsatian religious community for the mediation of potential discord, as was done in Metz.[182] That the authorized rabbi had his position in Breisach also resulted from a dispute in which he granted a foreign teacher by the name of Moses permission to give lessons in the Ville Neuve and forbade Aron Levy, who lived there, from giving religious instruction, and also excommunicated him and his family.[183]

Levy complained to Bailiff Scherer in the Ville Neuve, who decided in his favor. Antagonized by that, the rabbi and a community delegation appealed to the intendant, arguing that, in accordance with various ordinances, only the rabbi himself had the right to speak among the Jews.[184] It appears that the aforementioned testament, issued on 23 June 1697 by the Breisach magistrate, was used as additional proof for the complaint.[185]

---

[182]REJ Vo. 67, p. 85 [in French]: " . . . by which it is forbidden to all Jews established in all the places of Lower Alsace generally to make use of another rabbi than that already established in Breisach by the Jews of Upper Alsace to regulate and end differences that survive between them the same as is practiced in Metz.

[183]M. Ginsburger, "Samuel Levy, ein Stiefsohn der Glueckel von Hameln," [Samuel Levy, a Stepson of Glueckel von Hameln] in *Monatsschrift für Geschichte u. Wissenschaft des Judentums*; Ville Neuf de Brisach is translated falsely as Neu-Breisach. The Neubreisach (Neuf Brisach) today developed first only in 1697. The report of the case written in French in REJ, Vol. 65, p. 275.

[184]Decree of 4/30/1685 and 6/17/1694

[185]Doubtless the manuscript of the attestat with signature no. 1833 is organized in the Breisach city archive by documents from 1753 as required evidence, that Jewry could have some control over its own matters and the magistrate could not force a parnus on it.

Aaron Levy appealed to the King's procurator Scheppelin in Breisach on 23 September 1697 and requested permission to give lessons.[186]

The petitioner claimed that he had already lived for four or five years in Ville Neuve de Brisac, pursuing his business and mainly teaching youth, whereas now the rabbi of the "ville haute" had forbidden the Jews from sending their children to him for instruction and furthermore had allowed a foreigner to teach the youth.

On the same day, Scheppelin requested that the Breisach rabbi respond to Aaron Levy's grievance within three days. After a hearing of the two parties, it was decided that permission to teach would be granted to Aaron Levi in consideration of the protection money he had paid. The foreign Jew would be permitted to stay further in Breisach if he paid protection money, but he could also be free of that obligation if he were employed by any individual Jews as a paid "Domestique."[187]

An imperial decision on 8 January 1698 concerning the initial complaint directed at Bailiff Scherer determined that he alone and not the rabbi was authorized to pass sentence on disputes among Jews. Around this time, Rabbi Arie Loeb Teomim may have ended his term in Breisach. His name is not mentioned in any Alsatian memory book.[188] He held office in Trier intermittently and published the first two writings (Deraschot) of his father R. Aaron Teomim in 1710.[189] After acting as dajan (assessor of the rabbinate) in Frankfurt am Main, he appeared again as rabbi in Bingen and died on 3 Ijar 1717 in Frankfurt.[190]

The Breisach Community in the 18th Century

After Breisach was again allotted to Austria in the peace treaty of Ryswick on October 30, 1697, all inhabitants were free to resettle on French ground. All had the right to leave the city, with their portable goods, within a year to go somewhere else as they wished, without payment of the usual emigration tax. Residents could either dispose of their land or keep it and hire someone

---

[186]REJ, Vol. 66, p. 125, *Pieces Justificatives* [in French]:
"To Mr. Scheppelin Councilor Proctor General of the King and subdelegate to the intendant of Alsace. Aaron Levy, 4 or 5 years in the Ville Neuve de Brisack, humbly requests . . . however, the rabbi of the upper city received a stranger. Regarding the gentleman in question, and given the information above, may it please you to permit the supplicant to instruct the children of the Jews.
Let the present request be communicated and let the rabbi respond to it in three days. Done in Breisach 23 September 1677 I am transported to the rabbi's home . . . (etc.) . . ."
Done in Breisach 23 September 1677

[187]*Monatsschrift*, p. 490

[188]M. Ginsburger, *Les Memoriaux Alsaciens*, REJ 41

[189]L. Loewenstein, *Gesch. d. Juden in Kurpfalz*, p. 139. After that his father Aaron Teomim was rabbi in Prague and Worms and was murdered in Krakow in 1691 as preacher—Loeb Teomim's son Aaron held office as rabbi in Bingen from 1721 to 1765.

[190]Magazin XIII, 61

else to manage it.[191] Among those who chose that part of Alsace remaining French, there were Jews and non-Jews.[192] Breisach again became Austrian on 11 April 1700. The city received the designation "Old Breisach." In the Jewish-German dialect appeared the expression *Alt-Maukem* (old place); one spoke more commonly of *Alt Bressisch*.

The fate of the island city Ville Neuve de Breisach was also sealed in the peace treaty: it was to be razed completely. The general population also had the option of resettlement in the French fortress Neubreisach (Neuf Brisach), which had stood since 1700—but, in a diplomatic fashion, the Jews were to be denied entry into the newly-built city. On 13 June 1700 La Houssaye wrote that it was not the intention of the king to admit a Jew into Neubreisach, one should shut them out under any pretext without exciting much spectacle ("... les en exclure sous quelque pretexte sans faire trop d'eclat.").[193]

The new political situation effectively instigated a partial withdrawal and thus a diminishing of the Jewish community of old Breisach and the complete dissolution of the considerably enlarged community of the Ville Neuve suburb. The numerous resettlers from both banks of the Rhine mostly found a new home in neighboring Alsatian locales. No more Jews are documented in the margravial uplands bordering Breisach around 1700. As a result of war, and especially after the French invasion of 1689, they were also exiled also from other regions on the right bank of the Rhine.[194] It remains unclear whether those families with the name Preisach who lived in Metz in 1739 descended from emigrants of this period.

On 16 November 1700 the Upper and Lower Alsatian Jews elected their new rabbi, Samuel Levy, son of Cerf (Hirsch) from Metz, at the residence of Alexander Doterle in Colmar.[195] On 20 January 1702 he was confirmed by a royal decree as religious leader of the Upper and Lower[196] Alsatian Jews, in place of (important because of the occupation of the Breisach rabbinate) and under the same conditions as Aron Worms, who resigned.[197] Thus, it is

---

[191]Haselier I, p. 474

[192]Joh. Scheppelin and a second mayor moved to Colmar (Haselier), Official Scherer from the Ville Neuve after Neufbrisach

[193]Colmar District Archive

[194]B. Rosenthal, *Heimatgeschichte*

[195]Samuel Levy was born in 1678 in Metz. He studied there and in Poland (M. Ginsburger, "Samuel Levy, ein Stiefsohn der Glueckel," in *Monatsschrift f. Gesch*). His wife Genendele bore him the sons Meir and Abraham, and also two daughters (*Revue* Vol. 65). Genendele was the daughter of Abraham Schwab-Grumbach, who died in Metz in 1704. The latter was the son of the influential Meier Abraham Schwab (who died in 1688), who led the Geschicke of the Metz community for 30 years. Abraham himself had eight children with his wife Jachet Gomperz from Cleve, who died in 1709. Rabbi Samuel Levy married into the family of the famous Glueckel von Hameln." He was her stepson.

[196]Revue, Vol 44, p. 105

[197]Revue 65, p. 276
Revue Vol. 66, p. 267 brings pieces of evidence: "The Jews residing in our province of Alsace have represented to us that after the dismissal of Aaron Worms their last rabbi elected Samuel Levy to take his place, etc. 1/20/1702."

clear that no rabbi was confirmed during the period from the expulsion of Aron Worms through the confirmation of Samuel Levy in 1702.

At the time the census of Jews in Metz on 14 August 1739, there were thirteen families with the surname Brisach, which could refer to their place of origin.[198]

Bernard Brisach, wife, 2 children, 2 dependents

Boruch ben Schlome Preisach

The wife of Aron Brisach (Scheinele bas Abraham Nordon)

Ephraim de Brisac, resident, wife, child

Widow of Salomon Brisac "owner"

(Schlomo b. Jakob Koppel Breisach, died 1731)

Moyse Brisach and his wife, 4 children (Mosche ben Nesanel)

Samuel Brisach (resident), wife, 2 children, one servant

Marx Brisac and wife (Mordechai bar Mosche Breisach)

Samuel Brisach or charé (resident), wife, 2 children (Samuel b. Gedalja ...)

Cerf Brisac or Ennesem (owner) (Ensisheim) and wife

Moyse Brisach with wife

Abraham Brisach with wife, 4 children (Abraham ben Meier Breisach, died 1775)

Widow of Mose Cahen, daughter of Moyse Brisach (Mosche Izchak ben Josef Jakauf), died 1739

Lazare Brisach and wife, 1 child (the old Elieser (Liebermann) ben Meier Breisach, died 18 Adar 1, 1764)

Widow of Josef Brisach, with a child, Josel (Josef) ben Elieser (Lipmann) Breisach (Josel died 2nd Passover Day, 1737)

Salomon Brisach, wife, 4 children (Schlome Salmon b. Josef (Josel) Breisach, died 3 Tamus 1741)

Lazarus Brisach, wife, 2 children, servants (Liebermann ben Josel) Breisach, died 1776 (?)

Raphael Brisac, widower, four children

David Brisach, wife, 1 child, servants

Abraham Brisach and wife.

Jewish families also moved to nearby Biesheim, to which already after 1700 farmers had already returned after 1700 from the vanished Strohstadt in order to rebuild the village that lain dormant

---

[198]From: *Revue des étude juives*

since 1638.[199] According to documents of the Neufbrisach notary (Colmar district archive), the following settlers[200] could be found in Biesheim from 1701 to 1707:

Judas Bloch ben Benjamin

David Bloch ben Jakob

Jakob Salomon (aka Joel bar Jekutiel or Jacques Salomon; he was still living in Strohstadt on 15 March 1700)

Jonas Cerf

Isaac Katz

Fasy (Uri-Feiss) Bloch (?) ben Jakob Benjamim

Isaac Kinsburg (residing in Biesheim in 1702, in Altbreisach in 1707)

Joseph Kreilsamer (Kresemer); Hebrew: Josi Joseph ben Leime hakohen[201]

Samuel Werth, in 1702 in Biesheim (previously Ville Neuve)

Wolff Bloch

Judel Bloch ben Jakob

Elias Bloch ben Jakob (later in Müllheim?)

Joseph Kreilsamer (aka Joseph ben Abraham Hakohen)

Isaac Scheillet (aka Jzchok ben Jeschaya)

According to Picard: Scheyele Wesch, Ribeauville, partner of Josef Greilsamer)

Samuel Kinsburg (named in the Quartier St. Jacques in Strohstadt in 1702)

One of the best-known Breisach personalities in the 17th century was Alexander Doterle, who had made his name through his extensive horse trade and as significant supplier to the French army. As is indicated in a record issued by the magistrate of the "Ancienne Ville de Brisach" (Ancient City of Breisach), he was born in French Breisach around 1644. His father Heymann (Chaim) Wormbser already lived there during the time of General von Erlach and, like his grandfather Marx Wormbser, also died in this city.[202] Some of Alexander Doterle's contracts demonstrate his trade with butchers and "captains" of troops in Breisach. One of his aristocratic debtors was the squire Louis Zorn de Bulach, Seigneur d'Osthouse.[203]

---

[199]Biesheim was still in Breisach City's possession. A synagogue erected later in Biesheim was "demolished" on higher order in 1726 because it was built without permission. (Breisach City Archive)

[200]Personal communication from Sal. Picard, Colmar 5/8/1973

[201]Joseph Kreilsamer-Katz led a trial against business owner Scheyele Wesch in Biesheim in 1702, who moved out of Ville Neuve and into Rappoltsweiler.

[202]Municipal Archives of Colmar

[203]Milly Notaryship, Colmar District Archives, Contract 12/14/1680; more delivery contacts of Alexander Doterle in this Notarybestand in 1682, 1683, 1687, and 1688.

As with others of the Jewish faith, the content of obligations issued in Doterle's favor is briefly summarized on the back side in Hebrew cursive but without the usual signature. In an petition of 6 December 1693 to the intendant de la Grange, the horse dealers Alexander Doterle and Isak Netter of Breisach complained because they had to quarter "military and horses," which contravened the legal agreement.[204]

Because the Breisach Altstadt was allotted to Austria in 1697, the supplier to the French army was understandably compelled to leave the city and establish himself on French soil. He was the first Jew since 1510, whom the city of Colmar permitted (on 22 February 1698) to live within its walls, likely at the request of the Marquis de Huxelles, who referred to Alexander Doterle's services performed for the benefit of the king.[205]

With his change of residence, he also altered his official signature from "Toderus Breisach" to "Toderus Breisach me-Colmar." He first rented a residence in the center of Colmar on Schlüsselgasse (Rue des Clefs), where subsequently many decisions were made regarding Jewish matters in the neighborhood. He bought a property with horse stable and yard for his extensive business.[206] In his house lived not only his immediate family but also his "domestics." Among the servants might also have been included his two brothers Marx and Jakob Wormbser and their dependents, who likewise re-settled in Colmar.[207]

Alexander Doterle lived with his son Wolf Alexander, born in Breisach, first named at the beginning of the 18th century and still living in Colmar in 1707.[208] He was married to Rosine, the daughter of the district representative Jaekle Reinau in Rappoltsweiler.[209] After the death of Jaekle in 1698, Alexander Doterle supposedly hoped that the honorary office of district representative would pass to him, but Count von Rappoltstein named Baruch Weil from Westhofen, with whom he had close business relations, as district representative.[210]

Consequently, jealously erupted and the army supplier tried to bring all possible means and his influence to bear in order to cause trouble for the count and the representative he had

---

[204]Colmar District Archive

[205]Colmar City Archive, *Communes et Convents* 1696-1701 (". . . obliged to retire from the City (Brisac) and establish ailleurs of under the domination of the king of the agreement of puissance of the province. He received the authorization to reside in Colmar by the Colmar municipality on the instance of Marquis de Huxelles for services used coming to the king.
Date 2/22/1698")

[206]Communes et Convents (Sale of the 1705 Liegenschftern on 5/5/1712 through three brother as co-heirs to Alexander Doterle).

[207]Colmar City Archive

[208]He died, like all of his siblings, before his father.

[209]Rosine Hirtz, widow of Wolf Alexander from Colmar and sister of Kumprecht and Isak Hirtz in Rappoltsweiler was married a second time, to Liebmann Weil von Westhoffen, living in Straßburg on 7/3/1710.

[210]Colmar District Archive: " . . . Birkenfeld stated that Count Ribeaupierre had always allowed the Jews to determine their own representative in Rappoltsweiler District. The last who was thus appointed was the aforementioned Jaekle, whose daughter had married the son of Alexander Doterle."

appointed. The count maintained that it was Alexander Doterle who had incited the Upper Alsatian Jews to complain to the king.[211] The result was that Baruch lost his title as district representative, by ordinance issued to him on 22 May 1700, a decision in which the Rappotsweiler community elders Jaekel "the Long" and Aron Honel were also in agreement. The latter became father-in-law to Lehmann Guenzburger of Breisach three years later.

An extensive appeal by the Count von Rappoltstein remained ineffective, and the refusal by supporters of Baruch Wiel to profess obedience to a new rabbi by the name of Samuel Levy and the now appointed representative Alex Doterle, ended on 12 August 1700 with an ordinance from the intendant Le Pelletier de Houssaye, according to which all decisions of this rabbi and the representative concerning matters in the Jewish community were to be followed.[212] With that, the influential Alexander Doterle was victorious.

At his residence in Colmar, delegates of the Alsatian Jewry decided on 16 November 1700 to appeal to the king to confirm Rabbi Samuel Levy from Metz, chosen by the Jews of Upper and Lower Alsace.[213] Among the signatures are many earlier residents of Breisach and its short-lived suburb:

Alexander Doterle from Colmar (previously Breisach), Aaron Weil (from Rappoltsweiler), Meyer Lazare (surely Meyer Mutzig, who at that time still lived in Ville Neufe [sic] or Biesheim), Abraham Raphael (from Ville Neufe or Biesheim), Samuel Verd (from Ville Neuve), Jacques Vayant (the same as Jakob Heymann Wormbser from Breisach), Raphael Moyses (from Bergheim), Mendle Bloch (surely from Sulz), Jacques Goetschel (from Rappoltsweiler), Jude Merx,

Jesaye Lazare, Lazare Moyse, Elkan Salomon, Aaron Moyses, Joel Salomon,[214] Benjamin Nathan, Jude Jacques, Lazare Kohen, Moyse Meyer, Jacques Lazare, Samson Lehmann Koheim, and Isak Koheim.

In an imperial decree of 20 January 1702, the petitioners were allowed to appoint their chosen Rabbi Samuel Levy in place of the previous rabbi, Ahron Worms, who had resigned.[215] Soon after the death of Alexander Doterle, the city of Colmar requested in August 1709 that his brothers Marx and Jacques Wormbser and their large families, who lived with him as "domestics," as well as all other Jewish residents, had to leave the city within a month's time, with the justification that the privilege of 28 February 1698 was granted only to the army

---

[211]M. Ginsburger, "Samuel Levy, ein Stiefsohn der Glueckel von Hameln," [Samuel Levy, a Stepson of Glueckel von Hameln] in *Monatsschrift für Geschichte u. Wissenschaft des Judentums.*

[212]*Monatsschrift*, p. 492

[213]Archives du Haut Rhin, Colmar E 1627

[214]The Salomon family settled in Biesheim. According to a marriage contract deployed on 12/2/1756 by the Greffe de Biesheim in the Colmar District Archive, a grandson Jacob Salomon (Joel ben Leib), son of Representative Leon Salomon (Jehudo Leib ben Joel. . .) married Helen Mock (Elle bas Hirtz, born in Breisach, daughter of Hirtz Mock and Sarele Aron Jakob. Helen was accompanied by Jonas Aron, in the name of the brothers Nathan and Joseph, uncle and Vormund from Phalsburg.

[215]The Jews residing in our Province of Alsace have represented to us that after the dismissal of Aaron Worms, their last rabbi, they chose Samuel Levy to take his place.

supplier and his immediate family.[216] His children had already died before him in Colmar.[217] On request of the "Fiscal Procuror" of Colmar, the intendant for Alsace and the Rhine Army likewise issued a directive for expulsion on 13 August 1709.[218]

On 5 May 1712 Marx Wormser, living again in Altbreisach, as well as Jacob and Moises Wormser, then resident in Wintzenheim,[219] as co-heirs of their brother Alexander Doterle, sold the following property in Colmar:

The house belonging to their brother with yard, cellar, horse stalls, well, and other attachments for 6500 livres tournois Alsatian money.

The properties located behind the "Tribune des Laboreurs" (today Zunftkeller, Vauban Street) were, according to the content of the receipt, originally sold by Jean Christophe Bart, Community Secretary from Ste. Croix (south of Colmar) on 12 June 1705.

The brothers' three signatures in Hebrew again indicate that their father was called Chaim (Heymann). They acknowledge sale to the buyer Nicolas Haxo, "procureur au conseil souverain" (procuror to the sovereign council).[220] Marx Wormser went to Colmar again on 14 June 1724 to sell a horse stall and yard.

It is strange the learn from the Aub memory book that a rabbi from the uplands officiating in Bavaria was buried in Breisach in 1702. This was Jeremiahu, son of Gump from Schnaittach, formerly rabbi in the Ansbach and Würzbug District with a seat in Aub.[221] He was indeed a son of Max Schnaittacher (Schneittacher), who became a house owner on 8 August 1643 and was mentioned in 1673 by the name Marx (aka Meier, Gump) as one of six Breisach heads of household.

The Jewish tradesman Marx Guenzburger, who appeared multiple times as a plaintiff before the Breisach Council, seems to have not left the city following the change of government. Around this time, the Jew Hayum, imperial provisioner, is also mentioned: at his request, a flour

---

[216]Colmar City Archive, AA 174 No 88 (8/9/1709); the Beilage AA 174 No. 90, dated 7/31/1709, describes the origin of Alexander Doterle: The magistrate of the "ancient city of Brisach" proves that on this day Jean Jacques Disching, first mayor, Laurent Lamprecht, Rat, and Francois Goldtman, citizen of Breisach City, on the basis of good and sufficient knowledge, state that the late Alexander Doterle, "living Jew" who lived in Colmar in the above-mentioned city Breisach, was born some 65 years ago, that he was the son of the dead Heymann and grandson of the deceased Marx, that both Jews were established and died in this said city.

[217]AA 174 No. 97 (9 August 1709)
In the disappeared Balbronn memory book there was a Todros Breisach, whose son Naphtali Hirz was also mentioned (Communication of the Historian Robery Weyl, Straβburg)

[218]AA 174 No. 93

[219]Heirat Not. Besson Colmar 7/21/1750 Moyse ben Heymann ben Mosche s'l' Wormser, Wintzenheim with Matel T.D.Meyer Isac Westhoffen; with that the abovementioned Moises (born in Breisach) would have died already before 1725.

[220]Colmar District Archive

[221]Dr. Med. Weinberg, Entry No. 100 in Aub memory book, p. 181: Chief rabbi of the Würzburg and Ansbach District, Jirmijahu ben Gump from Schnaittach, buried in Breisach, died 1 Jan. 1702.

scale was made available to him.[222] The tax share of the Jewry at that time ran to 125 guilder according to the council report of 27 October 1701.

If one assumes a just distribution quota, this sum suggests a not too small community, because small dependencies were burdened only 40 guilder each.[223] The aforementioned Joseph Kreyllsamer, also called Joseph Katz, living in the dependency of Biesheim, appears in December 1701 as plaintiff in a charge against a Breisach citizen.[224] In the Quartier St. Jacques, in the left-bank region of St. Jakobsschanze before Breisach, lived Samuel Kinsburg (1702).[225]

While many Jewish residents preferred to leave the city at the departure of the French, they were also willing to return to their old *Heimat* after reoccupation by the French on 6 September 1703. "Isac Noeter, Coschel Lehmann, Isac and Lehmann Guenzburger, Jews, request permission to establish themselves here as before, together with their families."[226]

Further requests for settlement by Emanuel Levy von Bollweiler bei Gebweiler and Samuel Oettinger von Issenheim, who still appears in 1695 in the "ville de Paille," were approved by the city council on 15 November 1703.[227] More precise information about the family of Lehmann Guenzburger can be found in a Colmar document[228]: Aaron Honel (son of Elchanan Reinau, nephew of Jaeckel Reinau and grandson of Hirz Reinau, who died in 1672 in Schlettstadt), whose protection in Rappoltsweiler (Ribeauville) was approved on 18 March 1678 (ADHR Colmar: E 1625/88), petitioned for the protection of his son-in-law Lehmann Guenzburger on 21 March 1703.

He "had married one of his daughters about three weeks ago" to Lehmann, and, Honel communicated further, Lehmann was a "*widower* from Altbreysach," who had already "lived half a year or so here and there," but was now compelled "to seek a permanent place now that he was married again" (ADHR Colmar: E 1625/102). The appeal for protection was granted on 3 May 1703.

---

[222]City Council of 4/29/1700 (Haselier)

[223]Council Report of 5/21/1700 (Haselier)

[224]Council report of 12/19/1701. The family members differently writing changed at the beginning of the 19th century to the standardized name Greilsamer

[225]Personal communication from Mr. Picard, Colmar 8/15/1973

[226]Council report v. 10/12/1703 (Haselier)
Isac Netter had his central office in the "Vielle Ville" (old village), according to documents from 12/30/1698 and 12/6/1693, but also a house in the Ville Neuve, where he was one of the representatives. Isac Guenzburger of Brisach (Renker Notary, Colmar District Archives 2/2/1696) moved to Alsace and still lived in Biesheim in 1702. From 1703 to 1707 the notary documents speak of Isak Kinsburg as living in Altbreisach. Maybe he is the same as Isak Guenzburger, son of Meier, who was one of the first settlers in Rixheim, died there 1746 and was buried in Jungholz Cemetery (M. Ginsbuerger). Lehmann Guenzburger, who married young, may have lived a short while in Rappoltsweiler, where his father-in-law Aron Honel eingab his settlement on 5/3/1703.

[227]Council report of 11/15/1703

[228]ADHR Colmar: E 1625/102; attempts by G. Boll on 20 February 1986

Rappoltsweiler (Rapperswir), which became the seat of office of Rabbi Samuel Levy,[229] as well as Wintzenheim and Oberehnheim (Obernai) were at that time important Jewish communities in Alsace, which Breisach emigrants chose as new places to live.[230]

A list from 23 December 1710 includes, aside from the rabbi, thirty Jewish heads of household, cantors, and others employed in the Breisach community:

1. Marx Guenzburger[231]
2. Joseph Guenzburger[232]
3. Isaak Netter[233]
4. Mosche Levi
5. Marx Wormbser[234]
6. Simon Guenzburger[235]
7. Isaac Guenzburger[236]
8. Moyses Libel
9. Marx Geismar
10. Nathan Mock
11. Sieskind Geismar[237]

[229]The activities of Rabbi Samuel Levy stirred much discussion. He lived in Metz in 1709, where he became financially successful and Schatzmeister of Duke Leopold von Lothringen. On the basis of bad business decisions, he was later sent to prison (Revue, Vol. 44)

[230]Scheye Wesch (Jische ben Abraham s'l' von Westhausen, born in Oberehnheim, lived a time in Breisach and moved in 1700 as business partner of Joseph Katz in Biesheim to Rappoltsweiler. Lehmann Guenzberger switched his *Heimat*, which had become Austrian, likewise Ribeauville, where his father-in-law Aron Honel was living and on his behalf requested protection Aufnahme on 5/3/1703 (Colmar District Archie). The settlement was indeed bewilligt, but Guenzburger stayed hardly half a year. After the French again occupied Altbreisach (9/6/1703), he requested an appeal on 10/12/1703, to be allowed to go back there (Breisach Council Report).
From later population lists from Wintzenheim, it arose that some person in Breisach Strohstadt was born. In Oberehnheim lived Zadok Weil, father-in-law of the rich horse trader and Parnus Josel Guenzburger.

[231]A Marx G. from Breisach, "cousin" of the influential Josel G., settled in Müllheim in 1719; maybe identical with Marum ben Josef, named in the Eichstetten cemetery book in 1734

[232]born around 1660, representative in Breisach, married to Resle Weyl, daughter of Zadok

[233]Resettler in Breisach in 1703, the same as Isak von Bergheim, born about 1648, named in the 1684 notary, horse trader

[234]Marx, son of Heimann Wormser (Mordchai ben Chaim), named in 1694 notary records, born about 1658

[235]Simon ben Jakob Ruben David

[236]In Breisach before 1698, resettled there in 1703

[237]Son of Moses Geismar; Mosche ben Schneior Siskind, named in Eichstetter cemetery book in 1734, is a member of the Emmendinger District cemetery

12. Paule Risser[238]

13. Paule Metz[239]

14. Heimann Geissmar

15. Lehmann Guenzburger[240]

16. Samuel Riesser[241]

17. Samuel Ettinger[242]

18. Mayer Netter

19. Abraham Netter

20. Jacob Wormbser[243]

21. Doderle Wormbser[244]

22. Marx Geismar

23. Nathan Geissmar

24. Hirsch Geissmar

25. Samuel Levi[245]

26. Lehmann Levi

27. Emanuel Levi[246]

28. Josef Guenzburger[247]

29. David Guenzburger

---

[238]Raphael Risser

[239]Rafael ben Elieser, died in Breisach in 1734, buried in Emmendingen, wife Feia, already in Breisach in 1704. The surname points to the city with the same name in Lothringen, where the name "Brisach" also appears. Most rabbis came from or studied until then in Metz and were bound to the synagogue rituals and the religious laws of Metz.

[240]In Breisach before 1698, resettled there in 1703

[241]Samuel and Isak riesser, sons of Alexander Doterle

[242]In Breisach before 1698, then to Isenheim; resettled there in 1703

[243]Jacob-Jaecklin Heymann (son of Chaim) born in 1656

[244]Dotterle's son Elieser Liebermann ben Todres, named in the Emmendingen cemetery book in 1734

[245]Samuel Levi Bauer, died 17 Nissan 1744, buried in Emmendingen

[246]Came from Bollweiler (Alsace) in 1703

[247]Married to Bella, daughter of Toder Aron Rothenburger from Egisheim

30.   Bernhard Levi[248]

In the council reports Jews, like the businessman Marx Guenzburger, frequently appear as plaintiffs.[249] On his petition, a flour scale was made available to the imperial provisioner Hajum.[250] Along with the guilds and dependencies, the council also enlisted the "Jewry" on 27 October 1701 for 125 guilders for the raising of a tax. The Biesheim Jew Joseph Kreyllsammer brought a suit against a citizen of Breisach before the council on December 19, 1701, concerning a debt.[251]

The council tolerated Jews, but emphatically demanded their conversion from Judaism to the Catholic faith. When the wife of the Jew Vasi Bloch left her husband, taking all their portable goods as well, and then wanted to become a Christian, the council decided on 11 September 1702:

"When the Jewess resolves to be baptized, she should be helped in every way, but that such should happen in accordance with Catholic custom and the Jewess's promise to stay Catholic. But regarding the stolen goods, a settlement should thus be reached among the parties, namely Vasi Bloch and his former wife." And when this woman, née Metz, had married Feldwebel, for whose sake she had left her man, and complained about having to surrender her six-year-old daughter from the Jewish marriage, the council decided further: "Thus as has been very clearly and beneficially determined in spiritual matters, when one member of a married Jewish couple converts to the true Christian Catholic faith, any minor children conceived in Judaism are to be assigned to the convert; so in response to the desire and request of Maria Elisabeth Metzin, Vasi Bloch is hereby ordered to hand over the daughter conceived with said Metzin in Judaism, without any delay."[252]

A young teacher who worked in Altbreisach in 1707 was Zwi (Hirsch) from Krakau, son of the scholar Oscher (Anschel) Halevi, patriarch of the scholarly family of Levi Schopflich, which had settled in Alsace.[253] The government demonstrated somewhat more regard for the independence

---

[248]Married to Lipud (Elisabeth), daugher of obigen Simon Guenzburger

[249]Council report of 4/29/1700 (Haselier)

[250]Council report of 5/21/1700

[251]Council report of 12/19/1701

[252]Council report of 10/27/1702

[253]M. Jakobowits, *Vier Generationen der Rabbinerfamilie Levi Schopflich* [Four Generations of the Rabbi Family Levi Schopflich], (Straßburg 1938): In a Talmud exemplar from Amsterdam (Printer Immanuel Benevisti, 1645), on finds on the innenseite of the title page a feather drawing in 1707, the portrait of a young teacher in three-corner hat and long wig. Beneath it is written: "Thus speak the small and young among the thousands of Israel, who is named Zwi, who is called Hirsch, the son of my father, of the educated Oscher Anschel (of blessed memory) from the holy Krakow community (may they be protected from all evil), scholar (may his work be useful), here in Breisach, which

of the city with an inquiry to the magistrate: "whether the local protected Jews are useful to the city, how strong each household is, and what each has previously paid in protection money." After the French occupation of Breisach, numerous Jews, mostly from Alsace, migrated to the city. The Austrian government may have sought their departure. The diplomatically worded response declares that the Jews are "more harmful than useful to the city and commonwealth; if their number were reduced to six households, they would finally be tolerated, as long as an honorable council, which would be charged with accepting or rejecting Jews, found it good."[254]

An incident in 1718 may be appropriate to explain why the relationship between the city and Jews unfortunately had to be so problematic. An ungrateful music student who was daily accommodated in the Freiburg Augustinian Monastery, had stolen a silver chalice there and sold it to a Breisach Jew. The chalice was returned with the help of the Breisach magistrate. The thief had also however also purloined a ritual vessel from the Freiburg Dominicans, a silver incense burner, which likewise was returned to its rightful owners.[255] It is telling that the thief sought to move stolen goods among the Breisach Jewry, because in Freiburg there were no Jews at that time.

Authorities in Breisach may have become agitated about the trade in stolen goods among protected Jews, particularly as the stolen item in question was a religious object. But was it not the social relations of the time that turned the Jews into a "problem group?" In the High Middle Ages they had been highly respected and lived among Christians. Since the persecutions of the fourteenth century they were without rights, could even be "removed" at any time now, had to live in a ghetto against their will, and access to most respectable professions was denied them.

Given that suppression was possible at that time, the Jewish minority could survive only if its members had enough money to arrange, through bribery or gift-giving, to be left in peace and tolerated in the city. They devoted themselves perforce to cattle dealing or any other possible commerce, because the practice of respected trades was also denied them. Even higher education was not possible for them under the given conditions. In this way the pressure of survival determined the lifestyle of this minority, promoted its tendency to stay together, and was also the cause of their sometimes vexing business practices. Only the granting of citizenship rights, the so-called emancipation of the Jews in the nineteenth century, altered their economic and social standing to the extent that they still constituted a minority only with respect to religion.

In Rappoltsweiler (Ribeauville), at the foot of the Vosges, stood the cradle of the future Breisach rabbi David Kahn.[256] His father Jakob Caan (1640–1722) was likewise rabbi in Rappoltsweiler and rests in the cemetery in Schlettstadt established in 1622. His ancestors emigrated through Italy to Bohemia and settled in Alsace in the sixteenth century. A Yiches letter (letter of ancestry) that got lost during the chaos of the 1848 revolution in Dürmenach, testified

---

lies next to the Rhine river. In the year (may it be blessed . . . = 467 = 1707). Underneath is again the following signature: So speaks Zwi Segall in the Münsterland Province.

[254]Council report of 3/20/1715

[255]Freiburg Augustine chronicles p. 162

[256]Ludwig D. Kahn, *Die Familie Kahn von Sulzburg in Baden* (1963)

to the descent from Esra Hasofer, who served at the court of the Persian king Artaxerxes in the middle of the 5th century BCE and organized a return migration to the holy land.

After his marriage to Beyele Wormser, David Kahn resided for approximately one year in Winzenheim at the home of his father-in-law Moyse Wormser from Breisach. Kahn's son Isaak was born there around 1712.[257] The rabbi's call to and settlement in Vieux Brisach could have occurred in 1713.[258] It is related to the fact that his father-in-law Moses Wormser, and his brother Marx Wormser, who migrated back from Colmar to Altbreisach, influenced the employment of R. David Caan. The rabbinic family moved into the house of the village mayor Josel Guenzburger, the famous horse trader.[259]

One of the best-known personalities among Breisach Jews was Josle Breisach (Gintzburger), a wealthy, reputable horse dealer who signed documents as Joseph Gintzburger.[260] He was a parnus (representative) and advocate for the Jewry of Breisach and the surrounding area, and undertook much service for the fortunes of his community.[261] He had great influence in the government as a financier for Margrave Karl Wilhelm von Baden-Durlach. It was to his credit that seventeen Jewish families, who had fled from Switzerland and other places, received permission on 4 May 1716 to settle in the upper and lower districts (in the Rötteln and Hochberg offices) of Margravate Baden-Durlach.

First, five families in Emmendingen received protection, as did four families in each of Sulzburg, Müllheim, and Lörrach. But by September 1716, not all of them had moved to their approved destinations yet.[262] In the following years some families, mostly newcomers from Alsace, were permitted to settle in Eichstetten, Ihringen, Kirchen, Opfingen, and Tumringen.

---

[257]Colmar City Archive, Dossier JJCCB 605 Winzenheim 1763, treated an appeal with some Bescheinigungen for Hirtzel Hakn, son of Rabbi Isaak, to be allowed to live in Winzenheim. Behind that an Attestat of the magistrate of Altbreisach from 4/13/1763 can be found, in which Isaak Kahn, Rabbi from Vieux Brisach, who is legitimate son of David Kahn, to the former rabbi of Vieux Brisach, which Isaak of Winzenheim comes, that he with his father came from there and the former something more than 30 years was rabbi in Vieux Brisach, that Hirsch Kahn the legitimate son of Isaak Kahn is and that Hirschel married the daughter of Alexander Bloch from Winzenheim one and a half years earlier in Biesheim. A second document is a travel permission from October 15, 1762, valid for Hirtz Kahn, 23 years old, his wife Reisel, and their child, with personal description. In Dossier JJCCB 605B there is another Beschinigung of Nacharn von Moyse Wormser, wherein the wife of David Kahn is the daughter of Moyse Wormser in Winzenheim with the name Beyele. Parnus Meyer Levy of Winzenheim shows on August 22, 1763, that David Caan, grandfather of Hirsch Caan, had lived with his father-in-law Moyse Wormser in Winzenheim about a year vorübergehend, that during this time, Isaac Caan, father of Hirsch Caan, was born, that David Caan soon after that moved with his family to Vieux Brisach and that Hirtz Caan was born in Sulzburg. According to a marriage contract issued on 8/19/1761 in the notary office Callot, Colmar District Archive, Hirtz Neftali ben Isaak Kan, Sulzburg, married Reisel bas Alexander ben Benjamin Bloch in Winzenheim and Leye bas Koschel from Winzenheim.

[258]GLA

[259]Communication from Sal. Picard, Colmar

[260]M Ginsburger, *Die Guenzburger im Elsaß,* Gebweiler. p. 7. Josel G. is first mentioned in various documents of the Colmar District Archive, Renker Notary, Box 9, Nr. 22 from the years 1696 and 1697, in which he is also named Joseph Kuenzbourger or Joesslin Kindtsburger and the like; his father was named Marx Guenzburger.

[261]Leop. Lowenstein, *Blätter für Jüd. Geschichte und Literatur*

[262]Zehnter, p. 640

Almost all were servants or relatives of Joseph Guenzburger, who himself had the protection of old Further Austria. He "verakkordierte" (agreed) with the margravial government to accepting them and was responsible for the payment of their protection money.[263] In a petition he styled himself "Oberherr" (overlord). He had housed his dependents in the margravate so that they might foster his extensive business relations.[264]

In Breisach, Hirsch Isak, born in Opfingen around 1740, established a family[265] and took on the name Opfinger in 1809, while two other sons, Wolf Isak and Baer Isak in Emmendingen, took the surname Wertheimer.

The Relations with Neighboring Jewish Communities

Marx Geismar, apparently a close relative of Josel Guenzburger, could have been the first Jewish settler in the village of Ihringen, only a few kilometers from Breisach. He had to pay 25 florins in protection for his admission in 1717. Hamman Geismar followed in 1719. After another two years there were already seven families,[266] followed further by Jakob Geismar the elder, Abraham Wertheimer, Jakob Geismar the younger, and Lehmann Levi by 1727, and Salomon Geismar, Abraham Levi, and Veit Heilbronner by 1730.[267]

Samuel Weil and Moses Bloch, still documented on 20 August 1738, were, according to legend, exiles from Stühlingen. In 1735 Alexander Weil was permitted to relocate his residence from Emmendingen to Ihringen, but in 1744 he was living in Emmendingen again. At this time, the son-in-law of Jakob Geismar, Marx Guggenheim,[268] was also living in Ihringen, as was Samuel Loevel. Israel (Seligmann) Geismar was entitled to protection in Ihringen in 1748; later, his two sons Salomon (Bezalel) and Jakob settled in Breisach.[269]

The new settlers (1716) were again allowed to use the forest cemetery near Sulzburg created around 1550, but Josel of Breisach effected a burial site in Emmendingen[270] in 1717,

---

[263]GLA, Hochberg (Emmendingen): The late Old Herzel Wickert's backstanding protection money from 1716 to 1719 had to be given to his widow in *anno* 1720, so Joseph Guenzburger had to give 40 guilder in Altbreisach.

[264]B. Rosenthal, *Heimatgeschichte*

[265]Hirsch Isak's wife Marie Frank had already died by 1809; his second wife was named Hanna (b. 1744); children Jacob, b. in 1785 in Breisach, Keile (daughter of Maria), b. 1790, Sara, b. 1792. Heinrich Isak Opfinger, perhaps the oldest son of Hirsch Isak, b. 1774, married Meriam Geismar (b. 1784) with children: Jakob, b. 1806, Hanna, b. 1808

[266]This was mentioned by the founding of the communal cemetery in Emmendingen (Eichstetten community book).

[267]Supposedly the largest faction came from Alsace; the Geismars most likely came from Biesheim; there were also Heilbronners in the Lowlands.

[268]According to lore, he came from Switzerland.

[269]Seligmann, son of Jakob Geismar, was allegedly born in Biesheim and was buried in Emmendingen in 1779. In 1754 he pays protection money for the seventh time in Ihringen. His wife was Matel, daughter of David Guenzburger from Breisach.

[270]When a female Jew died in Emmendingen in March 1717, partly because of the Sabbath, partly because high entrance taxes demanded by the old Further Austrian authorities could not be spent on the cemetery toward Sulzburg, the Emmendingen Jews decided for the burial of the corpse "to buy a little piece of field secluded from the city (at that time), with the knowledge of the chief officer, to hereafter bury their dead." In May 1717, approval was

through permission of the margrave, for the Jews of Upper and Lower Emmendingen, Ihringen, and Eichstetten. With the Altbreisach rabbi, he signed decisions regarding the burial site in 1721,[271] where some people from Breisach also purchased graves much later. These stories were recorded[272] in an old Eichstetten community book that can no longer be found, with the following introduction:

"Book of the Community attached to the cemetery, which is under the authority of Emmendingen under the rule of the duke, our Lord—may G"d increase his brilliance—the Margrave von Durlach. The same was designed though a meeting of the representatives and notables of the territory in association with the representative and leader, the regional advocate, the respected gentleman Jausle Breisach, and with the agreement of the *Landrabbiner* David Hakohen. Therein are listed all particulars regarding said cemetery (recorded 481, that is, 1721)."

Per the decisions of 1721, one gabbai (advocate) for the cemetery was appointed each from Ihringen, Eichstetten, and Emmendingen; §5 of the provisions states: "It is to be known and it is listed in this book, who belongs to the cemetery and has the privilege:

1. The rabbi, our teacher David Hakohen

2. The representative Rab. Josle Breisach and his son

3. The most esteemed Rab. David

4. The esteemed representative R. Jechiel of Eichstetten etc."[273]

---

granted (Zehnter, p. 665). It was put next to the train platform and the margravial school, on today's Neubronn Street south of the city. Because a lower part laid out by the entrance was swampy and often stood under water, this piece remained unused and in 1899 a new cemetery was created on top of the "enclosurre" on the hill.

[271]Leopold Loewenstein, *Beiträge zur Geschichte der Juden in Deutschland II*, Nathanael Weil and his family, p. 6

[272]The former Eichstetten cantor L. Mirwis gave further excerpts of the above-mentioned archive documents in a family tree finished around 1929. The earlier district rabbi Dr. Adolf Lewin procured the translations of Hebrew documents and writings from the years 1721 to 1728. These, like the reports and lists, carried the signatures of gabbaim, who were confirmed as the cemetery commission from Emmendingen, Eichstetten, and Ihringen. In lists of "privileged people" the inherited right of individual members was registered and after the erection of a distinct grave site *anno* 1809 in Eichstetten, the particular synagogue council there carried on its deployment until 1880. Another list named the younger community members, who still had no right to the cemetery and therefore— according to a cemetery ordinance of 1728—with an imminent wedding at the cemetery had to buy into it. Another component of the Eichstetten community book listed Jews of the three communities all together on the occasion of the posting of their contributions. After that, in 1721, the Eichstetten community counted six families, Emmendingen seven, and Ihringen seven. In later years, some Jews from Breisach were still named, who bought into the aforementioned communal cemetery. As a result of this conscientious registration, writes Mirwis, in the community book started in 1721, a permanent list of names of Jews who lived in the period 1721-1809 in Hochberg, or Eichstetten, County, was created, in which the continuity between the ancestry in the 18th century and the same families today can be ascertained. Unfortunately, this valuable book, along with the whole Eichstetten community library, went missing with the Thirty Years' War.

[273]An extensive list in the works of Cantor Mirwis, who gives only ideas about his finished family tree of the families Epstein, Burger, and Wertheimer of Eichstetten.

The content of §5 is known from a 1728 report, which states by way of introduction:

"Today on 12 Ijar of the year 5488 (1728) the gabbaim gathered in the presence of the representative and leader, and of the regional advocate, David Guentzburger, son of the eternally respected gentleman Josle, who occupies the place of his fathers, and with agreement of the Rabbi David Hakohen of Rappoltsweiler,[274] to confer on the stipulations for the cemetery, of which §5 states ..." (see above).

The elaborations quoted by Kantor Mirwis in 1927 from page two of the Eichstetten community book are revealing; the same are taken up by B. Rosenthal on pages 202 and 240 of his own *Heimat* history. The "upper and lower district" referred to below are the Baden-Durlach offices Röteln and Hochberg.

"G-d was with Joseph, so he was a man who brought good fortune, who with the abundance of his wisdom and influence advocated to the margrave, on behalf of the refugees of Israel driven from Switzerland and other places, to take up these rejected ones in our residences in the upper and lower district. The spirit of Jakob returned to life, the spirit of the holy sheep that were tossed about and pushed from persecution to persecution, sick, disturbed, and plundered. The languishing people found peace and their foot became light. May G-d remember his (Guenzberger's) services, that his offspring be like him."

According to Eichstetten documents, the jurisdiction of Breisach Rabbi David Caan, even if unofficial, extended to the margravial Hochberg office. On 14 May 1720, the Jewish businessman Joseph Guentzburger reported in Altbreisach that the Jews of Hochberg and Badenweiler had long wished for a rabbi to give instruction in Jewish doctrine and laws and for mediation of Jewish business affairs; and that he, Guentzburger, could now "help out [with] such [a] matter" and the margrave could appoint David Kahn of Altbreisach as rabbi for the uplands Jewry. The uplands Jews themselves made the same request, and Kahn was then appointed as rabbi for the upper margravate as well and was granted instruction for the conduct of his office.[275] His commission came into effect on 25 February 1727.[276] The rabbi's seat of office initially remained in Altbreisach, but a change was brought about by the following circumstances: some Karlsruhe Jews, among them also their sheriff Mayer, made the request to the margrave that the upland Jewry be placed under jurisdiction of the lowland rabbi and the sheriff there, so that no one else would need go outside the area because of the rabbi, or need to call a foreign rabbi into the area. The contributions for the upkeep of just one *Landrabbiner* would then come to less. However, the entire upland Jewry repudiated this request on grounds that the lowland authorities lived too far away. At the same time they requested that David Guentzburger of Breisach, the oldest son of Josef Guentzburger, who had died in the meantime, might be returned to them as sheriff just as his father had been sheriff by permission of the government. He could also be their advocate with the government of old Further Austria and otherwise be of good service to the high authorities. The government at first refused this request, on 26 May 1727, because the Jews had already had an authority in Austrian Breisach with Rabbi

---

[274]Rabbi Kahn, at that time settled in Breisach, was elected on 2/27/1727 at the same time as Rabbi of the Upper Margravate.

[275]GLA 74/3728

[276]According to Zehnter, Gesch., p. 662, followed the confirmation on 13 May 1720.

Kahn and did not still need a sheriff, who likewise lived outside the area. After renewed applications, David Guentzburger was nevertheless instated as sheriff by decree on June 19, 1727 and, like his father, had to take charge of the guarantee of the protection money from upland Jews as well as other levies.[277]

Salomon Mayer,[278] the representative of the lowland Jews, would have liked to see his relative Samuel Elias Heilbronner as upland rabbi and petitioned the government again on 21 August 1730 to appoint this man instead of Rabbi David Kahn, who lived in Breisach.[279]

He suggested Eichstetten or Müllheim as the seat of office. He added that the appointment of Guentzburger and Kahn as superiors in the Baden Jewish community in Altbreisach might be cause for concern to the margravial rulers, because it could easily come about that the Austrian government or the city of Breisach claim the future right of the margravial Jews of the upland to be under the authority of the sheriff and rabbi of Altbreisach, without consideration for whether these latter had been appointed by the margrave or by Austria. The government therefore should find it in its own interest to dismiss David Guentzbuerger and his rabbi and to appoint the upland Jewish officials of the region.

Instead of the representative David Guentzburger, with whom he had differences, he proposed Moses Weil[280] of Sulzburg as a suitable person, or Daniel Heilbronner of Eichstetten, who however should serve only as lawyer for the settlement of small Jewish business matters in the upper territories. The government might appoint him, the petitioner Mayer, as chief sheriff for the entire margravate to handle all of the more important Jewish affairs. The privy council opposed this extension of his authority over the upland area, but indicated to Rabbi David Kahn in Altbreisach that another rabbi would be appointed if he did not transfer his residency to the margravial territory as soon as possible. Kahn subsequently took up residence in Sulzburg.

---

[277]Zehnter, p. 662

[278]As Jewish elder and court Jew in Karlsruhe, Salomon Mayer tried without lasting success, to build a form of central authority for the Jews of the uplands and lowlands at the beginning of the 18th century (*Jewish Lexicon*, 1928). He was born in 1693 in Oberwesel in Trierischen, lived in Pforzheim in 1717, where he married Fratel, the daughter of Model, who was a court Jew from Ansbach. In 1724 Salomon Mayer, also called Salomon Wesel, relocated to the young city Karlsruhe, where he became court Jew and Jewish sheriff. In the Swabian war, he managed a considerable fortune, proved by his elaborate will and the "Model'sche Foundation." He died in Karlsruhe in 1774. Baer Salomon Wesel, one of his five sonss, born in Karlsruhe in 1725, settled in Sulzburg, where he married Beile, daughter of Moses Weil. Descendants of this couple also lived in Breisach after 1820, as well as in Eichstetten, Müllheim, and Alsace.

[279]Samuel Elias Heilbronner, born in Sprendlingen, was engaged in 1730 to the daughter of Salomon Mayer's brother, who lived in Oberwesel. From 1733 on he held office as Storesschreiber (could mean a warehouse clerk, as as mix of French words and German) in Karlsruhe.

[280]The wealthy Moses Weil, born in 1688 in Stühlingen, was a brother of the upland rabbi Nathanael Weil in Karlsruhe and became Jewish protection money collecter in Sulzburg in 1728. He was the silver supplier to the margrave. His daughter Schoenle married Rabb. Isack Kahn in Sulzburg, son of the Breisach *Landrabbiner* David Kahn. Another daughter of Moses Weil became the wife of Baer Salomon (Wesel), born in Karlsruhe in 1725 in Sulzburg, son oe the aforementioned Jewish sheriff Salomon Mayer in Karsruhe; Hirschel, son of Moses Weil, was representative in Sulzburg 1775-1800. The ancestors of the Weil family were traced back to the 14th century by Rabb. Leopold Loewenstein in *Nathanael Weil, Oberlandrabbiner in Karsruhe und seine Familie.*

The Question of Protection Money

To counteract the increase of Jews in the margravate, it was ordered on 10 December 1729 that Jews who had not paid their protection money by the time of expiration should have their protection terminated and be expelled from the region. No additional Jew was to be taken under protection who could not demonstrate a fortune of at least eight hundred guilder. The charge for protection was raised to 75 florins for cities and 40 florins for villages. Again it was Sheriff David Guentzburger in Breisach who resisted this in a first petition on 4 December 1731 in the name of the upland Jewry.[281] A further, collective objection was raised by both Sheriff David Guentzburger and Sheriff Salomon Mayer (Karlsruhe), on 10 December 1731, in the name of all the Jews. They declared themselves in agreement with the proof of a minimum fortune for the admission of foreign Jews, so that not so many poor Jews would enter the region; but they found the raising of the protection fee unjustified given the poor economic circumstances of most Jews, not least as the amount was already much higher than in neighboring communities.[282] The request was rejected, but reduction of the protection fee was permitted for the entry of the children of Jews living in the region, in individual cases according to circumstance.

In February 1733 the representative for the Jews, David Guentzburger, appeared in person before the margrave in Karlsruhe seeking suspension of the ordinance concerning the evidence of fortune and to effect a decrease in the protection fee. By command of the margrave, he made his request in a petitionary letter dated 18 February 1733 in which he argued that, among many other reasons, he hoped that his request would be complied with all the more, given that he had been rendering for some time, and still rendered, considerable services for the margrave not only in the fruit trade but also in other respects. Thus, for example, he had recently increased the *Ohmgeld* (alcohol tax) to 600 florins annually through his debut in office in Badenweiler, but since he entered office in Rötteln the *Ohmgeld* amounted to as much as 1000 florins, not to mention the benefits soon to be seen from the sale of fruit.

The secret council supported Guenzberger's request, insofar as it recognized his services in the sovereign interest, namely the leasing of the *Ohmgeld* (alcohol tax). It thought, however, that the Jews should be charged a fee of 300 florins anyway for changing the ordinance. It was subsequently commanded in a decree of 3 March 1733 that the ordinance of 10 December 1729 regarding proof of a fortune of 800 florins and the increase in the protection fee to 40 and 75 florins in the upland should apply only to newly arrived foreign Jews. On the other hand, evidence of wealth would no longer to be required for admitting the sons of inland Jews into protection and the old protection fees of 25 and 40 florins would still apply. Guentzburger's payment of the 300 florin fee was recorded on 22 April 1733 and receipted in Margrave Karl Wilhelm's own hand.

At first both sheriffs, Salomon Mayer and David Guentzburger, submitted a communal petition to the court counselor on 8 January 1739 in which they demanded, among other things, the suspension of the ordinance of 16 October 1735 of the late Margrave Karl Wilhelm concerning the decrease of the interest rate to 5%. They explained that the lower interest rate

---

[281]Zehnter in *Zeitschrift f. Gesch. des Oberrheins*, Band 15

[282]In the royal and in Altbreisach the Jew pays only 10 fl. in protection money.

would not be in the interests of the subjects, because the Jews themselves had to pay an interest rate of 8 to 10% on the money they loaned. If the lowered rate remained and the Christian subjects were brought to foreclosure because they received no money from the Jews when paying their taxes, then the enforcement costs would come to more than the original interest. The Jews could not possibly procure high amounts of protection money with so low an interest rate. In the old letters of protection, they were granted an interest rate of one palsgravial heller weekly per guilder on loans up to 50 florins, which has amounted to 20% for the year. Everywhere in Germany the Jews were granted a higher interest rate than the Christians; it was already a common saying that it is the Jewish interest rate and this is field and plow to the Jews. The petitioner requested that the Jews uniformly be allowed 10%.

Soon thereafter Sheriff Mayer filed a new, extensive petition on this matter in the name of the lowland Jews, detailing further desires. He also mentioned that it was not the will of the late Margrave Karl Wilhelm to raise the amount of the protection money of the lowlanders. Already in 1730 he commanded that the ordinance concerning the raising of protection money rates should apply only to the uplands, "where many Jews had clandestinely come in through the assistance of the sheriff David Guentzburger. For that reason alone the uplands Jews would have also had to pay 300 florins for the modification of the law in 1733."

Again in 1747 the sheriffs Guentzburger and Mayer requested to no avail that the unfavorable ordinances of 1729, 1733, and 1739 be changed. The lower protection rates of 40 florins and 25 florins would apply not only to sons of inland Jews but also to foreign Jews who would marry the daughter of an inland Jew.[283] The sheriffs again requested the suspension of the ordinance of 10 March 1738, according to which only one additional child could gain protection in the future. Where, they asked, should a Jew go with his children if they are not tolerated in his fatherland and not allowed to find happiness in marriage? The ordinance should therefore be repealed. To prevent any abuse, though, one might indeed determine the number of Jews to let in, but this number should be higher than previously.

Finally, the sheriffs demanded that the protection money, which had already been decreased by the ordinance of 3 March 1733 to the old amounts of 25 and 40 florins for upland Jews, provided they were the children of inland Jews,[284] should also be decreased in the same way for low land areas. They demanded likewise for the lowlands, as had occurred in the uplands by the ordinance of 3 March 1733, that the sons of inland Jews be received without regard for proof of fortune. Nevertheless, the authorities had no luck with these wishes; they were turned away by the court counselor on 27 January 1739.

In 1732 David Guentzburger became court Jew to the Imperial General Field Marshall Count von Hohenzollern in Freiburg. He is designated in a document as a refined, wealthy Jew (See L. Loewenstein, *Beiträge zur Geschichte der Juden in Deutschland II* [Contributions to History of the Jews in Germany II], p. 6). As supplier to the imperial army, he had achieved great prosperity.

There were many disputes between Guentzburger and the uplands Jews. Paul Zifi of Müllheim and the Jewish collector Moses Weil of Sulzburg were Guentzburger's primary

---

[283]Zehnter, p. 52

[284]Zehnter, *Zeitschrift f. Gesch. d. Oberrh.* N.F. XV, p. 50

opponents. They accused him of engendering too many costs to the Jews and of deceiving them; of living outside the area, contributing nothing to the levy of the Jews; and bringing no benefit to the sovereign interests either, precisely because he lived outside of the area. Already in fall 1738, when Zifi and Weil had traveled to Karlsruhe to confer with the lowland Jews about a present for the merciful chief guardianship and the regional state administration, they requested in writing and in person at the government the removal of Guentzburger from the office of sheriff. They allegedly spoke on behalf of the entire Jewish community. When they returned to Karlsruhe in January 1739 for the purpose of presenting the gift of silver that had arrived from Augsburg, they repeated their demands. In no other sovereign territory, they claimed, did it happen that the Jewish sheriff lived abroad; moreover, the upland Jews did not need their own sheriff; the sovereign officials to whom the Jews gladly subjugated themselves were sheriffs enough, but if they wanted their own sheriff, at least one should be appointed from within the region, not outside of it (Zehnter, *Gesch.*, p. 581). Guentzburger, for his part, was not inactive in the face of this campaign. He traveled among the uplands Jews, and when the officials were commissioned, as a result of Zifi and Weil's objections, to hear the Jews' complaints against Guentzburger, the Jews declared immediately that they had nothing against him. The consequence was a penalty for Zifi and Weil. But Guentzburger, as well as the collector, Weil, were required to give an account their entire time in office.

In 1739 David Guentzburger also received a letter of safe conduct for Sulzburg; apparently he never took up residence there, because he was still residing in Breisach in 1747.

The title page of the fascicle[285] about the uplanders' accusations against David Guentzburger and their wish for back payments to *Landrabbiner* Isaac Kahn reads as follows: "The petition of the upland Jewish community, that the Jews' sheriff Davidt Guenzburger of Alt Breysach be removed from office for the reasons presented herein, that said office be occupied by two community leaders chosen from each upper office, and that the Jesish Rabbi Isaac Kaan of Sultzburg receive his delinquent pay, anno 1747, 1748."

Disputes

The Breisach Jews, under Austrian protection since 1714, won the right on 2 October 1717 to conduct free horse and cattle trade in the margravate Hochberg for three years, together with the right to collect debts. For this, each family had to pay 10 florins annually. The accounts indicate that twenty families were involved in 1720, yielding an income of 200 florins in Hochberg.[286]

By an agreement of 1 July 1732, the Breisach Jewry paid 150 florins yearly for free business dealings and travel in the Hochberg margravate, from which "12 fl. are deducted on account of the Jewish Sheriff Guenzburger."[287] The city of Breisach was little disturbed by the War of Polish Succession that began in late 1733 because it was protected by a strong Austrian garrison, but indirectly it was very encumbered by the task of supplying hay, oats, and straw. A

---

[285]GLA 74/3735

[286]Accounts, Hochberg office (endeavors by B. Rosenthal in the GLA, 1938)

[287]Breisach City Archive, Fasc. 1832. Surely David Guenzburger had it agreed that he could deduct 12 guilder annually for his troubles.

transcript describes the trade in Alsace. Mayor and council of Altbreisach certified on 3 January 1738 with an "Attestatum for all local Jews to the Royal Domain concerning the escort in Alsace," that of twenty-three Jewish families only eight have a regular business there.[288] In 1744 the Breisach Jewry was still paying the yearly 150 florins for protection in Hochberg: "of which 12 fl. was refunded to Representative David Guenzburger."[289]

The council report of 28 June 1745 included an unusual complaint. A representative appearing on behalf of the city apothecary Riethammer accused the following debtors:

David Isaac Guenzburger p(uncto)	19 fl.	11 ½	xr.	thereafter
Joseph Simon Guenzburger	2 fl.	8	xr.	
Alexander Guenzburger's heirs	7 fl.	41	xr.	
Jacob Schwab	10 fl.	1	xr.	
Daniel Wormser	30 fl.	30	xr.	
Salomon Wormser	10 fl.	43	xr.	
Lazarus Mez	23 fl.	32	xr.	
Paul Mez's heirs	3 fl.	46	xr.	
Joseph Levi on behalf of				
Alexander Simon (taken ill)	3 fl.	8	xr.	
and Emanuel Weil	8 fl.	21	xr.	

all for different medications acquired over several years. Defendants, who despite amicable summons had not remitted any payment and despite summons had not appeared, would now be addressed *in contumaciam* (in absentia). The records report a fight that happened in the Breisach *shul* between the rabbi (Isaac Weil) and David Marx Guenzburger.[290] The parnus (David Josel Guenzburger) then ordered that Jacob Grailsamer, Joseph Levi, and Isaac Levi (community deputies) gather in the house of vice parnus Hirz Mock for the purpose of reconciliation, which took place on 27 September 1745. The rabbi was also enlisted, and in the course of the discussion he reproached Hirz Mock, to which Mock took offense and then turned in an extensive report on December 7 to the "most excellent and wise Magistrate and Council of the Imperial and Royal City Alt Breysach" to obtain reparations.

---

[288]Breisach City Archive, Fasc. 1832. (Jewish convoy 1651-1756)

[289]Hochberg Office accounts (Emmendingen): in 1744, 3 fl. of burial money are listed, which Lazarus Greilsheimer from Altbreisach paid for the transfer of a little boy to the Emmendingen cemetery.

[290]Breisach City archive, Fasc. 1861

"We reproached the rabbi, in a well-intentioned manner, that it is not the duty of just anyone but his particular duty to maintain the unity of a community and to not view a (supposed) mistake as such that in reality is not one." "Consequently," Mock continued, "he (the rabbi) held forth against me with these words: that I am the cause of the fighting between him and other Jews and as the cause I must be seen as the instigator and ringleader, reproaches which speak against my behavior in the past forty years living here and severely tarnish my honor…. So my humble request to Your Grace and Favor to order the above-named rabbi to undergo examination in this matter (to render evidence of the charges), and, however, should he not be able to produce evidence that he be sentenced to render just satisfaction as well as costs and compensation,…"

The document is signed by Hirtz Mock, who died before 1748.

Documents for advocates of both sides of the fight were brought to the Breisach office on the morning of 2 November 1746. These documents may have been crucial in determining the fate of Rabbi Isaak Weil, appointed by his father-in-law David Joseph Guentzburger.[291] The Protected Jews Hirz Mock, Philipp Guentzburger, David Leman, Alexander Simon, David Isaac, Senter Raffel, Marx Cahn, and Simon David turned in a document to Mayor Schesmartin in the presence of chancellery officials with the remark that it had been faithfully translated from Hebrew into German. It includes the demand that Rabbi Isaac Weyl be promptly deposed, and requests the support of the authorities.

The document reads as follows: "We undersigned recognize by dint of this current authority Hertz Mock, Jacob Greylsheimer, and Philipp Guentzburger, as our elected authorities of the Jews have announced that they called in the Rabi Isaac, rabbi from there, the 12th of this month, and enjoined him to give 50 royal thaler this morning for the disputed expenses of summoning a foreign rabbi and in the present conflicts with Rabi Leman Guenzburger. Also imposed on Leman, he agree to make a payment, and in fact did so by depositing two rings. Nevertheless, Rabi Isaac has asked three, four, five times whether he, in the case that he does not want to pay the deposit of 50 royal thaler, should deposit just 20 royal thaler until more regulation has passed. Because he also does not agree to this, we find this as a sign of subordination and recalcitrance against the Jews. With that our only choice is to explain his rabbi position to him until the next regulation and that none of us undersigned should recognize him as Rabbi. For security we have signed below with our own hands. Thursday the 13th in the month Cheshvan 507.

Hertz Mock, Philipp Guentzburger, David Leman, Allexander Simon, David Isaac, Senter Raffel, Marx Cahn, Simon David.

(Note:) These two rings that served as Leman payment were deposited through the signet of Philipp Guentzburger by Hertz Moch."

The following questions were now put to a vote:

1. whether they wanted to file a complaint against their rabbi, Isaac Weyl, and what things should be included?

[291]Breisach City archive, Nr. 1846

2. whether they had any complaint about the rabbi's conduct and what?

3. whether they asked that the rabbi be released from his office or whether they approved Isaac Weyl as their rabbi?

Of the fourteen heads of household summoned, ten appeared, who wrote their opinions and signatures individually, sometimes also in Hebrew. They voted unanimously in favor of Rabbi Weil, about whose performance they had no objection.

The following persons were entitled to vote:

1. Lazarus Wormser

2. Alexander Wurmser (Sender ben Todres s'l')

3. Emanuel Weyl (absent)

4. Daniel Wurmser

5. Salomon Wurmser (Scholom b. Mordchai s'l')

6. Jakob Greilsamer

7. Joseph Levi

8. Moyses Geismar (Mosche b. Schneiur s'l')

9. Lazarus Grailsamer

10. Joseph Simon (absent)

11. Isaac David

12. Lazarus Mez (absent)

13. Isaac Neder (absent)

14. Isaac Levi

Appended to the document is another in Hebrew cursive, in which Menle Weil and Izik bar Avrohom s'l' approve Isaac Weil as their rabbi.

In 1744 *Landrabbiner* David Kahn died in Sulzburg after more than thirty years of service; he is also buried in the old sacred grave site. The simple inscription on his gravestone at the Jewish cemetery in Sulzburg reads:

Here is buried the *Landrabbiner* David Kahn,

Son of the great Rabbi Jakob (Hakohen),

Died and buried in good name

On Monday Erev Rosch Chodesch (the evening before the new moon) Sivan 504

(May 1744), here in Sulzburg.

May his soul enter into the bond of eternal life.

The still well-preserved stone has survived the storms of time. It has the usual half-round form of the Roman stele. His son Isaak Kahn was born around 1712 in Wintzenheim, grew up with his parents in Breisach, and likewise became a rabbi. Many document fascicles preserved in the regional and city archives of Sulzburg and Müllheim provide information about his life and activities.[292] In 1736 Isaak Kahn entered the bon of marriage with Schoenle (Jeanette) Weil, the daughter of Moses Weil, the richest Jew of Sulzburg.[293]

For her wedding, Schoenle Weil received from her father a dowry of 1450 guilders in cash, 500 guilders in clothes, and 500 guilders in jewelry, a significant sum for that time. The "well-endowed" father-in-law and also the father permitted Isaak Kahn after his wedding, to spend the years 1736 to 1739 in Frankfurt am Main "perfecting himself in Jewish studies" and to prepare for the rabbinate in Sulzburg, which his father had already occupied.[294] Isaak's father then requested that his newly married son might be taken into protection in Sulzburg.[295]

On 10 July 1736, Bailiff Saltzer responded to "His Serene Highness the Margrave," to whom the appeal for protection had to be forwarded, that "Sulzburg is full of Jews. If now the Highest among the same is against increasing number of this people, then it is your decision whether to turn away or accept those requesting to come in." The appeal was finally granted after much back and forth, after the father of the petitioner, Rabbi David Kahn, Jewish rabbi of Altbreisach and Sulzburg, had affirmed to "His Serene Highness the Margrave" on 14 November 1736, that his aforementioned son and future rabbi:

1.   had a very wealthy father-in-law, who would help with the purchase of a house (in Sulzburg the Jews were allowed land ownership, in contrast to other communities also in Switzerland, like Endingen and Lengnau);

2.   would pursue no business, either with wares or anything else;

3.   would "dedicate himself purely to studies"; and finally

4.   would "over time would bring many valuable goods from me into the region, and would also inherit something substantial from his father-in-law, on which he would be able to survive without burdening anyone else."

Isaak Kahn was granted Jewish protection from Sulzburg for a payment of thirty guilder, having to pay this fee like others in contrast to his Alsatian ancestors, who were free from paying protection money because they were religious officials.

On 24 July 1742 he was appointed as adjunct rabbi to his very elderly father, at the instigation of his father-in-law, Moses Weil.[296] He became *Landrabbiner* on 26 May 1744, after

---

[292]Ludwig Kahn, *Gesch. und Genealogie der Familie Kahn*, 1963, p. 23

[293]Moses Weil, born in 1688 in Stühlingen (Baden), played –formerly residence of the Baden margrave—in Thirty Years' War

[294]L. Kahn, Gesch. p. 23

[295]GLA, Abt. 229/103724

[296]GLA, Abt. 229/103724 v. 13.1.1744

the death of his father, for Sulzburg, Breisach, Ihringen, Emmendingen, Eichstetten, Müllheim, and Lörrach. This happened very much against the wishes of David Guenzburger, who would have liked to see his son-in-law Isaak Weil as rabbi of the upland Jews; he had in the meantime imposed him on the Breisach community.

There quickly arose arguments between Rabbi Isaak Kahn and Guenzburger. Kahn had already filed complaints previously, as a result of which the government felt compelled to admonish Guenzburger to order and good conduct. On 14 August 1747, however, Sheriff Mayer in Karlsruhe again accused Guenzburger, in the name of Rabbi Kahn and the upland Jews: that he was continuing to deal with the rabbi, raising false accusations against him, and seeking to end his post and his income, all of which was occurring only from personal motives, because Guenzburger had a son-in-law who was wrongly assuming the role of rabbi.[297] Guenzburger was also said to be appropriating money unfairly and even laying his hands on the fortunes of wards and orphans. Furthermore, Guenzburger was accused of having harmed the Jews in that he caused the Austrian government to raise the safety-escort fee to 80 florins, whereupon he was also twice unable to pay the sum ("fallit").

It was therefore desired that Guenzburger be removed from office and that two representatives be appointed in each high office, who could mediate Jewish affairs with the rabbi and observe the Jewish ceremonies.[298] At the hearing of the Jews by the high officials it also arose that Mayer had no right to act on behalf of upland Jews. The Jews explained that they did not have anything substantial to bring against Guenzburger, they also did not know that he had been *fallit*.[299] Whether or not he remained sheriff did not matter too much to them, they had not appointed him and did not want to depose him either. They didn't actually need a private sheriff; rather, they preferred to report directly to the officials—the sheriff just caused them expenses. But if it were preferred to put a representative in each high office instead of the sheriff, one would suffice in each office.[300]

Tensions and complaints against community representatives also arose in Breisach. There followed longstanding trials between David Guenzburger and Isaak Weil on one side and the Altbreisach Jewish community on the other, concerning the position of rabbi. They ended only through a settlement in 1752, in which Isaak Weil gave up the post for all times.[301] This was co-

---

[297]This son-in-law of David G. was Isaak Weile, born in Uhlfeld, was rabbi in Bruchsal from 1740 to 1743. Cf. Loewenstein (According to B. Rosenthal, *Heimatgeschichte*, p. 139, had at first effected Weil just as house rabbi at the Suessel parnus in Bruchsal).

[298]Zehnter, p. 582

[299]Compare with Breisach City Archie, fasc. 2869 on David G.'s failure.

[300]In July 1753, the uplands Jews requested permission for two representatives (Jewish sheriffs), who would manage Jewish matters together with the rabbi. For the Badenweiler high office, Elias Bloch was then elected and confirmed as representative in Müllheim in fall 1753 for three years. Subsequently, these others appear as representatives: Lazarus Braunschweig (1758-1775) in the Lörrach high office, Kusel Moses (1765) in the Emmendingen high offfice, and Joseph Mayer in the Müllheim high office (1765).

[301]Zehnter, Gesch. Baden-Durlach, p. 583

signed by Isak Weil, Philipp Guenzburger (additionally, in Hebrew, Lipmann Breisach), Jacob Greylsamer, Isac Lefi (additionally, in Hebrew, Izchak Segal Mi Breisach).[302]

After David Guenzburger had lost his dogged fight against the community, he had himself baptized Catholic in the Freiburg Cathedral. According to the entry of 27 October 1752, he was already a widower at the time.[303]

He received the new names Judas Thadaeus Ferdinandus.[304] The baptizand Ferdinand Guenzburger lived from then on as tariff collector in Guenzburg in Swabia and appealed again in 1754 to the "most honorable representation for his son-in-law's reinstatement in the aforementioned Rabbinical Office in Breisach."

On 1 February 1745 Hirtz Mock became the new vice parnus in Breisach. After a turbulent and fateful stay in Breisach with his young family, Isac Weil found a new sphere of influence as *Landrabbiner* in the princely Loewenstein-Wertheim lands, thereafter belonging to the Count of Erbach.[305] For reasons unknown, he had himself, his wife, as well as his eleven-year-old daughter and twelve-year-old son baptized in the Lutheran faith in Darmstadt City church.[306] Thereafter he called himself Ludwig Wilhelm Weyland and became a servant of the church and bellringer; his wife took the name Maria Carolina Christina. The daughter later married the surgeon Westermacher, and through further marriages there developed familial relations with the Merck house in Darmstadt.

In Breisach itself, difficult and chaotic circumstances reigned at that time. Around 1740, the Rhine current changed course and caused the Breisach fortifications such damage that they were abandoned and partially demolished,[307] and Maria Theresia, the new successor to the throne, gave orders to de-fortify the whole city. The fortifications were demolished and the garrison removed. The impoverished city could no longer afford the government's demands to

---

[302]Breisach City Archive, fasc. 1847

[303]In the "Hildesheimer Relations-Courier" *anno* 1752, Nr. 136 (11/16/1752) the following report can be read from "Freyburg the 28th of October":
"The day before yesterday, the sheriff of all the Brissgau Jews, David Guentzburger from Alt-Brisach, as the eldest and most eminent of this family, aged some 50 years, was baptized in the local cathedral church by the City Priest, Professor of the holy scripture and episcopalian comission, in the presence of the local nobility and other countless onlookers. The same, baptized man was given the name Ferdinand Judas Thaddeus, the president of the knighthood, Baron von Sigging, Baroness von Summerau"
(From: *Blätter für jüd, Geschichte und Literatur*, publ. by Dr. L. Loewensein, Jahrgang III, 1902 Mainz "Ein Täufling aus der Familie Guenzburg vor 150 Jahren" by Dr. Lewinski).
Likewise Loewenstein: Nathanael Weil, p. 1 and 6

[304]Ferdinand was the first name of the first godfather Baron von Sickingen

[305]Paul Arnsberg, *Die Jüdischen Gemeinden in Hessen* [The Jewish Communities in Hessen], see Michelstadt, p. 85

[306]Excerpt from the baptismal register of the Darmstadt Civil Community from 1759, pp. 68 and 69. Another daughter was born on September 30, 1759. Isak's wife, the daughter of David Guenzburger, the former Court Jew at Freiburg, was buried on 21 October 1760 at the age of 33 years, 3 months, and 15 days. She was therefore born in Breisach in 1727. He was 80 years and 7 months at the time of his burial on October 25, 1790. There were four children from his second marriage, who all were born in Darmstadt.

[307]Haselier, p. 53

pay its debts. The city was prosecuted and burdened with additional, heavy enforcement costs. A city investment fund was established under the initial direction of guild master Johann Mury, and from 1747 on, the investment Extanzien (the investment fund residual or receivable) in particular were audited. There were various quarrels over the disproportionate distribution of the account to guilds, the Jewish community, and small towns.

In 1743 citizens and guilds complained. The tensions dragged out over 1745 and 1746, when the French returned to the city, now without fortifications, and occupied it for almost a year. Waldshut was the refuge for the government of old Further Austria. A complaint to a temporary commission reveals that David Guenzburger of Breisach had gone bankrupt and a female plaintiff had lost 500 guilder that she had lent him in 1737 at a 6% interest rate. In a debt claim, the magistrate ruled sufficiently in her favor.[308] The city of Breisach was indebted to Jacob Grailsamer and knew through accounting activity to oppose his claims with counterclaims.[309] The Breisach Jewry was obliged to remove the enormous protection burden of the city in addition to its own problems getting rid of the unauthorized parnus and Rabbi Weil, who had been imposed upon the community.

Subsequently no one was prepared to take over the responsibilities of the representative's office, and the magistrate saw itself forced to confirm as parnus Isak Levi, a deputy of the community.[310] In a written protest of 13 February 1753,[311] a panel turned to the "high, imperious and merciful Lords of the city":

"We appear in the name of all local Jews with the subject's request that you hear us out.

A while ago a decree from the praiseworthy magistrate and council was sent to us from this date,

where it says that Isac Levi is named as parnus; but it goes against our right, that we already elected the parnus years ago and ratified him in the time of your praiseworthy magistrate and council. Therefore our supplicant's request is that Your Grace might take back this decree and leave us to our long-standing privilege of choosing one by majority vote, as a guild can freely choose its master.

"But we have just cause: Because the whole Jewry must be responsible for paying money both to the merciful local rulers and also to the praiseworthy city, it is also proper, when we have to be responsible to a parnus, that we know whether he will be solvent. The issue that since then we could not vote for anyone who was qualified, is such that does not want to be tied together with the fact that already for many years we are followed by a strong duty in the account and so that all local citizenry would stumble into this big labyrinth.

That the beginning of the settlement showed right away that we do not owe more duties, but what is for us still a considerable sum that we, too much paid, owed, now request in supplication to the high-esteem. guild master and collector Mury that he balance accounts with

---

[308]Breisach City Archive; Fasc. 2869 (Haselier II, p. 39)

[309]Fasc. 3513 (Haselier II, p. 51)

[310]Isak, son of Eliakim Levi in Breisach, had a son Gotschalk, who married Ella Bernheim from Soultz in early 1747. She was the daughter of the late Isaac B and Veronica (Frumel) Reinau.

[311]Breisach City Archive; Fasc. 1845

us, what we already made good on in the previous settlement, thereafter to subtract the current amount and pay us the rest and in the future to spare us the debt. Then we will choose a parnus according to the usual means and request merciful ratification from the proper place.

Lehmann Gintzburger (Leime ben Josel s'l')

Jakob Greylsamer (Jschai ben Josef K"z")

Joseph Levy (Jschi S'gan L')

David Lehmann (Dovid ben Jehudo s'l')

Leopold Mock

Lazarus Greylsamer (Hebrew: Alexander Siskind)

Joseph Lemburger (Joseph Lewuw)

Lebolt Levy (Leib Segal)

Marc Kaim

Marigs Joseb[312] (Hebrew: Jekel bar Mordechai[313])

Philipp Guenzburger (Lipmann Breisach)."

By command of "gracious authority," the Breisach Jewry appears to elect Parnus Lehmann Guenzburger out of four suitable owners on the 11th of August 1754. "Per old custom, man by man is heard about it" and the following *paterfamilias*, each with four of their voting choices named in the documents:

Philipp Guenzburger, Jacob Greilsamer, Isac Levi, Leopold Mock, David Lehmann, Salomon Wurmser, Joseph Limburger, Lazarus Greilsamer, Jacob Geismar, Alexander Simon, Marx Kahn, Leopold Levi, David Wurmser, Mayor Weil, Marx Joseph, Isac David, Moyses Geismar, Alexander Wurmser (absent, but he left behind a written opinion in which he named: Philipp Guenzburger, Marx Kahn, Isac Levi, and Lazarus Wurmser), Lazarus Wurmser, Gotschalk Levi Simon David, Joseph Levi, Lehmann Guenzburger, the parnus.[314] (He chose Philipp Guenzburger, Jakob Greilsamer, Isac Levi, and Leopold Mock). "Signed by me, Chief Cantor of representative vote, declared along with the certified Jews.

sig: Lehmann Gintzburger (attached beneath it in Hebrew: Leime ben horaf Reb Jeissle s'l')

---

[312]Marx, son of Joseph Guenzburger

[313]Jakob Geismar, son of Marx

[314]Unexpectedly, the news came that the former community representative and parnus Lehmann Guenzburger had in old age turned his back on Judaism. He undersigned the baptism with Johann Josel Guenzburger.

In the death register of the Breisach parish, an entry written in Latin says that "Johannes Baptista Guenzburger, deceased in God, baptized Jew, with holy sacramant richly provided, died on 14 December 1771 in Bürgerspital. He was buried next to the gravedigger Franciscus Belmer in the parish's own cemetery of St. Stephan's Church.

sig: Victor Moyses, Chief Cantor

The following ten community members received votes:

Simon David (suggested only by Alexander Simon and Leopold Mock), Jacob Greilsamer, Philipp Guenzburger, Marx Kahn, Isak Levy, Joseph Levy, Joseph Limburger (received only one vote from Philipp Guenzburger), Leopold Mock, Alexander Wurmser, Lazarus Wurmser. Ultimately, most votes went to Philipp Guenzburger, Isac Levy, Jacob Greilsamer, and Leopold Mock—results still in need of ratification. Upon inquiry with the district office in Waldkirch, the mayor and council of the city of Breisach received not only an affirming answer, on 11 October 1754, but also the indirect notice that the "High Representation" in Constance would have objections to the four and no concern about ratifying them, "although in such a way that neither the parous nor his granted assistants would intervene in that city magistrate's deserved jurisdiction."

Thus, on 11 August 1754 the following protected Jews with voting privileges were in Breisach:

1. Philipp Guenzburger
2. Jacob Greilsamer
3. Isaac Levi
4. Leopold Mock
5. David Lehmann
6. Salomon Wurmser
7. Joseph Limburger
8. Lazarus Greilsamer
9. Jacob Geismar
10. Alexander Simon
11. Marx Kahn[315]
12. Leopold Levi
13. Daniel Wurmser
14. Mayer Weil
15. Marx Joseph
16. Isaac David
17. Moyses Geismar
18. Alexander Wurmser (absent)

---

[315]R. Marx Kahn, brother of *Landrabbiner* Isaac Kahn in Sulzburg, was schoolteacher in Breisach. In this time, Rabbi Josph Hirsch came to the city as the second "shul servant," also carrying the title of rabbi and married Gittel, the daughter of David ben Lehmann Guenzburger.

19.   Lazarus Wurmser

20.   Gotschalk Levi

21.   Simon David

22.   Joseph Levi

23.   Sig. Lehmann Guenzburger, the parnus (Leime ben haraf Reb Jeissles'l')

24.   Sig. Victor Moyses, Chief Cantor

Whether for political or economic reasons or owing to family relations, some candidates for marriage in Altbreisach looked particularly to Rixheim in Alsace. When Jakob Wurmser, brother of Lazarus of Breisach, married Reichel, a daughter of David Levi in Rixheim, in 1745, he promised in the marriage contract to live in Rixheim.[316] Samuel Sanvil Guenzburger of Altbreisach was already living in Rixheim in 1748 when he married Bluemlen Bomsel of Oberhagenthal.[317] David Rieser, son of Isaak of Vieux Brisach, also settled in this village near Müllhausen in Alsace with his young wife Jendel, daughter of Marx Machol of Sulzburg, after his marriage on 29 May 1740.[318]

Around 1751, the Rixheim population complained that a number of foreign Jews from Altbreisach, Poland, and other foreign lands had been settling and buying houses in Rixheim for a number of years. Among them was likely also Isaak Guenzburger, one of the first Rixheim settlers, who had already previously come from Breisach. In 1708 he assumed responsibility for tax collection there, and later he also undertook rabbinical duties. His wife was Marie Haas of Rixheim. His stepson, supposedly from a second marriage, was Baruch Elias of Epfig, later parnus in Rixheim; on 11 July 1740 in Rixheim he married Regina, daughter of David Guenzburger and Schoenle Wurmser of Altbreisach. The bride was represented by her uncle Lehmann, son of Joseph Guenzburger of Breisach (Colmar District Archive Landser Notary). It seems that Keille, wife of Lazarus Bernheim in Rixheim and daughter of R. Meir Guenzburger, who died before 1745, also came from this city on the Rhine (Ginsburger, p. 13), as did David Marx Guenzburger, brother and heir to the aforementioned Isaak, whose son Raphael, born in Rixheim in 1737, married the Breisacher Leye Levy, daughter of Joseph (Jische) and sister of Hirsch Levy, according to the marriage contact deposited with the Landser notary on 28 July 1768. Hirsch Levy moved again after his marriage in 1772, to Tuerckheim, where he held office as "Commis Rabin" (assistant rabbi). Sara, daughter of David (ben Jehuda s'l') Guenzburger of Breisach, married Elieser, a son of Joseph Benjamin Levi Haas of Rixheim, according to the Landser notary contract dated 9 July 1759. According to a contract registered on 22 February

---

[316]Marriage contract of 1/28/1746 deployed in the Landser notaryship, Colmar district archive. A Waise, daughter of Merle Wurmser, when she married Peretz, son of Gerschon Wurmser, on 5/22/1772 in Issenheim with witness of Lazarus Wurmser of Breisach (Elieser ben Todres).

[317]When a daughter Judith entered marriage with Simon Bloch of Biesheim on 1/2/1778, she was given away by Jakob Bernheim of Zillisheim, because her father Samuel was no longer living.

[318]Offspring lived in Müllheim and Sulzburg.

1722 at the Neuf Brisach notary, Colmar District Archive, Reignine, daughter of Raphael ben Elieser Metz and Feiele from Vieux Brisach, married a Joseph Levy in Rixheim.

Aron Guenzburger[319] came from Altbreisach to Hagenau (Alsace) in 1756 and became engaged to Schoenel (b. 1749), daughter of Aron Feistel Mock,[320] whose wife Jentel, born 1721, also came from Breisach. The wedding took place in 1764. Aron died before 1784.[321]

Through marriage, the Guenzburger family established close relations to the Jewish scholarly families of the time. Reichle, the oldest daughter of the wealthy Josel Guentzberger of Breisach, was married to the Moravian *Landesrabbiner* Moses Lewuw, who died on 28 December 1757[322]; she herself died on 2 March 1748 (2 Aadar II 1748). On her grave stone[323] she is remembered as an entirely pious and intelligent woman. On her mother's side, she was the granddaughter of the deceased superintendent (Gaon and Stadlan godaul) Zadok Weil of Oberehnheim, and her father-in-law, Aaron, son of R. Moses Lewuw of Lemberg, held office as rabbi initially in Trier and from 1693 in Westhofen, where he was buried on 26 November 1712. A half brother of R. Moses Lewuw (1704–1757) was Rabbi Josua Heschel Lewuw (1693–1771), also born in Westhofen, whose wife Merle was a daughter of Rabbi Isak Aaron Worms, who lived a short time in Breisach in 1681.

In a dispute with Lazarus Wormbser [sic], Representative Wolf Mock composed a "true, written instead of oral account" on 22 January 1776.[324] After his brother Beer Mock, who had served as collector of Jewish monies and been paid 12 florins, moved away, Wolf was to look for a replacement and, together with the assessor, he selected four well-off Jews, had them draw lots in the presence of Joseph Hirsch, auxiliary rabbi, and then entered in the Jewry book the order in which the four newly elected collectors would hold office in the coming four years at a "Salaria"

---

[319]The same as Philipp Guenzburger, who called himself Lippmann Breisach in Hebrew.

[320]The members of the wealthy Mock family living in Hagenau (Alsace), could have stood in close relationship to the Mock in Breisach. Aron Feistel Mock in Hagenau, born in 1715, married Jentel in 1736, who was born in Breisach in 1721. Of their children, Marx, born in 1755, Marum, born in 1757, the eldest at the age of 14 got engaged to Aron Gentburger in 1763, who came from Breisach in 1757, who lived since then in subtenancy by Aron Feistel Mock. The wedding took place in 1764 in Hagenau. Aron's father Lippmann is the same as the big merchant and community deputy Philyps Guenzburger.

[321]According to enumeration, his widow Schoenle and four daughters—Reisel, Merle, Riechele, and Zerle—were still living at that time in 1784.

[322]M. Ginsburger, *Die Guenzburger i. Elsass*, p. 8, also *Feuchtwang, Epitaphien mährischer Landesrabbiner u. Localrabbiner in Nickolsburg* (Kaufmann memory book)

[323]Reichle bas jakozin Josel Ginzburg. . .
The wealthy Josef Guenzburg was therefore married to the daughter of Zadok Weill and could have been born around 1660.David, son of Josel, was already a father in 1727; Josel himself died in 1727. Another Josef Guenzburger, who in 1710 in Breisach sat in protection, married Beila Rothenburger, daughter of Toder Aaron Rothenburger. The latter was, as was the mentioned Joseph (Jeisle), no longer living in *anno* 1745. The widow Beile accompanied her son Meier, named Marx or Mahrum under the chuppah in Horburg in this year and arranged a Chalizah for her then still single son David Guenzburer. Another daughter Elizabeth (Lipud) married Joseph Hirtz von Soulzmatt in 1753. Bella (Beile) was still living at that time.

[324]Breisach City Archive, Fasc. No.

of 5 ½ florins. Marx Guenzburger was chosen for the year 1776. Some days later, Lazarus Wormser and his brother, as well as Lazarus Greilsammer, had some poor Jews come into the house of Joseph Hirsch and

"sent the Jewish messenger to me as a joke, that I" should go there. Lazarus Wormser had already prepared the gathering for a fight, but I betook myself there despite the usual custom. Lazarus Wormser confronted me with the idea that the Jews would not be happy paying a collector. But I countered him that without payment, it would be of interest to nobody whether or not the cameral money arrived. I would have all the responsibility on my back and remained determined to hire the collectors. Regardless of this, they made Lazarus Wormser collector (*Einnehmer*) and deployed Joseph Hirsch only as a money collector (*Geldeinzüger*) with 2 florins 45 crowns salary. The assessor promised to pay one week after the next visit." The Jewry now had to pay the 350 fl. that were due the previous year to the General Collectors; but, "because of bad intentions," hardly 100 florins had been gathered. Representative Mock does not, despite all of this, want to involve himself in this matter, although he can see from the beginning that the monies will be very poorly paid.

Each assessor would have been concerned only to complete his weekly rounds but not to collect money. Joseph Hirsch could legitimate to the assessor with his own handwritten signature that he was made collector but not really Schultermann at the mentioned meeting. "If I had not kept quiet about everything, it would come to punches because of this Wormser, when Nathan Geissmar, who also was called by Wormser, said to me: 'That is a nice parnus, we don't need such a parnus.' He uttered more bad words, but I didn't give any response."

On Sunday, the fourteenth ds., Lazarus Wormser again sent word by the Jewish messenger that I was to go to Jos. Hirsch's house and instructed him to summon his poor consorts. I responded that I was unwell, but also that he should not think me a fool whom he could summon at his leisure; if he had something to say to me, he knew where I lived. I commanded the messenger to summon no one else, upon which Wormser and his brother, as well as Grailsammer, came anyway. I asked what they wanted, to which he answered:

"To settle accounts with his brother Alexander," who produced a 4- or 5-year bill according to which he would demand 20 florins from the Jews. It became clear, on the contrary, that this amount had already been cleared and that he was owed the Jews several debts. Wormser responded: 'I don't let myself be put down like you have put down my son-in-law.'[325] Lazarus Wormser, who had come to fight and bicker, then abruptly took up his brother by the side and said: 'I have to slap your hand again, as I already have. Do you not know that you have been charged 9 florins in expenses by the praiseworthy Commission because of your thievings? You have hitherto handed in a bill.'

"I want to bring your thievery to light again, you thief: You no longer have more power than 30 crowns to give out . . ." I answered that he should shut up or I'd show him the door. He continued, however: "You imp. You thief!" I opened the door and said he should get out of my room; I did not have to listen to this in my house; I would report this to the authorities. But he not only did not want to leave the house, he also carried on with his evil language that I found myself forced to lead him out by the ear. In the meantime my son Hertz came and heard Lazarus Wormbser confronted me, his father, so impertinently and still didn't want to leave the room, so

---

[325]Surely Sisskind Levi or Löb Dreifus in Endingen (Switzerland).

he tried to drag him out, but his face got so scratched that no cat in the world could have done such damage.

Your Grace and Favor should therefore intercept if inclined, based on this true fact shown by these four, who were in my room at that time, and should mercifully recognize how large the paration [probably from Greek, related to *parat* = making business; see Grimm Dictionary] of that time and always will be achieved against me by that banal Lazarus Wormbser. It is also well to remember the same inclination that his withheld expenses of 9 fl. are imposed on me by the praiseworthy commission not because of the thieving or the crime committed but only because the unauthorized will before God is recognized, which can be seen in the commission report at that time, as the most supplicating and obedient, which requests not only him alone, Lazarus Wormbser, to discontinue his habitually loose tongue, but for me also to depart from a pleasurable satisfaction to me and consider him the accused in these costs, in whose pleasure I console myself and in all submission I remain.

Your Magnificence Grace and Favor's most supplicating and obedient Wolf Mock"

Funerals at the Jewish Cemetery Mackenheim

It is possible to show that the Breisach Jewry also used a Jewish burial place lying on an earlier branch of the Rhine near Mackenheim in lower Alsace during an unknown period before 1755, and the deceased were brought there by ship heading down the Rhine.[326] An addition to the Jews of Mackenheim and Breisach, the forest cemetery, already in use since 1608,[327] also served the Jews of Biesheim, Marckolsheim, Riedwihr, Diebolsheim, Boesenbiesen (also called Kleinbiesen), Grussenheim, and Gerstheim. It had to be expanded in different ways, especially in 1629, when the unregulated Rhine current washed away a part of it. The frequent flooding meant that the oldest grave stones disappeared or sank into the wet ground. Often only poor land was allocated for Jewish graves—sandy, wet, or hilly.

From about forty entirely or partially preserved gravestones from 1669 to 1752, at least fourteen belong to graves of Breisach Jews.[328] The influential Joseph Guenzburger was buried here on 4 April 1727, although he had been registered since 1721 as a privileged person of the Emmendingen cemetery established in the same year. In April 1733 his wife Resle was buried next to him. Her father Zadok Weil was representative of Ehnheim. The parents of Joseph Guenzburger and at least four other members of this wealthy Breisach family were also buried in the Mackenheim community cemetery between 1707 and 1752.

Gravestone Inscriptions[329]

1. Gaon, the AW Bet Din, our teacher and rabbi Jeremia, son of R. Jehuda sl.,[i] on 14 Ellul 445 (Thursday, 13 September 1685)."

---

[326]Joseph Luedaescher, *Gesch. des Dorfes Mackenheim*, Strasbourg 1922

[327]Mention of cemetery 9/25/1608 (Archive Department Strasbourg G 1358)

[328]Communication from Mr. Günter Boll, Müllheim-Feldberg 1985, who undertook an enormous investigation of the Mackenheimer cemetery.

[329]Discoveries by Mr. G. Boll, Müllheim, before 1986

2.	Frau Gele, daughter of the martyr David ah., who died on 10 Elul 453 (= Friday, 11 September 1693). And may her resting place be in the Garden of Eden with the righteous. May her soul be bound in the bond of eternal life. Amen. Sela.

3.	Here is buried Mrs. Sara Jentele, daughter of Josef sl. She was the wife of Mr. Salman von Gravehusen (= Grafenhausen) and would be buried on Tuesday, 5 Schwat 456 (= Monday, 9 January 1696). May her soul be bound in the bond of eternal life.

4.	A righteous and able man, the Mr. Jehuda Abraham Schlomo, son of Pinchas, died with a good name on Wednesday, Erev Sukkhot 457 (= 10 October 1696). May his soul be bound in the heavenly bond with the soul of Abraham, Jizchak and Jakob, who are in the Garden of Eden. Amen. May his soul be bound in the bond of eternal life.

5.	A competent and reliable man, Mr. Liebmann, son of R. Rafael szl., who left his world on Saturday, 4 Tischri 461 (=Friday, 17 September 1700). And may his soul be bound in the bond of eternal life with the rest of the righteous, who are in the Garden of Eden. Amen.

6.	The G"d-fearing Mr. Alexander, son of M (aertyrer?) Schmuel of Altbreisich (= Altbreisach), died on Tuesday, 2 Schwat 464 (= 8 January 1704). May his soul be bound in the bond of eternal life with the rest of the righteous in the Garden of Eden. Amen.

7.	The eulogized lady, Lady Ela, daughter of Jakob sl., wife of Kazin, Parnus of Manhig Mr. Izik Breisach, who came to the world and left it in good name on Rosch Chodesch Tamus 465 (1. Tamus 465 – Tuesday, 23 June 1705). May her soul be bound in the bond of eternal life.

8.	Isaak Netter, community representative in the Ville Neuve de Brisach, died 20 May 1714. The righteous and able man, the "Aluf and Kazin" (Hebr. for Chief), Parnus u-Manjig Mr. Izik Netter sl. of Breisach jzv. And he went into his world the first day of the Feast of Weeks and was buried on the second day of the Feast of Weeks 474.

9.	Mayer Netter of Breisach, died June 1714, a righteous and reliable man. The beloved Mr. Meir, son of Kazin, Parnus u-Manhig Mr. Jizchak, from the Breisich (Breisach) holy community, died with a good name on Wednesday, 11 Tamus 474 (11 Tamus 474 was a Sunday).

10.	Mrs. Hinle, daughter of R. Jizchak sl., from Turlach (Durlach), wife of the Parnus u-Manhig R. M. Maharam Breisach, (died) on holy Sabbath, 14 Elul 467 (Sunday, September 11, 1707).

11.   Gemar Reichel, daughter of Mr. Jeischaia schljt. . . . Here was buried the esteemed and lauded wife, the beloved wife . . . Reichel, daughter of Mr. Jeschaia schljt., wife of Mr. Menel Segal, from Breisach, who went to her world on Friday, 9 Ijar 470 (= May 9, 1710).

12.   Here was interred a respected and reliable man. His house was always open, and a good reputation is better than oil: the Kazin, Parnus u-Manhig Mr. Koschel Mosche Jehuda ha-Levi sl., from Breisach, who went to his world on Sunday, 10 Adar 471 (= 1 March 1711). May his soul be bound in the bond of eternal life.

13.   Mr. Süsskind Breisach, and he went to his world on holy Sabbath and was buried on Sunday, 16 Schwat 473 (born 11 February 1713, buried 12 February 1713), and his wife, Mrs. Mirjam, and she went to her world on Wednesday and was buried on Thursday, 20 Schwat 473 (died 15 February 1713, buried 16 February 1713). May their souls be bound in the bond of eternal life.

14.   He was wise and knew the sense of all his doings. They were done with talent. He walked pure and dealt fairly and righteously, the Aluf, Parnus u-Manhig R. Maharam, son of the Parnus u-Manhig David szl. Ginsburg, who went to his world on the eve of the holy Sabbath, 9 Ijar 473 (= May 5, 1713). May his soul be bound in the bond (of eternal life).

15.   The venerable, the aged and honorable Mr. Jehuda, son of R. Zwi, buried on Thursday, Erev Rosch Chodesch Adar 480 (29 Schwat 480—Thursday, February 8, 1720). May his soul be bound in the bond of eternal life.

16.   Mrs. Sarle, daughter of the Kazin, Parnus u-Manhig and shtadlan [advocate for the Jews to non-Jews], r. Maharam sl., from Breisach, died on Sunday, 2 Adar 480 (= 11 February 1720). May her soul be bound in the bond of eternal life.

17.   Mrs. Merle, wife of the Kazin, Parnus u-Manhig Mr. R. Maharam sl., from Breisach, died on Sunday 12 Ijar 480 (= Monday, 20 May 1720). May her soul be bound in the bond of eternal life.

18.   A reliable man . . . (. . . like a Hirsch. . .) . . . Mr. Naftali Hirsch (. . .). And he went to his world (. . . 481) died 1720/21.

19.   Moses Libel?

Mosche bar Mosche Jehuda sl., from Breisach, (died on) 5 Schwat 481 (= 2/2/1721)

20.   Abraham Netter, who must have died a violent death and was buried near Koppel Dreyfus of Diebolsheim, who was murdered in 1712:

ha-Kadosch Abraham ben Parnus u-Manhig Jizchak s'l of Breisach, died on Sunday, 15 Kislew 484 (= 12/12/1723).

21.   Grave inscription of Josef Guenzburger:

G"d was with Joseph, so he became a successful man. (Genesis 39:2). Here lies rescued in peace the lamp of Israel, the Kazin, the Shtadlan, Parnus u-Manhig, known at the gates of his time. He was protector and shield of the people in affliction. As wall he protected them. His house was wide open for the Torah scholars; his table was set. R. Josef Josle, son of R. Maharam sl. Guenzburg, from Breisach, of high renown was prayed to the heavens [people prayed for his safe journey to the afterlife] on Friday, 13 Nissan 487 (= 4 April 1727). May his soul be bound in the bond of eternal life.

22.   A righteous and able man, the Kazin, Parnus u-Manhig, the benevolent Mr. Joel, son of Jekutiel sl, from the holy community Biese (Biesheim), died and was buried with a good name on Sunday, 11 Nissan 489 (= 10 April 1729). May his soul be bound in the bond of eternal life.

23.   Mrs. Jachet, daughter of the Kazin, Parnus u-Manhig, Mr. Mahafram Schdilingen (= Stühlingen), wife of the Kazin Mr. Schalom Breisach jzv. And she went to her world on the holy Sabbath and was buried on Sunday, Erev R(osch Chodesch) Nissan of the year "Salvation" (29 Adar 490 = Saturday, 18 March 1730 = 1 Nissan 490 = Sunday, 19 March 1730).May her soul be bound in the bond of eternal life.

24.   Grave inscription of Resle Guenzburger née Weil:

The virtuous woman, righteous and pleasant, of distinguished and famous heritage, a wealthy and wise lady, Mrs. Resle, daughter of the Kazin, Parnus u-Manhig, of the reputable R. Zadok Weil, wife of the Parnus u-Manhig and Shtadlan R. Josle Breisach. Her soul rose to heaven on Thursday, Erev Rosch Chodesch Ijar 493 (30. Nissan 493 = Wednesday, 15 April 1773). May her soul be bound in the bond of eternal life.

25.   Nathan Moch (or Nathan Geismmar?):

ha-Aluf Nathan bar Elieser s'l of Breisach, died on Wednesday, 8 Elul 496 (= 8/15/1736). Back side: Nate Breisach

26.   Scheine, single daughter of Hirz Mock:

ha-Betula Scheine bat Hirz Breisach jz'v (= G"tt protect him), died (on 10/6/1738 =) Schemimi Azeret and buried (on 10/7/1738 =) Simchat Thora 499

27.   Doderle Wormbser:

ha-Aluf, ha-Rosch and ha-Kazin Totros ben Parnas u-Manhig Mordechai s'l of Breisach, buried on Sunday, 16 Schwat 502 (= 1/21/1742)

28.   Scheine Guenzburger born Wormser of Breisach, died 5 May 1749, the respected and lauded woman, the virtuous Kezina Mrs. Scheine, wife of Aluf and Kazin, Parnus u-Manhig R. David Guenzburger jzv., of Breisach. And she went to her world on Monday, 17 Ijar 509.

29.   Benjamin bar Jehuda von Biesheim, died May 2, 1750. A virtuous man, Benjamin, son of Yehuda schlijt., from Biesse (Biesheim). He went into his world on holy Sabbath, 26 Nissan 510.

30. The esteemed lady, the Kezina Lady Esther, daughter of Aluf and Kazin, Parnus u-d Manhig R. Hirz Levi sl., from the holy community Metz, wife of Aluf and Kazin R. Leima Ginzburger of Breisach jzv. And she went to her world on Thursday, 18 Schwat 512 (died 3 February 1752, buried 4 February 1752). May her soul be bound in the bond of eternal life.

Gravestones of Breisach Jews in the Schlettstadt Cemetery

Among the oldest gravestones of the cemetery near Schlettstadt, which was laid out around 1620 and used mostly by lower Alsace Jews (Ribeauville, Bergheim, etc.), can be found some epitaphs belonging to the Breisach community:[330]

1)   The boy Schlomo Mosche Schaul Naftali, son of Parnus u-Manhig R. Totros (yesterday on) Sunday, 8 Tamus 459 (= 5/7/1699)[331]

2)   Jakob Seev Wolf, son of Parnus u-Manhig r. Todros, from Colmar (died on) Wednesday, 20 Siwan 469 (= 5/29/1709)[332]

---

[330]Investigations and commentary by Mr. Günter Boll, Müllheim-Feldberg, from Feb. 20, 1986

[331]Naftali, son of horse handler Alexander Doterle, was single. R. Moise Ginsburger in "Les Memoriaus alsaciens," REJ tome 41, p. 142 confused him with the famous Verfbeer of Strassbourg. This Naftali ben Totros was buried next to the representative of Rappoltstein Jewry, Jaeckel Reinau, who had died 12 days earlier on 6/23/1699 in Ribeauville.

[332]Wolf, who died before his father, was the young husband of Rosina Rheinau from Ribeauville.

3) A double gravestone memorializes two single children of Marx Wormbser of Breisach:

The boy Mosche Juda, named Leib, son of Kazin Mordechai Preisach, died on Friday, 17 Tewet 481 (= Thursday 1/16/1721).

The girl Rebekka Sarle, daughter of K(azin) Parnus u-Manhig Mordechai, from Preisach (died) on Thursday, 17 Siwan 481 (=5/12/1721)

4) Near this double grave, one can find the stone of Rabbi Jakob Caan, placed on an iron pond; he was the representative of the rabbi family Kahn from Breisach and Sulzburg:

Jakob Kahn, Rabbi and Aw Bet Dein in Rappoltsweiler, died on 1/11/1722 in Ribeauville, buried in Sélestat [Schlettstadt] at the Jewish cemetery at Giessen. The inscription of his gravestone was the following R. Jakob ha-Kohen . . . from Rappschwihr on Sunday, 22 Tewet 482, "bidden in the heavenly Yeshiva."

Burials at the Schmieheim-Wallburg Cemetery

1) The esteemed lady, Mrs. Sara Chana, daughter of David, wife of the beloved Mr. Liebermann Metz, from Breisich (= Breisach), died on Tuesday, 20 Schwat 463 (= February 6, 1703).

2) (Rizpa?) Rechle, daughter of the R. Meschullam sl., of Diedenhofen (= Thionville in Lothringen), wife of Josle, son of Salman, of Breisich (= Breisach), died on Monday, 23 Nissan 463 (= 9 April 1703) and buried on the above-mentioned day.

3) The esteemed lady, Mrs. Sara, daughter of Abraham sl., wife of the beloved Mr. Sender, of Breisach, died on holy Sabbath, 25 Siwan 463 (= 9 June 1703).

4) Josua Uffenheimer, who died with a good name, old and full of days, and was buried on the eve of the holy Sabbath, 12 Adar Rischon 546 (= 10 February 1786). Behind the name is the abbreviation of the surname . . . which is written out in a acrostic inscription. (He was the leader and founder of the floret silk factory in Breisach and Schuttern.)

The funeral of three Jewish Breisach women at the Schmieheim cemetery in the first half of 1703 occurred when the Upper Rhine region from Speyer to Hüningen was also the site of the Spanish War of Succession (1702-1714). The Jewish cemetery of Mackenheim on the left bank of the Rhine was probably not accessible to the Jews of the old Further Austrian city of Altbreisach from 18 April 1702, when Kaiser Leopold I declared war, until the transfer of the imperial Altbreisach fortress to King Louis XIV on 6 September 1703.

A similar situation likely also explains the burial of some Breisach Jews at the Emmendingen cemetery during the war years after 1733 and during the Austrian War of Succession (1740–1748). It is to be assumed that the Jews from Altbreisach were again, and without exception, buried in the Mackenheim cemetery following the Peace of Aachen, which was concluded on 18 October 1748, until the approval of a dedicated burial site on 4 June 1755.

Funerals at the Jewish Cemetery in Emmendingen

In 1734 the following payments were registered at the Hochberg office in Emmendingen for graves at the local cemetery:

Moyses Geismar of Alt-Breisach

for his wife (buried in Emmendingen)	6 fl. (guilder)
Paul Metz in Breisach (Refuel ben Elieser)	12 fl.
Alexander Wurmser's wife in Breisach	6 fl.

David Guenzburger, Jewish mayor in Breisach:

a little boy	3 fl.

In the account lists of the Eichstett Community Book (ca. 1730) the following names of Breisach cemetery members reappeared annually:

Mose ben Schneiur (Moses Geismar)

Liebermann ben Rephuel (Lazarus Metz)

Jausle ben Schimon (Joseph Simon)

Lieber ben Todres (presumably Lazarus Wormser)

Marum ben Josef (Marx Joseph Guenzburger?)

Isak Netter (died before 1748)

Samuel Levi (died in 1744).

Few graves in the oldest part of the Emmendingen cemetery stood the tests of time. The following inscriptions were recently still legible, indicating those from Altbreisach laid to rest here:

1)   The "Cantor"[ii] Refuel ben Elieser,

died . . . (by the end of 1734)[333]

His wife Feiele, died 9 Tewet 501 (28 December 1740)

2)   The "Cantor" Schemuel S'gal (halevi) from Breisach,

---

[333]Identical to Paul (= Raphael) Metz

died on the fifth day and buried on the sixth day on the eve of the holy sabbath, on 17 Nisan 504 (1744)[334]

3)   The "Cantor" (rich) Joseph ben Ischai hakohen

died Friday, buried Sunday the 28th of Adar 506 (1746)

(officially he was called Jakob Greilsamer von Breisach)

4)   Naftali Hirz ben Aron Mock von Breisach,

died Saturday, Schuschan Purim 507 (February 25) buried 2/26/1747

5)   Esriel Geismar (named Seligmann) died 1779.

Maier Weyl from Altbreisach paid 12 florins for a transit fee in 1754 to the margravial, high-mountain register in Emmendingen on the occasion of the funeral of his father-in-law Michel Dreyfuss, who was buried in the communal cemetery in Emmendingen.

The Breisach Jewish Cemeteries

According to a copy of a manuscript collated by the Breisach chancellery, the Parnus Lehmann Guenzburger and "the three Jewish community deputies" Jakob Greilsamer, Leopold Mock, and Isaak Levi turned to the old Further Austrian district office in Waldkirch in April 1755 and requested as a precaution "that our old custom of burying deceased Jews in the Alsace also be approved and sanctioned for the future" in the case that the Breisach magistrate should request more money than the Jewish community, living in great poverty, could pay for permission for cemeteries outside or in the city.[335] From another piece of the fascicle it is apparent that an agreement between the city and the Jewish community was eventually reached: "In an extra session of the council held today," as was communicated to the district office on 4 June 1755, it was decided that "the former gardens of David Guenzburger" be sanctioned as a Jewish cemetery "because it is fully separate from the inhabitants, as if in a corner, with a rather high wall surrounding it; also the baths for the Jewish women have already long since been installed there and the Jewish synagogue is next to it as well."

The following documents provide verbatim information on the efforts that the Breisach Jewish Community officers took to get their own cemetery in the city:

---

[334]Thorough description of this grave in a series article by Karl Guenther, "Der alte jüdische Friedhof in Emmendingen" [The Old Jewish Cemetery in Emmendingen]. (*Badische Zeitung*, 21 Nov. 1967 to 1 February 1968). The widow of Samuel Levi died in February 1748.

[335]Breisach City archive, Fasc. 1848

1)   Jewish Breisach to Constance Representation[336]

"For highly respected Representation at Constance October 3, 1754

In accordance with Your Excellence and Grace reminder, received with the rescript on September 14th about Your Excellencies and Grace's deigning to hear our plea, which was not send in as a letter but was made through other means, about the approval of a Jewish cemetery, we herewith give obligatory and submissive thanks, and also enclose a humble account of why the aforementioned permission is so worrisome to us; because each and every local inhabitant of worldly and spiritual standing expresses not a small abomination at the conditions of the funerals of the Jews who are dying, especially in the city itself. Especially in consideration of the demolition of the local strongholds, due to which the ditches in the lower city are mostly besieged with stones and fallen walls, so that running water is stalled, and one finds a constant morass of everything impure, carried along down from the upper city through rain, already tending toward disease, just as many years ago when the plague reigned here the lower city is stained with it. While the upper city remains fully clear of such problems, the lower city will perhaps be so much the sooner infected when this cemetery, graciously permitted, would be laid in the middle of Jew Street between the houses.

This is also the undoubted cause why the garrison itself, although referred to as a large cemetery in St. Joseph, exists in the lower city and faraway from all houses, its burials in the ground, laid outside the city, which is why this consequently has to be considered a wholly infeasible thing.

So that this dreadful state of affairs might be remedied and the local Jews helped, so have we, although Jews themselves, as they already applied for such concession during occupation times, and indeed outside the city, did not want to permitted such a one for above-alleged (cited) causes, nonetheless in the furthering of the highest arary (goods administration) interest come to the decision to request again, one laid near the city and more comfortable place to the rear way, but conceding the fee in exchange.

And because to Your Imperial Royal Majesty it can only be of no importance as to whether this buries in- or outside the city, when only the therefore to be paid Fahl from you is always paid to the highest sovereign atrium.

So we set on Your Excellence and Grace's most honorable good will our firm and most subservient trust, that for our onetime made decision, all further et cetera and objections against it, we will be supported to the fullest and thereupon no adverse fate can befall our minds, as the hopefully thought about permission will be granted to us in Grace and loyalty,

and with subservient respect remain

Your Excellence and Grace . . . ."

2) The Jewry to the administration of Constance early April 1755

"Highborn, illustrious highness, high-esteemed, nobles, reeve, provident and wise men, gracious and benevolent Gentlemen,

---

[336]Breisach City archive, Fasc. 1835

Yesterday, gracious and beneficial Gentlemen have inspected the original document, which was send in the name of the very laudable district office of Waldkirch to us and therefrom understood that we are to choose a place outside of the city as our cemetery and after we do so to declare it within 8 days.

Since we were given such a short time limit, we would like to offer to your gracious magistracy the humblest faith and would like to make a petition that perhaps the very same could deign to assist us with help and direction as we declare our intent: in humblest respect subordinate to you, to afore mentioned use, would ½ the acre on top the so called Mihlenwaasen, belonging to the laudable city, be sufficient.

Therefore urgently petitioning to grant us said plot or if noble lords deem it better to grant us the Wannotischen Garden, in consideration of our well known poverty, at a low price and to send us the decided upon conditions in an immediate resolution. Recognizing devoted, eminent grace and in addition to our obedient respect to the high Protection, we remain

your Grace's and Benevolence's humble obedient Jewry here at Altbreisach

Jacob Greisamer, Lehmann Guenzburger, Isac Lefie, Leopold Mock "

3) Jewry to the district office Waldkirch, 22 April 1755

"Copy of an report given on April 22 by the Parnass and three Jewish deputies of Jewish affairs Jakob Greilsamer, Leopold Mock and Isaak Levi in the name of all Jewry, concerning the to be chosen cemetery site.

Foremost we give our humblest, most obliged thanks to your Grace and Sponsor about the passing of the decree by an eminently respectable representation and chamber: At the same time we cannot avoid to lament the same and initiate our report about the cemetery. Since none of the Jewry is in possession of its own land in the area of Breisach, we appealed to our nearest authorities,--as attached vindication shows--, and asked that one of the two sites mentioned in the vindication would be granted to us in grace for a simple payment. Whereupon we were answered with a negative decree, but with the notice that we will receive, from an eminently respectable representation, a letter allotting to us a site to this end outside the city.

Regardless that both cited lots are outside the city, not adjacent to any road and one of them, namely the so called Mühlwasser, is in nobody's way and is not even in use or of use to any person.

So in this way the entire Jewry's plea reaches your Grace and Benign, if your Highnesses would be so gracious to consider, bearing in mind with how much time and effort we all work on the sovereign atrium to increase the interest in it, to make the decrees to be passed by an eminently respectable representation to us your concern and hope with most subservient reliance that the high Gentleman will have mercy with the hard-pressed Jewry, which with all efforts and pains is barely able to make enough for the daily bread, and would give their worthy city the order to grant us one of the lots, for a small fee, as it is fitting for prevalent times. Otherwise, that your highest Grace's and Patronage will second our petition with the eminently respectable representation, that in the future once a Jew is deceased he will be buried in the Alsace. For such received grace from your Highness' we would be willing to show ourselves at any time as the most willing servant. With our everlasting recommendation and persisting in humblest submission.

accredited by Chancellery Breisach (registry of Breisach)

4) District Office Waldkirch to the representation Constance, May 28th, 1755

"As the representatives can see from the report sent on April 25th, the Jewry has, due to the letter from the representation from March 22, suggested a different cemetery location—either the Mühlenwasen or the formerly Wannotischen,[337] today Philipp Guentzburger's garden.

Waldkirch received, according to their request, a report from Constance on April 29, about why one wasn't able or willing to allot to the Jewry one of the two lots, but instead one on the Faulen Waag or one in the Wolfhöhle, or why it was not allowed to buy a place above Hochstetten under the condition, that the Jewry would pay a recognition to the municipality and a toll to the parish church as was done before, for example when their synagogue was erected. It was therefore necessary, that the Jewry send in a reply until May 6th about above mentioned conditions. This, however, was not done until Ejus 27th (also 27th Iyyar/Ijjar 5515= May 8, 1755), due to Jewish holidays, and the letter was handed to us by Parnass Lehman Guentzburger and some of the deputies. The majority of the votes elected of the three from the government suggested lots the one in the Wolfshöhle, Still the Jewry would like to know the price and the district office would like to know what Constance has to say about the recognition sum and the annual Fahl sum, because the estates would ask the same.

So Waldkirch would like a secure report, so that later no objections can arise.

1.   If the selling of the lot in the Wolfshöhle indeed came to a conclusion

2.   What was asked for the lot beside the purchasing price and whether a recognition sum was demanded and

3.   What the Breisach church should receive from the annual Fahl? Whether this and anything else will be put into a contract, agreed on with the Jewry, or if any other arrangement should be agreed upon, for example the offered servitude, and then a detailed description.

Waldkirch, May 28, 2755"

Ultimately there was an agreement:

The garden of Philipp Guentzburger, formerly the Wannot garden, which was already bordered by a rather high wall, was established as Breisach Cemetery in 1755.

The first corpse buried in this cemetery was of a servant girl who died in February 1756 in the house of Philipp Guentzburger.[338]

The new Jewish cemetery, founded in 1875, is located on today's Isenbergstraße. A small street "am Mühlwasen" leads to the entrance in the northern enclosure wall before the gate; on both sides of the street stand trees at intervals of a few meters to mark the practice of lowering the coffin three times after it has been taken out by the horse-driven hearse.

To the right of the entrance, west of the middle path, only male bodies—with few exceptions—were buried initially after the cemetery's founding. The left-side field was intended

---

[337] Wannot was a tax collector, he died 1743
[338] Council protokol from Februray 6, 1756

for women and children at first, but married couples were also buried here after the First World War. All gravestones stand in a north-south orientation, in the direction of the former synagogue, as was the custom in the old cemetery. Only the double grave of Rabbi Moses Reiss and his wife and the single grave of Cantor Joseph Guggenheimer in the so-called men's section point to the east (Misrach). The oldest of the twelve gravestones in this first row in the north-east corner bears the name Scholem (Sales) Geismar. Tradition has it that the last one to have been buried at the old cemetery also bore the name Scholem.

The male section as well as the "women's and children's section "include stones along the south wall dating from the years 1926 and 1925 respectively. Both sections of sixteen rows each, divided by the middle path, are also cut across after the eighth row by a path running west to east. This path leads north to and ends at the "new section," a cemetery still 3/8 unused.

The newer section, also beginning along the northern enclosure, starts at the scrub boundary with the double stone of Theodor Model (died 1924).

With the deportation of the last Jewish citizen in October 1940 to the labor camp Gûrs in southern France, burial ceased for several years. After the Second World War, only few survivors could be buried in their native cemetery. Due to a new law, all iron grave fencing was removed in 1942 and transported to the salvage disposal as scrap.[339]

The Textile Merchant Josua Uffenheimer

In order to secure a rebound for the city during a period of crisis, the old Further Austrian government authorized a waste-silk-plant, which moved shortly after its founding into the large, empty rooms of the military infirmary on today's Kupfertorstraße.[340] This was followed by an expensive modification and in 1768 the Breisach penitentiary and workhouse was established therein.[341] Prisoners as well as free workers and orphans were used as laborers in the adjoining silk factory.

The factory management and its administration soon came into the hands of one Formaro. Despite several loans, even from the provincial estates, the company produce no profit and suggestions for improvement were made.[342] "There arrived an unexpected savior in the person of the Jew Josua Uffenheimer of Kippenheim," reported Haselier.[343]

This capable businessman was already well known to the old Further Austrian government. He had had a good-sized store in Kippenheim[344] around mid-century and brought much toll to the state treasury through his commission business with "Constance in Tirol" and with Switzerland. Among other things, this Josua Uffenheimer had the abbot of Ettenheimmünster, the city of Ettenheim, and three neighboring villages transfer to him for collection an outstanding debt of 4100 florins owing to a war shipment to the imperial army. It was thought better to consider the debt a loss than to wait any longer, lest there be no more money to hope for should war again break out. "There is no doubt that the Jew will win quite a

---

[339] Documents about prosecution, Kohlhammer-publishing (1966), p. 351
[340] Haselier II, p. 89ff
[341] GLA 196/198 (Haselier II, p. 90ff)
[342] Old Further Austrian country estates to the government, Freiburg 4.II 1768 (Haselier II, p. 98)
[343] Haselier, p. 93
[344] J.A. Zehnter Geschichte der Juden in der Markgrafschaft Baden-Baden" (history of Jews in the margravate Baden-Baden), p. 412. Uffenheimer played a 30 guilder annual lump sum for his axes on manufacturing, after an agreement with the margravial gov. in 1751.

bit;" said the rapporteur, "but the bribery will cost him some too."[345] In 1769 the government allowed the Jewish entrepreneur Uffenheimer to open a hemp-spinning and weaving mill in the city as well as in the workhouse.[346]

In 1769 he fought a tough fight for the lowering of wages, which the penitentiary and the workhouse demanded from him for the workers they allocated him.[347] In part he used the same arguments the estates had cited before as the reason for the unprofitability of the penitentiary business. In the end, Josua Uffenheimer proposed the conclusion of a ten-year contract that allowed him to set up and maintain a graduated labor rate for those workers allocated from the penitentiary and the workhouse.[348] The company changed to "Vorländische Florettseiden- u. Leinwandfabrik Kompanie" (Anterior floret silk and canvas factory).

Furthermore, Josua Uffenheimer was able to find a suitable instructor for the untrained workers in the person of Benedikt Herzog, a ribbon weaver from Weitenau in Aargau.[349] The result was that Uffenheimer was able, already in the first Breisach business year, to export goods to Italy and to Kolin in Bohemia.[350]

In an attestation from the abbot of cloister Schuttern from 27 July 1773, Uffenheimer is called a "Breysach factory sytstem entrepreneur," who erected a promising cotton spinning and weaving mill in Schuttern about six weeks prior. Uffenheimer sent the attestation to the government as attachment to an application "to transfer the seal, graciously allotted to the Alt-Breisach mill, also to Schuttern." The president of the three country estates understood this application as "a notification and request about the removal of Fornaro from the penitentiary and workhouse in Altbreisach" and remarked in a letter, which, however, was never dispatched, "that Fornaro would be removed, but that because it was said that very suspicious circumstances had emerged, it was impossible to look at this lightly, and thus other steps must be taken."

An accountant's report from 1773 on the Breisach penitentiary and workhouse mention "derangement and disarray." However, this did not concern the merchant Uffenheimer, but the old Further Austrian estates as legal representatives of the institution. Thus the interior conditions of the penitentiary are also severely criticized.[351] Grave allegations were brought forth against the penitentiary manager Fornaro, who was associate of the mill at the time and then was consequently impeached.[352]

---

[345]Rosenthal, p. 196 as well as more detailed in Th. Weiss, Bistum Straßburg

[346] old Further Austrian commerce assambly to Josua Uffenheimer, Freiburg May 30, 1769 (GLA 196/702). Haselier II, p. 99

[347] Protocol of the work payment for the Altbreisach workhouse and penitentiary, subject Freiburg, Junw 26, 1769 (GLA 196/702)

[348]Old Further Austrian gov. and chamber to the estates commerce about the lease of the Altbreisach workhouse and penitentiary to the Jew Uffenheimer, Freiburg 1769 (GLA 196/702)

[349]Josua Uffenheimer to the old Further Austrian gov and Chamber, Kippemheimer Dec. 13, 1769 (GLA 196/702)

[350] Correspondence of the Altbreisach's chancellery trustee Schuech with the old Further Austrian gov, and chamber about sending cotton material to Italy from the Altbreisach factory- December 1769. Schuech declared that he had given the Jew Uffenheimer a trade pass for silk fabric to Collin. Breisach December 16, 1769 (GLA 196/702). Haselier II, p. 100

[351]Report of the K.K. Court chamber in Vienna to the court chancellery, Vienna September, 20, 1773 (GLA 196/703) Haselier II, p. 101

[352]From a detailed report of the highest judical office Vienna, January 25, 1776 (Haselier II, p. 102)

In the meantime, from 1774 on, the Breisach mill is listed as "cotton mill of Josua Uffenheimer," who largely drove economic life in the seventies of the 18th century in the margravate of Baden as well as in old Further Austria.[353]

On January 4, 1775, the old Further Austrian government reported to the court chancellery in Vienna and stressed that Josua Uffenheimer was "simultaneously co-tenant of Hall, in Inntal, salt retail."[354] He was to have built a factory at the Breisach penitentiary and negotiated a 10-year lease agreement with the estates. He allegedly invested about 18,000–20,000 guilder in his factory and also procured earnings of around 50,000 guilder for "the public." According to accounting documents, the earnings for the public in 1773 alone came to 12,857 guilder and 48 kreutzer. The barons of Wittenbach and Bollschweil, as well as the estates' collector of Camuzi invested with 600, 800, and 1000 guilder in the business. in order to "jolly along Uffenheimer, who increasingly wanted to give up the mill because of aforementioned hassles." The baron of Wittenburg affirmed to Uffenheimer "that he had shown a special eagerness over many years, to the present, to establish trade in old Further Austria and had spent a great deal of personal capital for the attainment (of this)."

According to the list of protected citizens of Breisach from February 11, 1775, Abraham Marx Wertheimer worked as the accountant of the Altbreisach country estates penitentiary and workhouse factory during the past three years, since 1772.

In a letter from 6 June 1775, Uffenheimer informs the president of the old Further Austrian commerce assembly in Freiburg that since February he has employed an accountant and manager for the factory, Christian Friedrich Oechslin, who had previously worked as a clerk in Frankfurt. This man would start the production of "Bed fustian and Kölsch" with ten to twelve chairs [looms?]. From the same year 1775 comes a price list that informs the reader: "At Josua Uffenheimer's, who lives in Kippenheim, not far from Freiburg in Breisgau, entrepreneur of the imperial royal old Further Austrian privileged factories of Altbreisach, Schutter, Hausen upon Thann, the following goods can be purchased at a low price. . . ." Uffenheimer's range of goods comprised "bed fustian with red and blue stripes," embroidered and smooth Kelsch, cloak of light cotton, Brabant cloth and drilling, denim, waist silk handkerchiefs, cotton spinning works, waist silk spinning works, schappe silk, galette textiles Gelettame (Basiness), cushion, dry and wet nonwoven fabric, as well as Turkish cotton in whole bales and waist silk and stud ribbon. [355]

It can be seen from this product list that the waist silk weaving in Breisach continued under the new owner. Certainly Uffenheimer's enterprising endeavor was much less susceptible to risk than the Breisach waist silk mill had been. Uffenheimer was also able to tip off his customers that "these registered goods are all furnished with a highly commendable imperial royal old Further Austrian commercial seal, and thus, the buyer may freely peddle in the old Further Austrian province." That the waist silk mill at the Breisach penitentiary and workhouse was affiliated with the Uffenheimer enterprise lead to expansion: the business was not limited to waist silk, but opened into a general textile plant.[356]

---

[353] Haselier II, p. 93

[354] Old Further Austrian gov. and chamber to the court chancellery, Freiburg January 4, 1775 (GlA 196/ 703), Haselier II, p. 102

[355] A detailed price list from June 20, 1775, and especially a detailed report about the factory buisness is in the dissertation of Uffenheimer descendant Siegfried Bergheimer, 1923 (university library Freiburg in Br.)

[356] Haselier II, p. 94

After two years in operation, a small business consisting of seven workers, who through a secret process could dye cotton yarn into durable Turkish yarn, was integrated into Uffenheimer's factory. [357]

A thorough inspection of the penitentiary factory by a royal committee in 1775 effectuated a discharge of the indicted Fornaro, releasing him from custody due to lack of evidence. After that, any person in charge of the workhouse and penitentiary was prohibited from investing financially in the workhouse or penitentiary. The commission also suggested prematurely terminating the 10-year contract between the old Further Austrian estates and Uffenheimer, because it was disadvantageous to the country. [358]

The highest judicial office in Vienna and the court chancellery, and even Empress Maria Theresia herself, concerned themselves personally with the commission report. [359]

Josua Uffenheimer threatened the estates with a lawsuit should the contract held with him be terminated or changed.

At the end of 1783 an argument transpired between the entrepreneur Uffenheimer and the penitentiary management. In defense against reproaches by the administrative authority, Uffenheimer charged that he was hiring workers from the penitentiary for his personal house construction or in his fields and housework. [360] In order to get the prisoners away from work, he used several different excuses and "*finesse.*"

The factory management wants to use their precious time "for useful and important commercial activities, rather than for daily disturbance and quarrelsome things." So the prison authority now tries to blame the factory management for the fact that on 17 November 1783 around 4 pm, one of the prisoners sentenced to life, Natter, managed to break his chains and shackles and escape with the prisoner Geyer, sentenced to eight years."[*sic*]

When Josua Uffenheimer's 10-year contract expired in 1784, it was apparently extended or replaced by a new contract. [361]

Around 1785 Goetz (Gedeon) Uffenheimer leased the penitentiary in Breisach and built a hemp and linen spinnery.

Simultaneously, he employed around 330 free workers in the Austrian villages upon Kaiserstuhl. Also in the Baar, this enterprising man sought to trespass—and succeeded—in partially opening a leather trade. Although not allowed to enter Freiburg, he had power over hundreds of workers just outside its gates. [362]

The bailiff of Neustadt in the Black Forest also communicated with him in 1756 regarding the establishment of a cottage industry for cotton weaving in that district.

---

[357] From Siegfried Bergheimer's dissertaion, Chapter 3, p. 77, Freiburg in. Br. 1923

[358] From the report of the highest judicial authority, vienna, january 25, 1776 (GLA 196/703), Haselier II, p. 102

[359] Counrt chancellery letter March 9, 1776 (GLA 196/703), Haselier II, p. 103

[360] Josua Uffenheimer to the K.K. Appeal commission, Breisach december 4, 1783 (GLA 196/200), Haselier II, p. 104

[361] Haselier II, p.104

[362] E. Gothein, Commerce history of the black forest, Stasbourg 1892, p.756 and 761

The former district rabbi could say the following about Uffenheimer's wealth and work:[363]

In Kippenheim he owns buildings worth 6,450 guilder, "movable goods" worth 15,416 guilder and 37 ½ kreutzer; secure owings worth 30,100 guilder and 10 kreutzer. He is remarkable for his daring, with which he builds up factories and stands out above his contemporaries. In Altbreisach he built a "cotton factory" worth 8,070 guilder, 47 kreutzer and a "Lein et seide fabrique" (linen and silk factory) worth 11,195 guilder, 54 kreutzer. The "factory equipment" is reckoned to be 1,006 guilder and 8 kreutzer. The receivables add up to 14,457 guilder and 13 kreutzer. So in total his fortune adds up to about 88,000 guilder from which debts of 23,502 guilder and 31 kreutzer have to be deducted, leaving him with a fortune of about 65,000 guilder.

In summer 1792 precautions were taken for the evacuation of the prison in case of a hostile attack on Breisach. The prisoners should be transferred to the castle hill of Graz and the prisons of Innsbruck, Klagenfurt and Laibach.[364] At that time the Breisach penitentiary had 50 inmates.

Shortly before the bombardment of Breisach (Sept. 1793) extinguished the Breisach penitentiary and workhouse, an agreement between Josua Uffenheimer and the estates assembly had been reached concerning the mutual claim from the lease of 3,632 guilder and 14½ kreutzer.

Josua Uffenheimer died in 1786 and was buried in Schmieheim; his wife Braeunle died about 1797.

The conditions should have taken place already before 1790 and it seems that Josua Uffenheimer retired after the end of his contract.

At the Close of the 18th Century

At the beginning of 1778, the "several protected Jewry at Altbreisach" turned to the "Ew. (Your Magnificence, address for an abbot) Excellencies and Graces" and thanked them for the local protection granted in past years. The reason that the consignation due in 1773, and the current one from 1778, were not yet arranged must be pinned on the Parnus Wolf Mock, because he is again unauthorized, as was the case last year, to assign a rating for the payment of the protection duty.[365]

Accordingly, persons like Coppel Mayer and others should pay, although they are excused from payment by the government. In contrast, the discharged auxiliary rabbi Joseph Hirsch was listed as a school employee, so he would not have to pay protection duty.

The Jewry took Mock to task for the irregular provisions. Since Joseph Hirsch, according with the high decree of Sept. 24 last year, was dismissed from the government and was directed to earn his living elsewhere, it goes without saying that he is no longer a school employee.

---

[363] Adolf Lewin, history of the Baden Jews 1738-1909, p. 19, data about weath was taken from a document in the possion of the former county synagoge Freiburg.
[364] Haselier II, p. 105
[365] GLA 196/246

The second point in the document elaborates this further: ". . . the planned investigation and written reports about this Joseph Hirsch by Chief Rabbi Isaac Kahn may also enlighten upon his character and merits: It would be the greatest shame and disgrace for us to employ him at the school or even at a lower position after he kept house—according to the rabbinical reports—in a very disgusting and punishable way for wholesome businesses of charity and brotherhood, as well as for affairs of widows and common Jewry. Furthermore, he lived with an advantage only for himself and Wolf Mock, and with a strong disadvantage for the Jewry; he cannot explain himself in any circumstance. And hence thirdly, because this Joseph Hirsch is anyhow to seek his living elsewhere, as instructed by the high decree from Sept. 24th (last year) by Your Magnificence, Excellence, and Grace, alone, through his wealth, estimated with this new tax draft at 450 Rhine guilder—not including his house, farm and furniture—he must be rich. But we are of the opinion that he owns many more assets, especially since his two sons—in Freiburg and in the countryside—and he himself in Breisach make business deals as well as, if not better than, others. And so living adversely to this situation, when one wanted to free oneself of such tax payment through employment as a school clerk and to cheat the interest of the highest imperial royal and baronial treasury. It was of no avail either with Chief Rabbi Isaac Kaans nor in speaking with Wolf Mock; he held fast to his contemptuous intent, and this is why the consignation is not to be approved.

"So that it (we) will not be seen as more negligent by Your Magnificence, Excellencies, and Graces, the highly gracious, common Jewry, in all subservience, terminate the eight hunted down and true consignations with the adherent, subservient, obedient request, your Highest would be so gracious as to condescend to grant protection to the highest sovereign as before. Until your highest remission, taking our leave with the deepest respect and remain forever."

A letter dated March 1, 1780, to the city of Altbreisach reports:

"Regarding enclosed petition from Joseph Hirsch, former auxiliary rabbi of that place: in granting a free escort, one expects that this Jew will abstain from business and merely through his own means feed (himself) and make ends meet.

"Excellencies Frey Reichs, [could refer to the Roman Empire or the Habsburger royalty lineage, which supplied most of the Roman Empire's local leaders] Nobles, Gracious Lords, Gentlemen! Joseph Hirsch, the former auxiliary rabbi of Altbreisach, presumes to report subserviently, to Your Excellencies and Graces, that the same has received the high mercy of free escort for the past 20 years by *decretum Excelsi Regiminis* [by decree of the excellent government/authority], excluding the usual tax, which he was until then instructed to pay annually. Given that from this day on, the same has signed over all his possessions to his children, because of age and weakness, from whom he receives his livelihood, particularly because he can neither take a single step outside the city nor conduct any business. The repeated prosecution of local Jews, which Your Excellency and Grace will have in good memory, had no little share in bringing about the afflictions and disabling him to befittingly provide his own food.

Thus, his most subservient imploring, Your Excellency and Grace would absolve, under consideration of above mentioned motive, the supplicant from the mentioned taxes of 40 kreutzer annually for the rest of his life.

For the hearing and the granting of the plea would I like to recommend myself with all merited submission and deepest respect to Your Excellencies and Graces.

Your Excellence and Grace's

most subservient Joseph Hirsch,

former Auxiliary Rabbi in Altbreisach."

His petition is rejected on December 12, 1781. In 1795 the Breisach council transcript refers to a lawsuit, probably of the former rabbi, who now had taken up trading:

"At today's council a decision was made concerning the complaint brought forth by local Protected Jew Joseph Hirsch against one Anton Heusler of Hartheimb. The damage done by the latter to the former was in slaughtering [or pommeling?] a cow. Moreover, in this matter, the ad hoc reeve of Hartheim recognized the following decree passed by the city court and on to the K.K. (commerce assembly) old Further Austrian city Altbreisach: Anton Hensler of Hartheim, because he disobeyed an order from the reeve not to slaughter a cow in Hartheim and knowingly and willingly caused a loss of 40 guilder and 30 kreutzer to the Jew Joseph Hirsch, who, with permission of the governor, also slaughtered a cow in Hartheim, is sentenced, firstly, to replace the said Jew's loss with 4 guilder and 30 kreutzer, along with expenses for the trial. Then secondly, to pay the reeve a Rhenish guilder for his coming to court, and thirdly, to atone for his disobedience to the reeve by serving a day in the tower of Hartheim."

The Tolerance Politics of Emperor Joseph II

Documents about Breisach[366] focus on the tolerance edict issued by Emperor Joseph II. On October 20, 1781, it was ordered that two years from Jan. 1, 1782, the Jewish language could be used only in church services. Elsewhere only language of the court should be used. Children must either be sent to the Christian school or be taught by Jewish teachers at the main synagogue. The teachers should be educated in Freiburg. Like the Christian schools, the (Jewish) schools should be under royal, imperial direction. Wealthy Jewish sons may attend universities "with the provision, however, that not only all business with other, Christian students cease, but that new Jewish books not be printed outside the hereditary lands, and moreover, that reading should be done only of books must be reading of books should written in accordance with the censorship guidelines."

They are allowed to lease property if they cultivate the land themselves and have wagons.

Craftsmen—tailors, shoemakers, bricklayers, carpenters—should study with Christian masters, "voluntarily, without having to commit to a guild." But they have to pay the same dues as guildsmen. If they have studied well, they are also allowed to be master builders, architects, cabinetmakers, painters, and sculptors, "thereby exercising the liberal arts." And [they may] do all factory work that requires expensive equipment, such as spinning, weaving, and taffeta making. Then they will be free to dress as they like, and to have a long or short beard or none at all.

The unrest in the Alsace induced a new branch of the Guenzburger to settle in Breisach shortly after 1780.[367] This branch was David, son of Nathan G., who came from Uffheim and

---

[366] A. Lewin, Jews in Freiburg

[367] Around this time the persecutions of Jews in Alsace were especially severe. A violent group traveled the land in 1779 and called on the Christians to cast the Jews out of the country. The eruption of the French Revolution changed little about these circumstances. Around the middle of 1790 the persecutions become very threatening, and many fled to cities like Mühlhausen, as well as sometimes to Basel and places right of the Rhine, among them, Breisach.

married Reichel, daughter of the Breisach Ashkenazim Wolf Mock and Hindel née Guenzberger.[368]

After the outbreak of the French Revolution, many Jews escaped Alsace for Baden, where they were taken in by protected Jews as servants. The presence of the emigrants led to some kinds of insalubrity (B. Rosenthal, "Heimatgeschichten der badischen Juden" [Stories of the Baden Jews], 1927, p. 234)

From complaints to the authorities, it can be inferred that dues to the Capuchin and the Augustinian monks from the Breisach parish were abolished by Emperor Joseph II.

From 1782 on, the circumstances for Austrian Jews generally took a turn for the better. From 23 December 1784 on, the day of the abolition of serfdom, no more levy was to be charged in the event of death. Nevertheless, the city of Breisach collected protection money from Jews who were incoming, as well as who were native, who wanted to establish their own households. The city likewise demanded a regular protection payment, which was 8 guilder, 20 kreutzer, for wealthy people and half that for the poor. The city took the position that only the protection money demands of the estates were overturned through the tolerance edict, not those of the city.

The church fond "Münster-fabrique" also demanded "recognition" (recognition sum = fee), which would be 3 guilder annually, "in addition to the thaler of the synagogue for the cemetery," all in all 18 guilder. The 10 guilder to the city priest for community rights "and all claims coming out of that," paid since 1755, now disappear.

In other regions discrimination against Jewish residents persisted for many more years:

1785 city council records show that protected Jews had to pay 20 guilder at their wedding for the admission of the bride if she was foreign.

According to the council records from 2/14/1785, this was the case, when Malcke, the daughter of Nathan of Lunéville, was accepted in marriage, since she brought her fiancé Joseph Hirsch "900 pounds dowry."[369]

Generally these foreign Jewish brides brought considerable dowries into the city. There were also impoverished Jews in the city. For example, "the very poor local Protected Jew Marx Guentzburger given grace on his debts of 7 guilder and 17 kreutzer until and including 1784, and also his future protection fee assessed at 10 kreutzer quarterly."[370]

The Breisach council opposed all attempts from Jews to acquire real estate apart from in the Judengasse,[371] which can be seen in the report from April 4,1785: "Since at today's meeting it was noticed, that at the auction of the house of the deceased widow Klorerin thither to August 23, 1784, the local Jew Parnus Wolf Mock was registered as the receiver; but because the Jewry here is not allowed to purchase houses at the Oberen Platz (high Place/square), as was resolved: via a fiat decree to the Jew parnus, it is not allowed for the local Jewry to purchase houses in the

---

[368] Dr. M. Ginsburger, Israeli weekly newspaper, publisher Dreyfuss, Gebweiler in Alsace, about Nathan Guenz. and family, as well as Ludwig Kahn, the descendants of Nathan Guenzburger from Uffheim (Basel 1971) (Publisher Leopold Loewenstein, "The Jews in Alsace before and during the Reign of Terror, in Pamphlet Nr.1, attachment to Nr. 97 of the "Israelit," Mainz)

[369] Haselier II, p.107

[370] Council report March 7, 1785

[371] Haselier II, p. 107

upper city and therefore an authoritative instruction is issued whereby he (himself) has to surrender the house."

Same happened to the Protected Jew Hirsch, Joseph,[372] who bought from Johann Hauri "a little house for 200 guilder near the Rhine gate at the so-called Langen Weg (long alley), but the authorities annulled instead of ratified the purchase and thereby prohibited any future Jew from buying anywhere else than in the Judengasse" (Council report July 18, 1785).

Civil Registry

We hear of Israeli civil record books first with the ranking of Jews as civil equals to Christians. But family records probably existed earlier, given that Jewish families were close and highly valued. A few remnants from Baden indicate this. In old Further Austrian Breisgau, Israeli civil records only became mandatory when in 1784 general prescriptions about record keeping were issued for Christian denominations.

The books were to be kept by the rabbis, who would then answer to the regional authorities.

When German became mandatory in 1787 for family and first names of Jews and for merchant books and other trade communications, Emperor Joseph II required German language also for birth and circumcision records, and extended it to death and marriage records as well. This meant that the records to be kept by the rabbis were now as public as the Christian records. Otherwise,

any decrees regarding Jewish civil records in Baden have been found only since the reorganization of the grand duchy law (May 29, 1809).

The rabbis were ordered to keep these records. In small villages where no rabbi lived, the oldest clergyman took over this task. In Breisach the task was reassigned to the catholic priest after complaints in 1817. [373]

The rabbis were free to keep civil records besides these. This arrangement lasted until 1870; after that, the rabbinate has kept records independently.

The death registry for the years 1784 to 1788, still in existence, gives partial information about the 15 deceased people on the parents, age, also the street number and the cause of death, like "rigidification of the abdomen," "typhus," "red hairiness" [Actually "red addiction": people with red hair, white skin, and freckles were believed to be related to vampires and werewolves, therefore in company with the devil], "short-winded stabbing," "at the doctor," "articular gaut," "cachexia," "smallpox," "big lump," "common," or "lump in the chest and typhus." The birth registry, also begun 1874, ends with the destruction of the city in 1793. During this period 84 children were born; at the end of each Jewish year the total, divided by boys and girls, is given. Girls' names in particular now took on first names that sounded of more German or Latin origin. A list of pupils "of children 6 to 12 years old" with age and details about the fathers, shows that with 38 pupils, the Jewish community has grown to a considerable size.

On November 2, 1793, the representatives of the Jewish community of Altbreisach send original documents to Sulzburg with the address "Most Worthy, Highly Educated, In particular to the Highly Honored Mr. Chief Rabbi Gideon Jakob Uffenheimer." Signed by the elected

---

[372] Propably Hirsch (naftali) Joseph is meant, whose family called themselves Weishaupt from 1809 on.
[373] Rabbi Moses Wurmer signed the entries until he moved in 1817; after that, the Catholic Priest Rosman continued with them.

"County Deputy Abraham Marx Wertheimer,"[374] those individuals here listed "after the highest decree from July 23 of the same year and beginning January 1788 to naming German first and last names." Gideon Jakob Uffenheimer, among others, signed as a community representative.

The Destruction of Breisach in 1793

On September 15, 1793, at 7 pm, still at twilight, the French bomb squad began its destruction. It was just the moment when the Jews gathered in prayer on the highest holiday. The bombardment began with four mortars and seven guns from the hostile Fort Mortier; soon afterward the cannery joined in, which was placed opposite the Rhine gate and Eckartsberg (Eckart Mountain).[375]

The Franciscan monastery, the *Radbrunnen* (wheel well), and the penitentiary behind the hill were hit first. Glowing bombs set the houses on fire and artillery shells followed, hitting the Judengasse. The terror impelled every resident to flee the city with just the necessities, to save their lives if not much else. The bright flames in the upper city served to orient residents as darkness broke, until soon the fire had spread and the entire city was ablaze. Because of its location in the back city, the Judengasse was especially vulnerable to the fire and bullets. The synagogue burned to the ground and the cemetery behind it was completely demolished. One girl was struck there by a bomb and died.

A servant girl at the tavern "Zu den drei Königen" ("At the three kings") hid in the rock cellar and suffocated there under the debris of the house. The French commander Lacoste succeeded in laying Breisach to rubble and ash and reported that the republican blitz had crushed the city. 577 houses, home to 2700 citizens, were vanished. The now homeless people had to seek a new home, and they found it with their fellow believers in near and far surroundings. Some Geismar, Levi, and Guenzburger had relatives in the nearby Ihringen. Eichstetten, Emmendingen and Sulzburg were possibilities for a large number of the Jewish refugees. The 1819 list of conscripts{military drafting medical examinations of 1819}, in which all Jews liable to enlist were named with detailed information, shows that some of the young men were born in these foreign places. Even Oberschaffenhausen at the Kaiserstuhl is named as a place of birth, where in the past no Jew had ever lived.

The newly adopted surnames Burgheimer, Eichstetter, Forchheimer and even Neuburger, appearing in 1809, likely came from evacuation towns. The newlywed teacher Isaak Guenzburger found a position in Sulzburg and intermittently also in Schmieheim.

The future Rabbi and private school student, David, son of Marx Guenzburger, fled to his relatives in Ihringen when he was young. There he married his cousin Voegel, daughter of the moneyed Chaim (Heinrich) Geismar, on 4 Adar 1797. Surely it was this David that was able to officiate as a rabbi in Altbreisach in 1797. After obtaining a *Kopulationsschein* (marriage license) from the *Landrabbiner* Kahn, he could perform weddings for a fee of 5 guilder 30 kreutzer.[376]

The distress and poverty caused much grief and sorrow among the homeless. Eight years after the 1793 destruction of the city, the Breisach Jews lived discouraged, unsettled, and flighty.[377]

---

[374] Wertheimer was employed as an account clerk at Josua Uffenheimer's waist silk factory since 1772.
[375] Gebhard Klein, *The Bombardment of Breisach* (Series of the History Club, Issue 1, February 1970)
[376] A. Lewin, *History of the Baden Jews*, p. 86
[377] Report from the poem of praise from Reb Alexander Ries, 1806.

A witness report of the bombing:[378]

Thoderle was the nickname of Theodor Geismar. I of course didn't know him, because he was already an old man in the forties of the past century. But my old uncle still knew him well and he told me:

I was still a little boy; but as memories from earlier youth are sometimes more vivid than those from later years, so I remember very clearly how old Thoderle, God bless his soul, sat on the stone bench in front of our house on the afternoon of Sabbath, how he put on his ear glasses of brass and read the "Zenne urenne" [collection of religious texts, stories, directions; for entertainment mainly written for women, who did not speak Hebrew and therefore could not read the Torah]. And afterward he often told us the story of how the city Breisach was destroyed by the French in 1793.

"So," he began, "it was Erev Yom Kippur 1793, Kol Nidre night; the plentiful dinner was over and the fast had begun. The children, however, would be provided for on the following day. Iron pots with rice and beans had been taken to the bakery. There they stayed in the oven until Yom Kippur midday, by which time they had cooked into a thick soup. When the whole congregation was gathered in the synagogue, the old blessed *chazzan* (cantor) climbed the *almemor* (pulpit). The men were dressed in snow-white shrouds; the women wore white caps. There were no benches at that time, but everyone had their own portable stand; and white mantles were placed on these stands, whereupon the *mahzorim* (prayer book) lay. Back then we had very large ones. And the many donated candles festively lit the synagogue. The Kol Nidre prayer was faded away; it had put the congregation into a reverent mood. After the Aron Kodesh (altar containing Torah scrolls) had been opened, the chazzan ceremoniously begins the Jaaleh [Aliyah?] prayer:

"May our prayer rise from night,

may our prayer come to you from morning,

and may our call be favorable to you until night."

and soon he begins the second verse:

"May our voices rise from night. . ."

But gets no further because a shock goes through the congregation; a grenade had exploded in the Judengasse. While all scattered every which way, deathly pale, concerned only with saving the lives of themselves and their loved ones, a second grenade flies over from Fort Mortier. The lights continued to burn undisturbed inside the empty synagogue and the *mahzorim* lay open on the white mantles. However, Thoderle and his father quickly took the *seforim* (Hebrew books) from the open Aron Kodesh and put then onto a hand cart. And with that they hastened out of the city, in the direction of Ihringen. That was well done, because just as the last book was loaded onto the wagon, boom, a grenade struck the synagogue—it was the third or fourth— and set it on fire. Then came the fifth

---

[378] Article of Otto Geismar, born 1873 in Breisach, deceased 1957 in London-Harrow, published in the Israeli weekly newspaper in Switzerland. The mentioned uncle was Maier Geismar, called Crutch Maier, born 1834 and died about 1920 in Breisach. The bringing back of the Torah scrolls could not have been on the next day, but much later, since the bombardment of the city lasted three days and nights and the Judengasse as well as the synagogue were nearly entirely destroyed by the fire.

shot, and the sixth and the twentieth and the hundredth, until the whole city had become one single heap of ruins. In the Judengasse nothing remained standing except two stories of a private home and the main part of the cheder. Whatever was not destroyed by grenade fell victim to the fire. But Thoderle and his father luckily brought the holy scrolls to Ihringen, one hour away, where there was a Jewish community.

Most of the congregation members had fled there as well; very few looked for safety further down the Rhine.

Everybody was in such a hurry because of the panic that one woman lost her little child, whom she had carried in her apron; luckily it was found the next day unharmed. That was on the way back— after *maariv* (evening prayer service) everybody hurried back home to look in the debris for anything that might be left of their wealth. Although fasting on Yom Kippur was voluntary, now came a time of involuntary starving and untold misery. The rich had as little to eat as the poor. Everybody first rushed to the ruins of the Jewish bakery. The oven was luckily intact and the food untouched. All swarmed around the rice, which had been meant for the children, and those who came last had the disadvantage. Two men were not to be seen at the oven: they were keeping watch by the Torah scrolls.

On the next day the starving and impoverished paterfamilias gathered to bring the seforim back into the city with a ceremonial procession. The hand cart was pulled by Thoderle and his father Mosche walked behind it. Both looked haggard, but their eyes gleamed with joy.

Otto Geismar

From Protected Jews to Citizens

One could also conclude from the records that a certain transformation in Breisach occurred regarding how Jews were valued. The Further Austrian constitution had hardly changed, but the Jews had come in relatively big numbers into the city, which was destroyed after the disaster of 1793, and they contributed to the revival of the economy through their orders for constructing houses: now it was not possible to regard them with the same suspicion and contempt as earlier. In April 1789 the magistrate demanded urgently a sum of 300–400 guilder to pursue a lawsuit concerning the island to the west of the Rhine: "the suggestion made by a few gentlemen to ask the Jewish representative Wolf Mock,[379] who had indeed deposited some funds in the registry, to advance the amount of 400 guilder to the city and forestry office for a few months. In return they would offer him 12 % and 300 bales [of cloth?]. He, however, flatly refused and was not afraid to leave the city without help in this matter; this action affected everyone—Christians as well as Jews. At this, some gentlemen turned to the local Protected Jew Gideon Uffenheimer, who had the generous altruism and charitable mindset to immediately advance this sum of 400 guilder for no more than 5%."[380] Maybe it correlates that on August 25 Gideon Uffenheimer was released

---

[379] Mock had requested resignation from the post in summer 1803
[380] Council report from 4/28/1798 (Haselier II, p. 172)

100

from paying protection fees for two quarters "due to special reasons known to the court."[381]

During a fire that broke out in Summer 1798, from unknown causes, three more Breisach Jews distinguished themselves: Kaspar Senft, Nathan Braunschweig, and the young Frommel Uffenheimer. The latter two had "let themselves be used as fire riders [men who warn others of fire or ride to a nearby town for help] at the most recent fire, laudably willing and speedy in extinguishing it." They were awarded a "decret of praise" for this.[382] At the end of 1798, during which time the magistrate had approved some 15 building applications and had charged several newly arrived Jews with the construction of a house, France again declared war on Austria.

For Jewish cattle traders, the significant event occurred on April 2, 1803: the "removal of the common pasture land." On January 1, 1804, both the "common pasture" as well as the common cattle herd were to be eliminated. People disregarded the immediate implementation of this regulation because Winter 1802/03 had been so hard and the feed supplies scarce. The municipal authorities took it as "generally shown and known that a common pasture is more trouble than useful." Therefore it should be made public "by drumbeats" "that each man should stock up on feed at appropriate times so that he can keep his cattle at home." Thus barn feeding was introduced in Breisach at the beginning of the previous century.

The Jewry in Breisach lost none of the stature it had regained since 1793. The longstanding Jewish parnus Wolf Mock had requested a release from his duties due to his age. The magistrate had to therefore "appoint another suitable representative for the Jewry from their midst." He requested, "according to custom," that the Jewry suggest to the magistrate within eight days "three of the most skilled and well-off men from among the Jewry," who are experienced in the German language in speaking and writing."[383]

The magistrate was inclined to treat the Jews fairly at that time. Thus he reduced the protected citizen's admission fee for the son of Breisach resident, Jew Nathan Levy to 18 guilder, "because he was the only Jew who didn't emigrate during the blockade of 1798 and thereby did service to the city and its citizens."[384]

At the council meeting of 24 September the Jewry were exhorted to suggest three names for the appointment of a new Jewish parnus, unsuccessfully, it appears, because the council chose a parnus.[385] Still, at the end of the year, the council permitted "the Jews to build a new synagogue, according to the submitted plan, in modified architectural style overseen by the court."[386] Translation of the song of praise to Baden by the Breisach rabbi Alexander Ris about the annexation of the city of Breisach on 15 April 1806[387]

Come brothers! let us be joyful,

The time of terror is over:

---

[381] Council report form 4/25/1798
[382] Council report form 4/25/1798
[383] Council report from 8/27/1803
[384] Council report from 8/27/1803
[385] Council report from 9/24/1803
[386] Council report from 12/24/1803
[387] Haselier II, p. 208

Bright is the future smiling at us.

From the bottoms of our hearts

We want to sing to G"d,

His wonders our lips should declare.

Do you still commemorate the former times of sadness?

Is Breisach's misfortune still imprinted on your hearts?

We were all like a parturient, all of us together,

Misery and hardship surrounded us from all sides.

Oh! Breisach's cry of angst. The superb,

Once magnificent ornament of the holy convention!

How she went to waste.

Encased in a blaze the obliterating blitz raged,

Consumptive fire,

Threatened her dissolution.

We despaired for our existence.

Our fortune vanished in the thousands

Despondent we saw ourselves bowed down.

Eight years we wandered erratically and fleetingly,

We drank fully the wormwood cup,

Our hearth resembled the transformation of Sodom and Gomorra.

This happened because of the Lord

His hand beat us,

He wanted to test our innermost,

But we—remain, abiding his help.

Sing to the Eternal, intone songs of praise for him.

He does not spurn the cries of the hard pressed.

As a reward for our pertinacity,

He did not let our hope turn to shame.

The Eternal destined us for this day

We speak of the same one: Now the Eternal has

let us forget all our suffering:

Under Carl Friedrich's mild scepter our destiny fell

How enviable our part,

How princely our fate.

Vivat! Long live our Prince!

Our eyes see the gloss of his holy see radiate

Hail! Hail! Hail the folk, whose shepherd he is.

His sleepless eye, his fatherly heart

Carries willingly the burden of his folk.

In his shade we can rest,

hearts with no sorrow.

The wakeful eye of his servant protects us from all unrest.

You, lovely singers, prepare for singing.

Sing a dulcet song to our casted lot.

Today our eyes see that benevolence has been

lavishly bestowed on the upstanding.

Hail! Hail! Hail to the folk!

That our eyes see

How virtue is rewarded,

How the scepter of Breisgau fell on Carl's pate.

How lovely our part is!

Jubilating and joyful shall our days flow.

Daughter of Breisach! People of *Jeschurun* rejoice,

Let timpani and trumpets ring out

To honor Carl Friedrich, our protector.

Delightful offspring of the House of Zähringen.

May your kingdom last as long as the moon.

And should one day rulers provoke you,

May you come, see, and conquer!

May G"d extend your years of life,

and your descendants be as numerous as the stars in the sky.

Most powerful prince, crown of beauty,

Of noble, blossoming stock.

Tarshish[388] and the furthest islands

bring you gifts.

From the ends of the world

Shevo and Svo lay their homage at your feet.

May God's help protect your rights

The years of your life flow gently and peacefully,

Govern your place of living unchallenged,

Untouched, like a confident lion—forever.

We saw how many Jews came to Breisach looking for protection after the destruction of the city, and to what extent they participated in its rebuilding. But the documents of the beginning of the 19th century show, in all clarity, not only the lower legal position of these protected citizens, but also a deplorable discord among them. Excluded from most trades, restricted mainly to business of necessity and cattle trades, and even dependent on illegal trade like usury, they lacked necessary unity. At the end of the Austrian period, council decrees warned the Jewry to obey the appointed representative.[389]

The building of a new synagogue in 1804/05[390] by Samual Metz also gave rise to conflict about the "places of men and women" in the new religious meeting room. It was demanded that a day's council be held to debate the arrangement proposed by Metz.[391]

In 1804, Wolf Levi complained about the interference of a foreign Jew in the school affairs in Breisach.[392] The basis of this was that several Jewish residents had their children taught by a foreign teacher instead of by Wolf Levi, the appointed teacher of Breisach.

---

[388] Tarshish-Levant coast or closer region of Israel
[389] Breisach city archive
[390] City archive Breisach: Fasz. 1863. 1866
[391] Dgl. Fasz. 1866
[392] Dgl. Fasz 1865

The right to operate a Jewish inn was also cause for some quarrel in 1807. Klara Wurmser and her husband Josef Isaak had given up their Jewish inn but, during a quarrel with the then current "Jew innkeepers" David Guenzburger and Salomon Geismar, wanted to regain permission for their own business again in 1807.[393]

June 4, 1808, took on special significance for the Jews of Baden.

Grand Duke Karl Friedrich passed the sixth constitutional decree concerning "the German constitutional law of estates."[394] His 19th paragraph[395] concerned the "rights of the Jews" and declared them to be "inheritance-free [allowed to pass on their land and other possessions to whom they want] citizens, who enjoy all common citizen rights, which, according to the first constitutional decree, are not excluded from the church constitution." In fact the edict did not give them the right to settle anywhere in the Grand Duchy of Baden "as long as they generally did not attain the same education about food and work as the Christian residents." In the places they had always settled, they should not be considered community citizens but citizens of protection, like Christians who were considered unfit for community rights and citizenship.

However, a certain, precisely defined legal status, which could no longer be diminished, only improved, was guaranteed to them by this edict. From now on Jewish citizens strove for permission to have their own "butchery" and general stores.[396] Naturally, the butchers' guild and gentlemen's guild met these desires with—ultimately unsuccessful—opposition.

After a complaint by the Jewry, the regional office declared invalid even the auction sale of the square of the Augustinian monastery, because the sale had been announced only at the Breisach Christian church and so little in advance that the Jewry learned of it too late and could not participate in it.[397]

That two of their Jewish brethren—the representative Gideon Uffenheimer and the tithe administrator from Reutlingen, Alexander Ries—and greatly excelling in education and competency, resided in the Upper Rhine city, was already mentioned; the acquisition of the right to collect the tithe by senior administrator Elkan Reutlinger likewise pointed to the Jewry's gain in prestige.

The 85 families who lived in Breisach in 1809 had 35 different surnames; according to the official designations we find 44 different names: 52 families with 23 surnames used earlier, kept the old names.[398] 33 families with 13 names changed to 16 names. The reasons for the adoption of certain family names can in many cases no longer be determined. Many named Levy rejected the name and were now called Levi-Breisacher, Levi-Burgheimer, Brumberg, Gradheimer, Levi-Kleefeld, Levi-Blotzheimer, Levi-Rosenberger, and Levi-Schwab. Wolf Wangen Levy (Loewy), school teacher, whose roots may have come from Wangen on Lake Constance, is curiously not a Levite, and his name probably derived from Loew. His widow changed her name to Foerschheimer for a short time, and his descendants changed it back to Levy, or Levi.

---

[393] Dgl. Fasz. 1864
[394] Grand duchy Baden gov. Pamp. VI (1809), p.145-146
[395] Haselier II, p. 165 ff
[396] City archive Breisach: Fasz. 1871
[397] GLA 196/453 (Haselier II, p.342)
[398] E. Dreyfuss. Die Familiennamen der Juden [The Family Names of the Jews] (1927)

It stands to reason that the bearers of the names Burgheimer and Foerschheimer lived in the cities of Burkheim at Kaiserstuhl and in Forchheim by Freiburg, after the destruction of the city in 1793. This is proved by the family Baer, who changed its name to Eichstetter, then back to the old name Baehr after a short time. The widow of Model, [could be a reference to a kind of builder, a loanword from the Roman builders who came into the country under Karl the Great] with her two sons born in Breisach, called themselves Neuburg beginning in 1809. Through oversight the modified surname Model is once again queried and interestingly retained officially a few years later. Isak Samuel calls himself Neumark, Hirsch Joseph changes to Weishaupt, and Levit becomes Felsenstein; the cantor Isaak Loeb becomes Freund.

Family members of the auxiliary rabbi Joseph Hirsch, deceased in 1805 and, according to lore, from the left side of the Rhine, took on the name Blum, which had long been established in the Alsace. But no familial relationship with the Alsace could be discovered.[399]

An explanation for the adoption of a new, previously unlisted name, is given in only one instance: Berel (Beierle), the widow of a different Isak Loeb and her children want to take on the name of her son Reichshofer living in France.

Starting November 2, 1811, the right of the Breisach township to tithe belonged without restriction to the privy council von Zentner, who received it as a gift from King Maximilian Joseph von Bayern for his services to the state. Von Zentner then sold the Breisach tithe as financial property on 30 November 1811 to the rich and esteemed Karlsruhe Jewish senior administrator and court agent Elkan Reutlinger.[400] He was probably the only non-Christian holder of a rights of tithe in Germany. In Breisach's neighboring parish Ihring alone he had possessions worth 893,000 guilder. This land ownership in Ihring may explain the interest in buying the Breisach's tithe. The government of the Middle Rhine province praised him in 1808 for his known support to the poor of all religions and for his many merits to the state, so that the grand duke appointed him as the chairman of the Israeli educational department for Baden in Karlsruhe, after it was established. Due to a financial crisis in 1814, he lost this post as chairman and died November 15, 1818.[401] His widow, born 1787 as Miss Ekla, had to fight a series of difficult lawsuits, and the Breisach right of tithe became part of the "Reutlinger's bankruptcy assets." Some unpleasant court disputes occurred between the city priest Pantaleon Rosmann in Breisach and the widow of Elkan Reutlinger.[402] As Manager of the tithe, Elkan Reutlinger had appointed Israelite Alexander Riess, known as the "country eldest." He had studied several years in Fürth and was considered one of the most highly educated Jews of the Upper Rhine province at that time.[403]

Troops from Baden and Alsace—and Jews—took part in Napoleon's 1812 campaign into Russia,[404] but several failures induced Grand Duke Karl of Baden and his troops to join the allied

---

[399] Interestingly enough the name Blum was also chosen by Jews in Breisach who did not belong to tribe of Levi

[400] Elkan (Elchanan), born in Karlsruhe, was a descendant of Emanuel (Menle) Reutlinger, who was born January 17, 166,9 and who moved in 1717 from Durlach to Karlsruhe, where he was the first sheriff. He died October 20, 1727, in Karlsruhe.

[401] Elkan, born January 14, 1769, became rich through military deliveries around 1800. In 1811 he married Ekla, who was born February 18, 1782. The marriage remained childless.

[402] From this period is the former clock at the Spector [some kind of tower or public building], which was donated by the Widow Reutlinger.

[403] RP 5, 1818, p. 129 (Haselier II, p. 307). Also A. Lewin, p. 141

[404] Isidor Lehmann from Randegg, born in Bischheim in Alsace, went as a troop provider into Russia with the large army.

forces. Breisach citizens were appointed to activities and to digging trenches in Höllental behind Freiburg. "Because the trench diggers in Höllental were to be relieved the following Thursday (March 3, 1814), and the earlier replacements had all been Breisach citizens alone under great sacrifice while the Jewry had been spared, it was resolved: The Jewry, by decree, was to provide the next 11 men trench diggers for the city of Breisach by next Thursday in Höllental without exception; otherwise, if they failed to do this, established punishment and threatened military impounding was to be transferred to the Jewish council" (RP May 26, 1814).[405]

On April 4, 1815, the widow of Lukas Joseph Blum, Beile, filed a petition with the grand ducal government of Baden on a pre-printed form to place her son Hirsch Lukas at the end of the reserves list. She said she needed her son to help her with her business. Detailed information about the family and its financial situation is included as well as the signatures of her aid Marx Guenzburger, Emanuel Weil as community merchant, Salomon Geismar as reeve for Hirsch Lukas Blum and the Jewish senior administrator Gedeon Jakob Uffenheimer.[406]

Also interesting is that a month earlier this man due for military service had gotten engaged to the daughter of Heinrich Geismar (his uncle), from whom he received at least 3,000 guilder as dowry, "without even having hoped for it." It was this Heinrich Geismar of Ihringen that loaned the city of Breisach 550 guilder when it was in need after the fire and then asked for it back in 1805.[407]

Even if the Jews in Baden Breisach were denied a certain right, a small step toward their equality was always connected to it at the same time. At the end of 1811 Fridolin Riedin went bankrupt. One of his most important creditors was the Jew Lehmann Wurmser, who, in order to save his claims, acquired the house of Riedin by way of an auction. The city council, which had to approve or reject this auctioning, discussed that "a Jew had never been allowed to buy Christian houses in the city, but especially not in the upper city, even though this had been permitted for some time in special circumstances in the lower city and in proximity to the Judengasse." The city council decided to relay the decision to the district authorities.[408]

This matter shows that the principle of confining the Jews to a Ghetto had been broken several times already. A list of the citizens of the upper city from 1827 shows that the Jew Elias Levi lived in this part of the city, among Christians, and was willing to pay four kreutzer to take water from the well.[409]

The slow improvement of the Breisach Jews' legal position was due on one hand to the legislation of the state of Baden and on the other to their financial power. There were also, however, "notoriously poor Jewish families" in the city with fewer economic means. When the fee for protection relatives was standardized to 2 guilder 24 kreutzer per Jewish family by a decree of the regional directorate in 1818, more than 20 Jewish heads of house, including three widows, were granted a reduction of fifty percent.[410]

---

[405] Haselier II, p. 223
[406] Jewish community archive Breisach (1938)
[407] City council report April 6, 1805 (Haselier II, p. 185)
[408] Rp. April 4, 1812, Haselier II, pg 342
[409] Rp. November 24, 1827, fol. 198-110. Elias Levi is listed under OZ 32 and fol. 109 with the comment: cannot write on the Sabbath.
[410] Rp. July 8, 1818, p. 99 ff

On February 3, 1819, "homage to the new local ruler Grand Duke Ludwig was paid according to the common and binding forms of the Jewry" in the Breisach synagogue. Invited and present were the "Israeli citizens" of Breisach and Ihringen. At 9 o'clock in the morning a few "Jewish authorities and community members picked up the prefect at his apartment and escorted him" to the appointed school (synagogue). At its entrance, the Israeli board of directors handed a list of the assembled Israelis to the officer. The ceremonial rite began with singing Psalm 72, after which the country eldest, Alexander Ries, gave a speech in which he pointed out the importance and sanctity of the oath in general and in particular of the duties of the local lord. The elder then moved on to a religious reprimand while mentioning various benefits received from the family of His Highness. The homage commissar also demanded unfeigned obedience, loyalty, and devotedness to the new ruler by briefly bringing to attention the good deeds of the Baden legislation, especially the good done by the new state constitution for all citizens of the state; he also pointed out the institutions that the citizens of the Mosaic denomination have to thank for their improved civic live. After the general, official rendering of homage and after the oath-taking had been recited by the whole congregation, a common occurrence or the Israelites, the country eldest Alexander Ries raised the Torah and pointed to those words that G"d revealed through Moses, on the scroll of law. After the oath was given the Rabbi Moses Wurmser took the Torah, blessed the local ruler, and began the prayer for the Serenest, Highest family. In conclusion Psalm 150 was sung.[411]

The text of the homage had the following established wording: "What was just read to us, which we heard and understood well, and surrendered our faith to, all of this we want to and should unwaveringly, ever solidly stand with, with the help of the Almighty of our forefathers Abraham, Isaak and Jakob and by the holiness of this law delivered to us by his servant Moses. Amen"

The minutes from this event were signed by the country eldest A. Riess, the Rabbi Moses Wurmser, the parnus Gideon Jacob Uffenheimer, also by Joseph Marx Bergheimer, Salomon Gaismer, Isaias Levy and Aron Mock.

It was of eminent importance to Breisach that an Israeli protected citizen, Joseph Marx Bergheimer, took over the local Rhine quay.[412] Since 1806 the steadily increasing Breisach Jewry had spilled out of the ghetto and demanded permission for regular trade. These wishes had been repeatedly opposed by the four Breisach traders. The frequent quarrels between the Breisach butchers' organization and the Jewish butchers can be ascribed to the fact that the Christian population was used to taking (commercial) advantage of the inferior rights for Jews.

That now a Jew was awarded the rights to the quay likely happened because no Christian took any serious interest in these rights. At the same time it demonstrates clearly that the Breisach Jews were on their way to emancipation. The economic power of the Breisach Jewry required the managers of the impoverished city to pay ever closer attention to them. Incidentally, among the young Breisach Jewish sons at that time was also the "Jewish theologian David Gaismar, son of Jacob Gaismar."[413]

---

[411] GLA 236/1777 (Haselier II, p. 282)

[412] R.P. July 8, 1818, p. 95 (Haselier II, p. 280)

[413] "Protection and marriage petition of the Jewish theologian David Gaismar, son of Jacob Gaismar" (RP: May 18, 1819, p. 283)

In 1820 David Marx Bergheimer was named lessee of the Rhine quay.[414]

The best solution, it was thought, to overcoming poverty and for the Jewish population to also overcome social isolation and discrimination was in the acquisition of an education. The 6th constitutional decree[415] stated clearly enough that the settling of Jews was to be restricted "as long as they generally did not attain the same education about food and work as the Christian residents."

The Jews made good use of this chance to improve their circumstances. We learn of the existence of an "Israeli school association" in Breisach through a petition of David Hirsch Marx Bergheimer, the lessee of the Rhine quay, "for some (citizen) wood to heat the schoolrooms at the usual price," since of late "the lessons of the Jewish children are conducted in two sections at the expense of the association, namely separately for boys and girls" and therefore the association needed a double amount of firewood. The city council approved "in each classroom 150 bundles from the city forest for payment of the logger and carrier."[416]

The city council treated the Jews properly. When the Israeli country eldest Alexander Ries wanted to marry his daughter Zierle to one Emanuel Mock of Breisach, the city council did not object to the marriage license and the adoption of the son-in-law as protected citizen.[417] This was in contrast to "the Jewish council's repeated rejection of attempts by Abraham Levy Kleefeld, unmarried son of a Jew, to take Braeunel Bloch of Emmendingen, unmarried daughter of a Jew, as a protected relative or as cohabitant [hintersässlich = someone living in a city/county either with no property at all or no property in that county/city, and nevertheless living from proceeds of that county] and to petition for a marriage license. The township defied the vote of the Jewish council and recommended to the district office that Kleefeld's petition be granted, among other reasons because the petitioner had acquired a considerable wealth, with which he supported his crippled mother and his siblings, and because in 1811 he participated in the physical examination of the Baden military. The district office acted on the vote of the community, and not the Jewish council, and commanded on May 1, 1822, that Kleefeld's "cohabitation" and marriage license be granted.[418]

The endeavor to escape isolation and join the general development of the city was expressed in several ways. For example, the highly esteemed Gideon Uffenheimer bequeathed the sum of 100 guilder to the Christian poverty institution in his testament. The city council decided "for the present that his heirs should receive the grateful sentiments of the city council for their blessed father's newly displayed pious nobleness as well as for his universal, altruistic deeds to the city and its inhabitants."[419]

With a closer approximation to the education level, conventions, and habits of the Christian population of the Upper Rhine city, the self-confidence of the Breisach Jews increased. It could have also been based on not insignificant financial contributions to the local community

---

[414] Son or nephew of the above-mentioned Joseph Bergheimer, according to list of name taking 1809.

[415] Grand duchy Baden gov. Pamp. VI (1808) p. 145-176

[416] RP. March 6, 1822 and from November 12, 1823 following 123 (Haselier II, p. 343)

[417] RP. March 27, 1822 (Haselier II, p. 343)

[418] RP. March 27, 1822 (Haselier II, p. 344)

[419] RP. February 18, 1824 following 148 f (Haselier II, p. 344) Gideon Jakob Uffenheimer died in Breisach January 21, 1824, 88 years old

and even on particular political accomplishments of individual Jews.[420] In the course of the year 1824 a few "disputes" arose "regarding money paid to the city for a long time by the local or native descendants of Jews who had previously been taken into the city as dependents."[421] The Jewish citizens of Breisach thus faced the same problem Christian citizens had faced earlier: namely, the question of why the legal status of the fathers as citizens, and really as protected citizens or *Hintersässe*, was not just passed down to the sons; instead they must pay again—though an amount much lower one than that for foreign citizen applications. The dispute was discussed and resolved at a "meeting" of the members of the city council and the Israeli council, where it was pointed out that descendants of Christian descendants must also pay another fee for citizen rights. In this matter, however, the amount that the *Hintersässe* should pay was reestablished.

The son of a *Hintersässe* with assets up to 1000 guilder must pay 15 guilder; assets 1000–2000 guilder must pay 20 guilder; and assets 2000 guilder and more must pay 30 guilder. In addition, a fire bucket should be supplied and an annual fee of 2 guilder and 26 kreutzer arranged, to be played in quarterly installments. Widowers who married a foreign woman for the second time should not have to pay a second fee, nor should the sons of Jews who married foreign women.

The continuing increase in fees for the Jewish son of the *Hintersässe* should remain, taking into consideration, however, the assets of the husband and wife.[422]

If the Breisach city council was conservative in admitting Jews to full citizenship, it was inevitable that the Jews would subsequently try to expand their rights and jurisdiction. At the council meeting on 21 March 1827, it was submitted "that the local Israeli council has so frequently intended to preside over judicial transactions that belong in the jurisdiction of the city council and mayor's office; for example, the same has allowed itself to sanction and put in place increases, inventory, retaining structures, etc." The city council was of the opinion that such actions diminished its own standing, were prejudicial, and the Israeli council would, if not stopped, "find itself driven to further absurdities." In an earlier period the city council would have simply forbidden the Jewish council from assuming such unlawful public authority.

But it is indicative of the new situation and legal status that the gentlemen decided on this occasion merely to "immediately file a complaint with the grand duchy's district office."[423]

For "old maukem," as the Breisach Jews lovingly called their hometown,[424] there was even an advantage to the conservative Baden community legislation of 1831, as it related to Jewish emancipation.

As the oldest and biggest Jewish community of Breisgau, Breisach had long had a local rabbi, even though it did not get to have one of the three Baden provincial synagogues, as Sulzburg did in 1812.

---

[420] The RP mentions once the accomplishments of a Biesheimer Jew in the enforcing of the Breisach reparation rights against France for cutting down the forest on the Rhine islands.

[421] RP June 25, 1824 fol. 11-13 (Haselier II, p. 348)

[422] RP (extra conference) February 19, 1826 (Haselier II, p. 349)

[423] RP March 21, 1827 fol. 19 (Haselier II, p. 349)

[424] The word maukem, from the Hebrew *moqum*—city, place, site. Compare with the relevant article in Wilhelm Gesenius, *Hebräisches und aramäisches Handwörterbuch über das Alte Testament* (*Hebrew and Aramaic Dictionary about the Old Testament*) (reprint of the 17th version ,1949, p. 455) and Siegmund A. Wolf, *Wörterbuch des Ratwelschen* (*Dictionary of the Council Argot*) 1956 # 3646, p. 219, therefore alt-mauchum = old city.

In 1806, Alexander Ries, composer of the Hebrew praise poem about the annexation of the city Breisach to Baden, was local rabbi;[425] in the homage list of Breisach city from 1811 Rabbi Moses Wormser[426] appears and in 1825 Benjamin Dispecker.[427] The three provincial synagogues, established through the edict of 13 January 1809, were, in the course of a re-organization of the clerical circumstances of Jews in 1827, abolished, and the Israeli communities of the country were merged to 14 district rabbinates or synagogues. From then on, Breisach was immediately subordinate to the high council in Karlsruhe.[428]

The Breisach district synagogue comprised the Jewish communities of Breisach, Eichstetten, Emmendingen including lower Emmendingen and Ihringen. When a Jewish community emerged in Freiburg in 1863, it also was allocated to the Breisach district synagogue, until 1886, when the district rabbinate was moved to the larger city Freiburg. Had a more Jewish-friendly municipal code allowed for the establishment of an Israeli community in Freiburg already in 1831, the district rabbinate would have probably been moved from the Upper Rhine city to Freiburg at a much earlier date than 1886. The population of Breisach, according to their census of December 1846, had to name eight electors.[429] To begin with, the city council prepared a "register of all eligible citizens in Breisach."[430] In addition there was still a "list of local Israelites eligible to vote in the election of a representative for the general national convention," which contained the names of 97 male Breisach Jews.[431] That the Jews were listed in a separate register probably had only practical reasons, because the name of Rabbi Reiss was not on the separate but on the first list. On both Thursday, April 13[432] and Friday, April 14[433], 200 eligible voters were invited by the apparitor; the remaining 264 eligible voters were invited for Saturday, April 15.[434] Strangely this latter group included the Israelites, who were not allowed to write on Saturdays according to their religious laws. A special "register of the ten local highest taxed citizens" contains no Jewish citizen.[435]

School conditions in the 19th century

The best way to raise the social status of the Jewry in the city was in improving the education of Breisach Jewish children. A report from the country eldest Alexander Ries on the Israeli school in Breisach[436] depicts its origins in a hardly favorable light. The schools, reports Ries, were in Breisach, as everywhere, "in a highly *pitiful* [Fr.] condition." Uneducated but trusted teachers, often without any elementary knowledge, had "usurped" the teaching positions.

---

[425] Haselier II, p. 351

[426] GLA 236/1654

[427] As co-signer of the "obedient application and plea of the village synagogue Breisach," 9/301825 (GLA 235/20710). Also: RP 4/271825 fol. 154, where the name Dischbecker is written.

[428] Lewin p. 226 ff Moses Reiss can be proven county Rabbi 1829-1869 in Brisach (GLA 235/20711). He was born in 1802 the son of merchant Seligmann Reiss in Karlsruhe and died in Breisach October 8, 1878, 76 years and 9 month old (entry in the burial log)

[429] County office to Breisach city April 1, 1848 (City archive; Fasz 3989), Haselier II, p. 509

[430] Register of all eligible citizens of Breisach (City archive; Fasz. 3989 fol. 4-16)

[431] Ibid. fol. 17-19

[432] Ibid. fol. 20-24

[433] Ibid. fol. 25-29

[434] Ibid. fol. 30-35

[435] Haselier II, p. 509, Anm. 39

[436] Obedient report of the country eldest Ries to the senior administration of the Israelite in Karlsruhe, about the Israeli school in Breisach, Breisach, November 17, 1823 (GLA 235/20710), Haselier II, p. 344

Family fathers had hired itinerant persons to teach, "without review, even without a certificate of good conduct," then fired them and replaced them with "others who were equally incompetent."

"School, teachers and pupils alternated, holding school also at home, where the teacher boarded, until the pupils reached the 13th year and left school as limited in knowledge as they were crippled in moral education."

With the admission of the teacher Marx Wertheimer around 1810, more stable conditions set in at the Breisach Israeli school; he presided over the school "with excellence." Throughout his time in office, "the ambulant army of foreign teachers was frightened away." The Dreisam district board of directors decided, after a school visitation and upon recommendation by the provincial deanery, "to entrust the teacher Wertheimer also with the political education of the Israelites." Since then there have been two classes in the Israeli school. The beginning students are to be taught by the teacher Nathan Levi in "Hebrew and Jewish-German reading; the more advanced pupils are taught by Wertheimer in Hebrew and German grammar, biblical translation, mathematics, reading and German writing."

Ries then describes how all possible "arts of Satan were tried and employed to destroy this charitable institution." The "charity society" revoked their contribution to the teacher Wertheimer's salary, in fact, "after the instigation of a man, who is now dressed in the cap of the rabbinate,[437] and who, during his short stay here (in Breisach) caused more harm than can be rectified in ten years, by inciting local Jews against each other and against their superiors, whose consequences we unfortunately feel most acutely; since then conflict and quarrel prevail in our community, which previously had not been known."[438]

The Breisach Jews sought to recoup the deficit of the charity's grant among themselves. In contrast, a few Jewish parents seized the tack of school walkout and hired for their children the private teacher Elias Weill, born in Bühl near Baden-Baden.[439] Surveyed on which of the two teachers the parents wanted employed as the official local teacher—Wertheimer or Weill—the Jewish parents voted that their children should attend the local Breisach school, but each father should be free to send his children to Wertheimer or to Weill for religious education. This vote came to pass under the influence of Parnus Seligman Geismar, an enemy of the teacher Wertheimer. A definite factor also in the mix was that Wertheimer had over the years become hard of hearing. That the Dreisam district board of directors enacted an order corresponding to the vote agitated Alexander Ries. Jewish religious education, given by someone "from whom we have never seen a single document from a Jewish authority!" Why, instead of asking experts about the qualifications of the teacher, were the parents simply allowed to decide? "Until that day, it was believed that an educated man and expert should be asked about this; but now, oxen merchants, stable hands, slowpokes, shoemakers should carry out this task!"

Ries also rejected that the district board imposed on the Jewish schoolchildren attending the local school "18 Kreutzer per month for the German lessons to the Breisach educational cash register." This would be against the decree from January 13, 1809, "in which it is explicitly stated that where no tuition is to be paid by the Christian children, no tuition should be paid by the Jewish ones." Lastly Ries presented another major issue: "But what the patriotic Israelite is

---

[437] Geismar
[438] Haselier II, p. 345
[439] Elias Weill, protected Jew in Bühl, was in the Spring of 1822 teacher in Altdorf, where his wife Beier Weil gave birth to a child Hirschel Weill, born March 15, 1822, according to local records in Altdorf.

most hurt by is the casualness with which religious education is handled, allowing fate to decide or employing a person who is declared neither worthy nor capable by any Jewish authority."[440]

By addressing the issue of religious education and also trying to explain some of the opposition toward the teacher Wertheimer, Ries brought to light the main feature of the Breisach school dispute. He and probably Wertheimer too belonged to the liberal side of Judaism, their opponents to the side of orthodoxy! Ries writes: "I found it appropriate and fitting already several years ago to reform this school according to the Zeitgeist and after the example of Frankfurt and Karlsruhe, grounded in the thorough study of Hebrew and German language. As all new and better things have to face opposition and attack, so was this new curriculum antagonized from all sides. It was not possible to bear that the right of the parents over their children should not extend to school."[441]

A submission by the teacher Marx Wertheimer from January 2, 1824, confirms all of this and shows how sharp the antagonisms within the Israeli community were.[442] The city community sympathized with Ries and Wertheimer.[443] But Elias Weill, called a "drunkard" by Wertheimer, fought these hostilities. At the Dreisam district board of directors, the exposé by Alexander Ries was met with utmost rejection.[444] In the end, Elisa Weill had to take an exam in front of the high Israeli authorities in Karlsruhe, in his opinion "a difficult exam, more appropriate for a candidate for the rabbinate or priesthood than for a teaching position."[445] On February 2, 1825, he complained in very flowery language to the highest authorities of Karlsruhe about Ries, who, in a "sinful deluge of November 17, 1823, drowned the highly praiseworthy District board of directors, the venerable Rabbi David Jakob Geismar, the gentleman Parnus Seligman and all of Israel."

He called Ries a "Tartuffe," a debaucher of the good Breisach people" and accused him of publicly hoisting the flag of outrage and lawlessness.[446]

With this attack on Alexander Ries, Elias Weill made himself totally ridiculous in Breisach. The Breisach district office investigated all charges brought against Weill—the investigation records ultimately amounted to eight fascicle—and lastly advised the high authorities to "consider the most speedy removal of Elisa Weill from the local educational service." The report of the county district justified Alexander Ries completely, without mentioning his name, by maligning Weill, inter alia, as "evil in character" and worse. Another role in this was his "improper behavior at the hysteric sick Haudel Kahn, which promoted superstition." The district office informed the senior directory that they would also send "a report

---

[440] Obedient report of the country eldest Ries to the senior administration of the Israelite in Karlsruhe, about the Israeli school in Breisach, Breisach November 17, 1823 (GLA 235/20710), Haselier II, p. 344

[441] Ibid. (Haselier II, p. 346)

[442] Marx Wertheimer to the senior administration of Israelis in Karlsruhe, Breisach January 20, 1824 (Ibid.); Haselier II, p. 347

[443] Report of the senior administration for Marx Wertheimer, Breisach January 20, 1823 (Ibid.)

[444] Dir. of the Dreisam District to the senior administration of the Israelites in Karlsruhe, Freiburg February 23, 1824 (Ibid.)

[445] Obedient report of Elias Weill of Altbreisach to the grand duchy senior administration of the Israelites, about his commission as teacher, Breisach, 9/101824 (Ibid.). The report of the senior county Rabbi Ascher Loew for Weill, Karlsruhe 8/15/1824 (Ibid.)

[446] Elias Weill to the senior administration of the Israelite in Karlsruhe, Breisach, February 2, 1825 (Ibid.)

from the community about the newly established local Israeli school and the compensation for the teacher to be hired."[447]

After these unpleasant disputes, which ended with the removal of Elias Weill, the local council of synagogues made efforts to establish an "Israeli village school," and succeeded in the spring of 1827. Until then the Jewish children had to attend class at the Christian school. In the new school, located in the former pub "Zum St. Peter" (To St. Peter) at the entrance to Judengasse at Kupfertorplatz (Copper Gate Place), teacher H.L. Bensbach from Mannheim functioned as the village teacher with a salary of 300 guilder; in addition to him, Nathan Levi of Breisach was employed but only provisionally.[448] The school came under the supervision of the senior administration of the Israelites in Karlsruhe, just like the (Christian) village school was supervised be the Catholic church section of the Ministry of the Interior. An account from the Israeli educational ministry on Breisach, July 5, 1829, shows that there were many things to be improved at this new school—with issues of people and space. With time its requirements were met and it satisfied the legal prescriptions, needs, and claims of the Breisach community, and two teachers at the educational establishment worked with a curriculum written by the ministry.

Already by February 22, 1827, the senior administration of Israelites in Karlsruhe praised the communities of Karlsruhe, Mannheim, Heidelberg, Breisach, and Pforzheim for the good standing of their public schools.[449] The Israeli school commission of Altbreisch sent the abovementioned "obedient account to the senior administration of the Israelites in Karlsruhe, the examination of the inner as well as outer structure of the Israeli religious and grade school," dated July 5, 1829, Breisach.[450]

The Israeli school in Breisach owes much also to its first teacher, its head teacher Heinrich Halle, appointed July 10, 1828.[451]

In his retirement request, the Israeli teacher Heinrich Halle included complaints about "the many mortifications and prosecutions, which I suffered during the ominous years 1848 and 1849 because of my loyal attitude and conduct, which I tried to always display on a daily basis, and which (the mortifications and prosecutions) likely led to my last sickness."[452]

The Naphtali-Epstein Society, which was founded in 1852 in Karlsruhe to assist needy teachers or their widows, also had various members in Breisach[453]

In 1909 there were   Hermann Blotzheimer

Samuel Geismar

Philipp Greilsamer

---

[447] District office Breisach to senior administration of the Israelite in Karlsruhe, Breisach, July 18, 1825 (Ibid.)

[448] Decision of the Grand Duchy Baden Senior Administrator of the Israelite—school conference—Karlsruhe, May 17, 1827 (Ibid.)

[449] Adolf Levin, History of the Baden Jews (1909), p. 217

[450] GLA 235/20711, Haselier II, p. 348

[451] Appointment decision of the senior administrator of the Israelite, Karlsruhe July 10, 1828 (GLA 235/20711)

[452] Heinrich Halle to the county office Breisach, Breisach, June 1, 1853 (GLA 235/20713), Haselier II, p. 56

[453] It was common at weddings and other festivities to auction off the *Benschen* (table prayer) and give the money to the society. In 1906 for example at the wedding of Julchen Geismar and Hermann Greilsamer. According to 1921 records, 70 marks were given to the society from the wedding of Bella Geismar and Arthur Kahn in Frankfurt, at the wedding of Berthold Breisacher and Hedwig Bildstein in Freiburg (June 26, 1921) the auction brought 50 marks.

Moses Kleefeld

Viktor Kleefeld

Emanuel Mock

Elkan Strauss, Head teacher

Adolf Uffenheimer

Max Uffenheimer

(In addition to those mentioned above, there was in 1908 Heinrich Guenzburger, and in 1906 Gedeon Uffenheimer)

The salary collector and arbitrator was Head Teacher Elkan Strauss. Members listed in 1921 were Hermann Blotzheimer, Samuel Geismar, Philipp Greilsamer, Elkan Strauss, Ad. Uffenheimer, Mrs. Rosel Geismar-Uffenheimer. (In 1919 also Max Uffenheimer, father of the last one.)

Outlook: The Last Years of the Breisach Community (1914–1940)

In the "Fight for the Vaterland" many Jewish Breisach citizens lost their lives. "For the honorable remembrance" was at one point a marble plate placed on the left, eastern wall in the synagogue, dedicated to the eight names of the fallen of 1914-1918, engraved in gold letters:

Robert Breisacher   15.4.1918[454]

Victor Breisacher   (? 6. Nissan 1887) - 6.7. 1918[455]

Ludwig Geismar   27.8.1918[456]

Josef Kahn   23.5.1892 - 22.10.1914[457]

Hugo Levy   24.1.1890 -15.2.1916[458]

Arthur Model   4.2.1882 - 25.5.1915[459]

Emanuel Weil   4.9.1881-14.8.1916[460]

Martin Max Wurmser   14.11.1879 - 8.10.1914[461]

Ludwig Floersheimer

12.11.1898 - 12.5.1920

(died in Mannheim due to a war injury)

---

[454] Robert and Victor were sons of David Breisacher of the fish hall
[455] See 452
[456] Ludwig Geismar, born 1894, son of Jakob G, fell in the last days of war in Ardennenwald in France
[457] Josef Kahn was single son of Nathan K.
[458] Son of Leopold L, Kupfertorplatz, was called Hugele
[459] Son of Ferdinand M.
[460] Called Mandi, son of Abraham
[461] Martin Max Wurmser, who married Frieda Weil from Emmendingen shortly before the outbreak of WW I, was among the first who fell

Gottfried Geismar (Nesanel ben Schneiur Sueskind) was likely born in Breisach on Yom Kippur 1880, although by the outbreak of the War was married in Berlin. He fell on October 5, 1916 by Buetow (Galicia).

Jakob Rosenberg, son of Heinrich, fought in the Battle of Verdun, was treated in different military hospitals for asthma and lung afflictions, but insufficiently, and succumbed to this sickness in 1929.

Hugo Geismar, son of Salomon, also suffered many years from a disease developed in the world war. At his burial in Breisach 1931/32, the military association honored him with the usual salutes.

Cantor Paul Weinberg could look back on a long ministry. Even into old age he practiced the profession of mohel. His last circumcision was on the late-born son of Sal. Kleefeld (Nois), who died due to complications from this procedure.

Even before Cantor Weinberg's death, the community hired a successor, who came from Danzig. He did not fit into the milieu and was unliked.[462]   It was Leo Halpern. During his term in Breisach his wife gave birth to one son Heinz and the then representative Isak Levi and his wife, Mrs. Klara (born Maier), assumed the role of godparents. Heinz emigrated to the Midwest of the U.S.A. and then died very young. His father survived him. (In 1977 he was living in the state of Ohio).

In 1933 about 80 Jewish families with 231 members lived in the town. They had restaurants and colonial goods stores, fabric and hardware stores; they were butchers and slaughtered meat according to Jewish ritual; they owned wholesale and mail-order businesses or they drove out to the country with horse and wagon directly to their customers. They were cattle and horse dealers, they ran clothing and dry good stores, they were real estate agents and worked in export businesses. There was one Jewish leather shop with supplies for shoemakers and a shoe store. They sold coal and wood, tobacco and cigars, flour and grains. Only a few were employees and officials.

Jews were members of different societies; they maintained a good relationship with other Breisach citizens. The first act of Nazi violence against Jews came on March 31, 1933, with a curfew of 9 pm. Already the day before, in a venture by some local high party members, some Breisach Jews coming home late from work with the train were apprehended and imprisoned at the Rhine gate and not set free until the next day.

---

[462] When he left after his 5-year contract with the community ended, he received a satirical poem, written by the humorous Hermann Kaufmann in Breisach "Yiddish-German:"

5 years you were in our town;
The fruits of your work:
you have mooched off the "Kehilla," [*kehile*: Jewish community]
Yet good deeds you did nowhere,
You did not belong to this sort,
The one who helps the needy.
The rich spittle you wanted,
But were a "Dalfen" yourself,
Therefore you are hated by us,
While packing you bags,
You never fit in with us,
You belong to the Polacks."

SA-guards stood in front of Jewish stores to prevent any shopping. Whoever shopped at Jewish stores had to count on public ridicule for being a friend of the Jews. From then on Jews were subject to personal harassment and bullying; some were also temporarily arrested. Still, until 1938 there were no riots in Breisach. From August 1938 on, every Jew had to have the name Israel or Sara on passports and any legal documents. Those who had relatives or acquaintances in the United States who signed a warrant could emigrate.

On the morning of November 10, 1938, an SA division from Freiburg under the leadership of a Breisach SA-Standartenführer (colonel of the SA), and with the help of some Breisach SA-men, burned the synagogue down. The windows of a Jewish store were broken. But Jewish dwellings were not destroyed. About 30 Jewish men were deported to the Dachau concentration camp. Jakob Bernheim died from abuse; Michael Eisemann could no longer cope with his emotional depression and took his life in 1939. The deported returned from Dachau three weeks later with shaved heads. Not one was willing to talk about the camp. Leopold Breisacher died on June 19, 1939, as the last Jew in the heimat. He was brought to the cemetery in a handcart by his family, because the city refused him the hearse.

At the beginning of the war, Jews were evacuated to Württemberg separately from the rest of the population. At the end of 1939, most returned to their heimat. Some remained in Württemberg and were deported to a death camp in the east in 1941/42. 14 people died there. After the German troops crossed the Rhine, the city administration independently sent all Breisach Jews in Summer 1940 (July 31–August 12[463]) to Ruffach and had them admitted to the local insane asylum.

After about four weeks they were returned to Breisach under the orders of a higher authority. In the meantime, many had their furniture, clothing, and food supplies stolen.

Their lot became worse every day; they could not or were not allowed to do any work. Most of those still remaining had to be supported by Jewish charity societies.

On October 22, 1940, the remaining 34 Jews in Breisach were, together with all Jews from Baden and the Pfalz, arrested and brought to the still unoccupied part of France. They could take as much hand luggage as they could carry, 100 marks of travel money and provisions for four days. At their deportation the Jews from Baden had to leave behind their account books, jewelry, and valuables, under the order of the leading local commander; their assets were seized and, through a decree passed on November 25, 1941, handed over to the Third Reich. Their furniture and other household things, along with their houses, were auctioned off, often under value. The original, Jewish property owners had their property reinstated to them after the end of the war during the restitution process, without compensation, and could sell them for the regular current rate to the former owners or foreigners.

The French government in Vichy placed the Jews deported from Germany, in the detention camp Gurs near the Pyrenees, which had originally been put up for refugees from the Spanish civil war. Some 70 Jews currently and formerly from Breisach met here at the camp. Men and women were separated in barracks of 60 people, children with their mothers. The provisions for the 6500 people was at first insufficient.

The exceptionally cold winter brought the flu: Snow, sludge, and rain turned the camp into marsh, so that many people, especially children and elderly, died from sickness and

---

[463] Record of Ludwig Blum, New York

exhaustion. In the course of 1941, many detained Jews were sent to different camps. Through the intervention of relatives and acquaintances who lived in foreign countries, some could emigrate; others hid in homes, cloisters, and with French families. 18 Breisach Jews died. Due to pressure from the Nazi regime the French government in Vichy handed over the Jewish refugees who were not nationalized, and so the deportation for 33 Breisach Jews to the death camp Auschwitz started in August 1942 during operation "Endlösung" (the Final Solution). After the retreat of the German troops in France in the summer of 1944, an American charity placed the Jews who were still in southern France into hotels in Lourdes, until they could be admitted into asylums. Almost all Breisach Jews remained in foreign countries; two women returned to Germany, one Jew returned to Breisach, and another went to Freiburg. One Jewish woman, in a so-called *mischehe* (mixed marriage), remained in Breisach; after the invasion, her husband[454] was appointed acting mayor of Breisach by the occupation troops.

---

[464] Albert Ziehler[454] sl. may mean "Segan Leviyah" (Levitical excellence, i.e., a Levite); jzv. may mean "May his Rock and Redeemer preserve him."
preserve him."

[454]"*Kozin*"

[454]"*Kozin*"

Appendix

Photo caption: According to the court registry of 1319, various Jews owned houses and property above the Phlegeler Gate (Hagenbach Tower) (Postcard around 1920, Breisach City Archive)

Appendix 1: Letter of Safe Conduct by the Breisach Governor for a [specific] Breisach Jew[455]

Gabriel De Cassagnet Seigneur de Tilladet, Governor and King's Lieutenant General for the city and fortress of Breisach and their dependent lands and places.

Per the previous identification of David N the Jew, who with his wife and children resort near Ichtingen[456] requests of us safe passage, for him alone . . . is allowed and authorized for a year. So with this, everyone is asked, with good intentions and according to rank, not only that the abovementioned Jew, together with his wife, children, and squire, during the abovementioned time, pass freely and safely through and back through this city and this government's district— but also to hold other inhabiting Jews the same way, where taxes are concerned, and to also let them grow their food without hindrance; this we are willing to sign, each according to his rank:

Breisach, dated 3 March 1651 Signed

Tilladet

It is herewith confirmed that David the Jew has an exemption from us and the subjects of the local government are charged to observe this in their capacity until the expiration date without exception.

Breisach, dated 20 August 1651

Charleroix

Appendix 2: Letter of Safe Conduct by the Further Austrian Forelands of the Hapsburg era for the Breisach Jews from 1686/88[457]

We, Rom. Emper. and also Roy. Maj. of Hungary and Bohemia, as Reigning Archdukes in Austr., Stateholders, Regents and Chamber Council V. Austr. lands, offer to all that this open edict would concern, our willing, friendly service and greetings and given to understand according to the entire Jewry living with us in Breisach, with names David Guenzburg, Alexander Doderle, M(arx) Guenzburg, Salomon Gaissmar, Simon Ginzburg, Sender, Lieberman, Jaeckle Geissmar, Marx Geissmar, Sussman, Moise(s) (Alex)ander, ?Rickh Isace?, Jaeckhle Alexander, Jsaekhle Schwarz, Samuel Alexander, Mayer Rabin, Koschel Levituss,[458] Schollum Salomon, Ahron Geissmar, Juda Wolf, Assur Levituss, Samuel Ra(fel?), Borich, Abraham Juda, Abraham Rafel, Wolf Juda, Binioman, Jsach der Jung, Mayer Jsach, Lazaruss Katz, through which J(ews) all represented in the delegation of the Austrian convoy, concerning payment of a certain bit of money demanded in fees, and us then not against their appeal: with registered deputies to

---

[455] GLA Karlsruhe
[456] today Jechtingen in Kaiserstuhl
[457] GLA Karlsruhe: 196/238
[458] as with Marx Alexander, Wölfle David, Jäckhel Levituss

contract such an Austrian convoy for a certain yearly amount, (and w)hen such a thing really occurs, that all the Jews requesting such an Austr. convoy remove the Christian tax from wares bargained for, which they in all cases should be owing: to pay 60 royal thaler in advance, in coins, annually to the V: A. Office of the Sangreal Captor.

Also, in granting such escorts annual entrance with supplementing fees of registration: and toward such comparable yearly 60 royal thalers at all V: A. toll stations, except those administered at ( ) and Villingen, and so not understood in this treatise, for the sake of the escorts or personally taxed individuals who should pass safe and free, come together in order of the planned agreement that the aforenamed Jewry really have paid the established 60 royal thaler for this current year 1686
(Side note: 1688 as calculated from today's date)

As we have communicated by this detailed document to them, to Jews of the present edict or general escorts, including all of them but each free escort privately signified with the Aust. coat of arms, that immediately, as in this current year 1686 (below: 1688), and regularly registered Breisach Jews, also the solitary households, with exclusion of all others, were contracted and freed, such generally and privately escorted also available no longer than the end of this time (Side note: + : that they again register immediately and pay the established 60 Thaler, or if adversely robbed of the agreement and everywhere that such people enter their effects be actually taken away) or in the future in the year following. To serve no others or Jews living outside Breisach: those who opt out should (not) understand that they can lend such a document to others or to practice another significant deception in avoiding punishment in such a case (at present). Giving witness of our heretofore imprinted signatures in Waldshut, the second March in sixteen hundred eighty-sixth year ./. (below: the first of January 1688.)

(2 signatures and 4 small official seals)

David Guentzburg	Koschel Levitus
Alexander Doderle	Marx Alexander
Marx Guentzburg	Woelfle David
Salomon Geissmar	Jaeckhel Levitus
Simon Guentzburg	Scholum Slomon
Sender	Ahron Geissmar
Lieberman	Juda Wolf
Jaeckle Geissmar	Assur Levitus
Marx Geissmar	Samuel Rafel Borich
Suessman	Abraham Juda
Moysses Alexander	Abraham Nafal
Isaac	Wolf Juda
Jaeckle Alexander	Biniomen
Isaeckle Schwartz	Isaac der Jung
Samuel Alexander	Mayer Isaac
Mayer Rabin	Lazarus Katz.

Appendix 3: Application for Protection by the Jews Meyer von Heiteren and Aaron Blum of Rixheim in the Ville Neuve de Brisach[459]

"March 22 1689

On this day have been received into protection the names Meyer the Jew of Heiteren and Aaron Bloume also Jew of Rixen from the new City, paying annually the usual and accustomed rights."

Appendix 4: Application of the Rabbi Arje Jehud Loeb Teomim[460]

"His Serene Duke,
Merciful Prince and Lord.

Your Prince, High and Serene, the undersigned servant has the end of wanting to remonstrate that he may immediately gain peace to move away from Breisach and into the Upper Alsace. When now, merciful prince, with things formed this way that the same person has decided to settle in Rappoltswyler: As it has reached Your Prince, High and Serene, those living there would like to mercif. be allowed to rest and be set up in prince. Hanau territory like the Rabbis, mercifully contracted, before such Grace of Your High Prince, he will forever remain in all indebted abject respect.
Your Prince, High and Serene

Most subserviant Loew Jud

To the High and Serene Prince and Lord
Lord Christian Pfaltzgraf bey Rhein,
Duke in Bavaria,
Count of Veldentz, Sponheim, and Rappoltsstein
Lord of Hoehnackh, my Noble Prince and Lord,
My most humble letter
Loew Jud"

"Decree

When Breisach is again given over to the Germans, subjects should be granted a year of residence in Rappoltsweyler;
Strassburg dated August 4, 1698.

Christian Pf(alz) g(raf)"

---

[459] ADHR Colmar: 1 E 80 No. 8
"Registre de la Police of the Ville neuve de Brisacde L'annee M DC Lxxxviii" (1688-1700)
[460] ADHR Colmar: E 1625/100

Appendix 5: Engagement Contract (*Tenaim*) between Marx Guenzburger from Altbreisach ['Old Breisach'] and Beile Bickart from Wintzenheim on August 12, 1745 in Horburg in Alsace[461]

Mazel tov. May the words of the covenant flourish and grow like a garden in the heavens, which were arranged as conditions on the occasion of the marriage (*chupah*) between the two parties, namely between the dear Mrs. Beile, the wife of the late Joseph Josle (Guenzburger), may his memory be blessed, from the holy community of Breisach, who appears in the name of her unwed (*bochur*) son, the bridegroom (*chossen*) Meier Mahren, on one side, and the dear Mrs. Rifka, wife of the late Jizchok Eisik (Isack) Bickart, may his memory be blessed, from Wintzenheim and her dear son Goetschel, who appear in the name of the daughter, or sister, Miss Beile, on the other side.

The single young man, the bridegroom Meier, marries Miss Beile by religious law and she consents to this.

And Meier Mahrum, the *Chossen*, brings to the marriage his entire fortune and also gifts.

And Mrs. Beile, wife of the late Joseph Guentzburger, the mother of the *Chossen*, gives as dowry half of the house where she now lives in Breisach, including the yard that belongs to it, all to go to the young pair after the death of Mrs. Beile. But during her lifetime, an apartment in the mentioned house will be given to the young pair at no cost. Likewise, half a Sepher Torah that she owns should belong to the couple and also the seat in the men's synagogue (in Breisach) and also the seat in the women's synagogue (*Esras Naschim*) should belong to the couple after her death. But during the lifetime of Mrs. Beile, the wife of the late Josel, the couple has no right to these things, and she has the same property right as beforehand. Still, efforts will be made for the couple to secure protection rights (*Esronit*) and residence (in Breisach), at the expense of the mother of the *chossen*. They will also be seen to for Mrs. Beile, daughter of the late Isaak (Eisik), a get a halitsa letter from her unwed son, the boy David ben Joseph.[462]

And Mrs. Rifka with her son Goetschel will give Miss Beile the sum of 600 livres as dowry, Strassburg currency, as well as gifts, etc. when possible, and she will also dress in dignified clothing also for Sabbath, Yom Tov, and work days, according to rank (L'phi Kwodo).

And from now on the couple will act in love and friendship and they will not leave each other, neither he her, nor she him, in no case, and they will live together.

In the case that they cannot agree—G"d forbid—and Meier has something against his wife Beile, and they go to Beth Jin (rabbinical court), he should then immediately give her 10 gold ducats in alimony, and he would give her this monthly as long as their disunity persists; likewise their clothing and jewelry. And he should go with her to Din Tora (rabbinical court) within two weeks after their summons. And after the settlement, she should go back again to the house of her husband.

In the event of Meier's death—G"d forbid—in the first year after the wedding without children, then Mrs. Beile will take everything that she had brought him, although nothing that she acquired.[463]

---

[461] Colmar District Archive, Notariat Drouineau

[462] Religious law stipulated that a single man marry the childless widow of his late brother, but this obligation could be dissolved through a certificate of renunciation (*halitsa*). (Leviratsehe)

[463] Voluntary, added-on sums, to treat the engaged persons as equals with equivalent values in the contract; one who is not as well-off should not be shamed by it.

In the event that it happens in the second year without children, Mrs. Beile will take everything that she brought to the marriage, in addition to half of what came about.

In the event that Mrs. Beile should die in the first year without children, Mr. Meier is obliged to give back to her heirs everything that she brought him.

In the event of her death in the second year without children, Meier must give her heirs half of what she brought him.

But from the third year on and later, the husband inherits the wife; or, if he dies, she will take her *kesubo* (basic amount according to the marriage contract) and the bonus that amounts to 600 Rhenish guilder.

All of the above obligations and conditions the two abovementioned parties have taken on and approved and agreed to, all above according to the commandments of our scholars, may their memories be blessed.

And we witness this accord between Meier and his wife and between all parties according to the transcript above.

Given and executed on 13 Aw (5) 505, according to the short calendar here in Horburg. All fast and enduring.

Oscher bar Alexander Bloch from Wintzenheim, as witness.
Leime bar Noson (sch'Lit 'long may he live'), as witness.
Nachum bar Jauseph (may his memory be blessed), groom.

Appendix 6: Discussion concerning the Rabbi Joseph Hirsch in Breisach 1777[464]

"1.   The Jewry in Altbreisach requests the opportunity to terminate the Rabbi and to suspend for the time being the Vice Rabbi.
Concl. to give the following, that in the matter of . . . extensive documentation was just delivered three days ago, and particularly because they could not be dealt with immediately owing to other important matters, they, the Jewry, keep calm under threat of punishment and leave everything as it is until discharge of the issue.

Sig. Mayer"

Government Report 24 September 1777

"16. The City of Altbreysach, date 19 and 21 September, recommends that the Vice Rabbi, Joseph Hirsch be retained. Concl: the Jews may absolutely refer to the order of the 10th.

17. By Secretary Stehle, date 30 Aug., gives a report with records of the various Jews in Altbreysach against their chief rabbi, Susel Enoch,[465] and whose substitute[466] Joseph Hirsch,

---

[464] Stuttgart Archive B 17, Volumen 328: Further Austr. Government Report 1. – 9/30/1777 (p. 6185, Cameralia), Actum, d. 10 September 1777
[465] Susel Enusch was reigning Chief Rabbi for Breisach at this time. His full name was Meschullom Sussel ben Moyse Enusch.

puncto amotionis, et respu diversorum:

18. Concl. R. the Jewry, regarding the particular complaints ad notam the same referent for the review of the parties involved, with the application of the act of removal—that, as
Suessel Enoch did not properly care for the Jewry, and did not appear when summoned to Cowenar and also acts contrary to order, that the contentious Jewry should leave the country for the preservation of justice, both the latter and his substitute Hirsch are to be dismissed, others to be chosen to replace them forthwith, and presented here for confirmation.
et
to order the city of Altbreysach: it should pay the 5-year-old debts of the deceased bridegroom Lehmann Levi without further delay [and nothing more], according to the order.
Vid. Mayer"

Appendix 7: Index of the Breisach Rabbis and Other Community Service People

Rabbis

1657	[467]R. Simon Blum, Rabbi in Breisach and Hochrhein[468]
before 1685	R. Jirmia, son of Juda, died 14th Ellul 1685, interred in the Mackhenheim cemetery
1681	R. Eisik Werd, son of Jakob Juda, rabbi in the holy Breisach community and Hochrhein (Upper and Lower Alsace), died 29 Cheshvan 1675.[469] R. Jirmja, son of Juda[470]
1681-1684	R. Aaron Worms, born in Metz,[471] appointment to king on 5/21/1681 with a location in Ville Neuf de Brisach (Breisach Strawtown).[472] Rabbis in the Breisach holy community and Hochrhein,[473] died after over 50 years of office tenure in Metz on July 25, 1722
1691	R. Juda Loeb, son of R. Isak Mosche Neuburg from Worms,[474] died 9. Tamus 1691 and buried in Breisach

---

From the marriage contract of his daughter Frumet, who married the widowered parnus Libmann Moyses in Bergheim on 8/3/1747, it is put forth that Susel Moyses was at that time Rabbi in Kreuznach a.d. Nahe and married to Sara, daughter of Simon Segal.
From 1754-1787 he served office as Rabbi of Upper Alsace with a position in Ribeauville (F. Raphael / R. Weyl, Strassburg, Regard Nouveaux, p. 22, 1980).
As a widower, he married the widow Keile Isaac Levi on 3/16/1772, but the marriage was then separated on 12/7/1772 in Ribeauville.
Simon Suessel, a son of the rabbi, married Sara of the well-known Netter Family in Bergheim on Feb. 1, 1776
[466] Joseph Hirsch was hence Deputy Rabbi of Upper Alsace and Local Rabbi in Breisach
[467] Th. Weiss, Die Juden im Bistum Strassburg, in Alemania, 23. Band, p. 108: Since 1657 the French King had always appointed a rabbi for all of Alsace.
[468] M. Ginsburger, Les Memoriaux Alsaciens [The Alsatian Memories], in REJ Vol. 41, P. 136 (Niederheim (Nidernai) memory book entries and Hagenau, as well as Endingen memory book, Switzerland)
[469] Hagenau and Nidernai memory book entries
[470] Nidernai memory book entry
[471] Encyclopedia Judaica 1928
[472] REJ 3 Vol. 8, p. 267 ff.
[473] REJ Vol. 41, p. 136
[474] Worms and Aub memory book entries

1694-1698	R. Arje Juda Loeb Teomim, also named Loeb Schnapper, served office in Breisach and surroundings as in Switzerland[475]
1702	R. Jeremiahu, son of Gump from Schnaittach, died 1/1/1702, buried in Breisach.[476]
1707	R. Zwi Hirsch Schopflich (Halevi), Teacher, son of R. Oscher Anschel from Krakau[477]
1712-1744	R. David Kahn, born around 1670 in Rappoltsweiler, came in 1712 to Altbreisach after a one-year job in Wintzenheim, was likewise official local rabbi for the margravial upland in 1727 and transferred in 1730 his residence to Sulzburg, where he died and was buried on May 26, 1744.[478]
1744-1752	R. Isak Weil, born in Uhlfeld (Bavaria), 1740-1743 in Bruchsal, was imposed upon by his stepfather, Parnus David Guenzburger, of the Breisach community, to relinquish his tenure after the death of Parnus David Kahn; in 1752 a release from his employment.[479]
1744-1797	R. Isak Kahn, uplands rabbi, born in Wintzenheim 1711, raised in Breisach, son of the aforementioned R. David Kahn. Marriage in 1736 in his later place of residence, Sulzburg.[480] Studies in Frankfurt am Main until 1739. In 1742 a rabbinate adjunct of his father in Sulzburg and, on 26 May 1744 after the death of his father, a successor as local rabbi for Breisach and the margravial uplands. He died in September 1797 in Sulzburg.
1757-1777	R. Joseph Hirsch, schoolmaster,[481] auxiliary rabbi, rabbi, born around 1735, protection in Breisach first in 1757, died 1805[482]
1784	Jakob Alexander Loew, school teacher and rabbi,[483] born around 1750, died supposedly before 1798
1797	*Landrabinner* Isak Kahn died in Sulzburg and was called to a meeting in the

---

[475] Dr. Ahilles Nordmann, MD, Der isr. Friedhof in Hegenheim, Basel [The Israeli Cemetary in Hegenheim, Basel] 1910, p. 105

[476] Dr. M Weinberg, Die Memorbücher in Bayern [The Memory Books in Bavaria], Aub memorybook, Entry 100. R Jeremia allegedly held office before his death in Breisach, because he is buried there. Earlier, he was a rabbi in the Ansbach and Würzburg districts with a seat in Aub.

[477] M. Jakobowits, Vier Generationen der Rabbinerfamilie Levi Schopflich [Generations of the rabbi family Levi Schopflich], Strassburg 1938. Listed note about R. Schopflich's works in Breisach in a 1707 Talmud exemplar.

[478] R. David Kahn, son of Rappoltsweil rabbi Jacob Caan, married Beyele in Wintzenheim, daughter of Moses Wurmser, who was from there but born in Breisach.

[479] R. Isak Weil later became local rabbi in the princely territory of the Loewenstein-Wertheimisch district. He and family were baptized in Darmstadt on 7/1/1759.

[480] Isak Kahn married Schoenle, daughter of the influential silver purveyor Moses Weil, in Sulzburg.

[481] Joseph Hirsch and Marx Kahn, brother of the parnus Isak K. in Sulzburg; both appear as "Schoolmaster" in the list of protected Jews from January 1761.

[482] Joseph Hirsch appears as rabbi in a document from May 1773 and he also dealt in trade. His title of *Morenu* also comes from the grave inscription of his widow Gitel, born Guenzburger, who was buried in Breisach in 1810. The families of the two sons and Gitel took the name Blum in 1809. Joseph Hirsh had to give up his rabbi post according to a decree of September 24, 1777. He made a plea to *Landrabbiner* Kahn to reinstate him in 1781, however.

[483] Jakob Alexander and Tilla's son Alexander Loew, born in Breisach on 11/27/1784; in the draft register it is noted: is a student, has crooked fingers and is crazy. Tilla Alexander, died 12/13/1784 in Breisach, House 474, 34 years (born 1750), Jakob Alexander Loew and Rachel, daughter Sara, born 5/12/1789, House 474.
1809 list: Jakob Loew widow calls herself Fratel Floersheim (born 1764) with daughter Boehla, born about 1790 and son Judas Loew, born about 1792. According to the Breisach *Standesbuch* (district registry), Fratel, wife of Alexander Jakob Loew, rabbi, died on 3/18/1819. Details and time of operation for the rabbi are not therefore apparent.

	uplands about choosing a new rabbi[484]
1797	"David of Breisach," performing marriage ceremonies,[485] supposedly David Guenzburger, rabbi, Ihringen
before 1808-1819	Rabbi Moses Wurmser, born Bollweiler, 1757[486]
1816-1854	Alexander Ris as local rabbi and country eldest, appointed in 1816. Born in Niederhagenthal[487] around 1775, studied in Fürth Rabb.; was mostly tradesman and farmer in Breisach, established the Jewish school, lawyer for the Elkan Reutlinger *Gantmasse* (right to church tithe). As of 1823, the local eldest, as of 1835, the council of the district synagogue for several years; died in Breisach in 1854
from Sept 1819 on	Rabbi Seligmann Gottschalk, born in 1770 in Niederehnheim, came in 1819 from Pfalzburg to Altbreisach[488] as a successor of R. Moses Wurmser
1823	David Jakob Geismar, "for a short time Rabbi of the community"[489]
1825-1828	Rabbi Benjamin Dispecker[490]
1828	Country eldest Reb Alexander Ries held office o 12/19/1828 as Rabbi Administrator[491]
1829-1878	District Rabbi Moses Reiss, born 12/11/1802 in Karlsruhe, died 10/8/1878 in Breisach. Last rabbi with position in Breisach (Moses ben Seligmann).[492]

---

[484] GLA Karlsruhe, Hochberg documents (according to Cantor Mirwis, Wertheim Genealogy, Eichstetten)

[485] Next to the newly elected Sulzburg *Landrabbiner* R. Abraham, son of Thia Weil, a David served as official in the destroyed Breisach; he also could perform weddings after getting a marriage license from the *Landrabbiner* for a fee of about 5 fl. 30 Kr. (Lewin, p. 86)

[486] R. Moses ben David Wurmser supposedly held office already by 1804, when the new Breisach synagogue was put into place. He ran the community civil register. In 1819 he Müllheim, where he died in 1826; he was buried in Sulzburg. According to the 1809 list, his wife Zerla (Sara) was born around 1762, daughter Keila in 1789, and son Raphael in 1795. The grave inscription in Sulzburg speaks of a long term in office in Breisach and Müllheim, though it is hardly legible. (Cf. David W. Bollweiller, 1784)

[487] Reb Sender Ries, son of the Swiss rabbi Raphael Abraham Ries from Niederhagenthal, respectively Endingen-Lengnau, came to Breisach as an educated rabbi around 1799 and married Zipora (born around 1773, died 1836), daughter of the parnus Gedeon Jakob Uffenheimer. Reb Sender Ries was also the author of a praise poem for the new prince, when Breisach became part of Baden in 1806.

[488] From a report of 8/12/1819, the Pfalzburg rabbi was asked to take over the Breisach rabbinical office at the departure of R. Moses Wurmser. He demanded some conditions, however, and stayed only a short time, because 1826-1832 R. Seligmann Godchaux Rabbi was in Hagenau; later Chief Rabbi of Hochrhein in Colmar, where he died on 7/29/1849.
(Joseph Block, Histoire de la Communaute Hagenau, as Godchaux's successor S. W. Klein in Colmar calls it); Information also in "Univers Israelite" 1849/50, p. 158, 215, 267

[489] He had inherited the rabbi title shortly before his Breisach position, and was hired presumably with the influence of his brother, Parnus Seligmann Geismar. He married Jette, daughter of Rabbi Falkenau in Fürth in 1819. The family was still living in Breisach in 1827. David later was District Rabbi in Sinsheim (Baden) and died on 12/22/1889 in Alzey bei Koblenz.

[490] The local Breisach synagogue, presumably supported by the Sulzburg provincial synagogue, comprised Rabbi B. Disp. and Sal. Geismar, country eldest (February 1825). After a short-lived marriage, Rabbi Dispecker died, leaving behind a son, Samuel, who emigrated to Fuffalo. The widow Jeanette, born Bloch in 1802 in Ihringen, married Wolf Bloch in Sulzburg.

[491] At the wedding of Salomon David Geismar and Marie Anna Guenzburger from Emmendingen (according to the Breisach *Standesbuch*)

[492] In 1844, with Rabb. Schott from Randegg, he was called to Frankfurt for a rabbinical meeting. Descendants lived in Breisach, Eichstetten, Emmendingen, USA. (GLA 235/20711-20715, Haselier II, p. 351). Moses Reiss married Babette (Beyerle) Levi Burger, born in Eichstetten 4/8/1813 and died in Breisach Tishri 1879. A daughter Fanny

	The Breisach District Rabbinate is suspended after the death of Rabb. Moses Reiss. In his place came the newly created district rabbinate of Freiburg's growing community.
1888-1909	Rabbi Adolf Lewin;[493] born 1843, was called out of Koblenz in 1885 and held office in Freiburg until 1909; died in Freiburg on 2/24/1910
1909-1910	Rabbi administrator Fr. Strassburg in Freiburg
1910-1912	Rabbi U. Eschelbacher in Freiburg
1912-1936	District Rabbi I. Zimels in Freiburg,[494] died in Israel, single.
1936-1938	Rabbi S. Scheuerman was successor for a short time in Freiburg[495] of R. Zimels and with Teacher Kaufmann expanded the Freiburg Israeli religious school, in order to, *i.a.*, teach the Breisach schoolchildren.

Teachers, Cantors, Synagogue Sextons

1745	Jakob ben Reb Jehuda s'l'shamash (synagogue sexton)[496]
1761	R. Marx Kahn, Schoolmaster, Marriage 1742, died in Breisach in 1770
1775	Joseph Hirsch, Koppel Meyer, Alexander Simon and son figure into the list of protected Jews from 11 February 1775 as school teacher
before 1780	Isak Loew, cantor, 30 years[497]
1788-1805	Wolf Wangen Loevy, teacher and mohel,[498] born around 1743, died in Breisach in 1805
1809, still 1827	Nathan Levi Breisacher,[499] teacher, born in Breisach 1775
1809	Isak Guenzburger, teacher,[500] born in 1755, son of Marx Nathan

---

Reiss, born 9/12/1839 in Breisach, died in Breisach on 7/31/1869 as the first wife of beer brewer Heinrich Guenzburger (1835-1908). She donated a mohel bench in memory of her firstborn little son Theodor Guenzburger, born on 2/12/1864 and died on 9/26/1864 in Breisach. According to the 1809 Karlsruhe list, Seligmann Reiss, born 6/25/1767, "Rabbi and little spices," was married to Frumet, born 1/15/1771 (6 children by 1809); Moses R. District rabbi in Breisach and Babette Burger were married in Breisach on 11/21/1855; Kaufmann Roos, rabbi, born in Lichtenau around 1807, died in Schmieheim in 1875 (son of Samuel Roos); 7 children

[493] A daughter Anna married Dornacher, Freiburg

[494] Rabbi I Zimmels came to Breisach during his last year in office for religious school examinations. He emigrated in 1936, unmarried, to Israel.

[495] He was a son of the Frankfurt rabbi Scheuermann and could emigrate to the USA, where he died young in North Carolina.

[496] He wrote the Hebrew marriage contract on 3/12/1745 for David Bernheim from Tiengen and bride Hendle Netter from Rosheim and added his name to "Shammosh here in Breisach"

[497] According to the 1809 list, Isak Loew's widow Berel, born on 1757, was still living with her family, who adopted the family name Reichshofer; also mentioned was that her husband was a cantor for 30 years.

[498] His mohel book was still in the possession of his great uncle Hermann Levi. The family doesn't belong to the Levite branch. Wolf Loevy's wife, named Marian (Miriam), born 1742, buried in Breisach in 1815, was the daughter of Rabbi (Hagaon) Isaac Kahn, Breisach-Sulzburg

[499] In the 1809 list appears the following: There are classes for children. Nathan Breisacher was still provisional teacher in 1827. His wife Haendel Kahn, born 1771, daughters Zipora (born around 1801) and Feya (born around 1803) were also later teachers

[500] After the 1793 destruction of the city, he was still working in 1798 as a schoolmaster in Sulzburg. Wife Gutta Oppenheimer was born in 1765.

	Braunschweig,[501] teacher, born 1767
1809-1814	Isak Loew Freund, cantor, bassist and singer, born 1773[502]
from 1810 on	Marx Wertheimer, hired as teacher at the Israeli school (born Breisach 1773),[503] appointed schoolmaster as of 1814, teacher of the upper classes in 1823, died in Breisach
1814	Isak Gerson, *Judenbott* [Jewish messenger?], born 1770[504]
1816, still 1823	Moses Geismar, *Judenbott*, born 1770[505]
1816, still 1823	Leon Weidenbach, cantor[506]
April 1815	Teachers:[507] Natanael Mock,[508] Nathan Levi,[509] Isaac Guenzburger,[510] Marx Wertheimer[511]
from 1822/23	Private teacher Elias Weil (orthodox), protected citizen from Bühl and earlier a teacher in Altdorf[512]
1823	Charity society founded[513]
1827	Teacher H. L. Bensbach from Mannheim and provisional teacher Nathan Levi worked in early 1827, when the Israeli community school was being erected[514] Already on 2/22/1827, the chief council of the Israelites in Karlsruhe praised the

---

[501] In 1809 he supported "with instruction of children" himself, wife Dina, born 1770

[502] Isak ben Jehudo, called Freund from 1809 on, died in Breisach on 5/15/1814, wife Elie, born 1779, sons Heymann, born 1792, and Elias, born 1779

[503] His father Abraham Marx Wertheimer came to Breisach in 1772 as a bookkeeper for the floret spinning business of Josua Uffenheimer. By 1809 Marx W. was still living as a single man in the house of his widowed mother Ella (born 1754) and his eight younger siblings. His wife Schoenle bore him a daughter Helena in 2/2/1816.

[504] According to the entry from 7/4/1814, when his son Abraham died

[505] According to the 1809 list, the wife is called Zierla, born 1767; son Isak, born 1799 and Roesele, born 1803; Moses G. witness at David Isak Blum's wedding (3/23/1823)

[506] First appointed on 6/2/1816, when his wife Reizle bore a daughter Gella: witness at David Blum's wedding 1823

[507] From the report of the representative Ged. Jakob Uffenheimer to the district office on 23 April 1815 with a list of the "local, eligible Israeli schoolchildren" (Münster Archive). After that is a list of 37 boys of school age, 6 to 13 years, and 33 girls ages 6 to 13 ½ years, totalling 70 schoolchildren.

[508] Mock was a teach of just 5 children from the families of Abr. Uffenheimer, Emanuel Weil, Reb. Al. Ries and Heinrich Geismar

[509] Nathan taught children younger than 10 years old. From 1809 on, the family Levi was called Breisacher

[510] Isaak Guenzburger, born 1755 in Breisach, son of Marx

[511] Aside from his stepchildren Loeb and Salomon Wurmser (10 and 7 years old), Marx W. was hired to teach older children

[512] According to the Altdorf *Standesbuch*, his wife Beier Wiel bore him a child there on 3/25/1822. In 1823 friction arose between him and the progressive teachers Marx Wertheimer and Reb Alexander Ries, so that an examination had to be taken for the Chief Rabbi Ascher Loew in Karlsruhe; testament dated 8/15/1824. Due to his difficulty hearing and also his official leave of duties, Weil had to later give up his post.

[513] It came about during the tenure of Parnus Seligmann Jakob Geismar and withdrew its support in 1823 for the teacher Marx Wertheimer

[514] In 1827 the ministry of the interior implemented through a petition of the chief council a classification of the Baden Jewish communities in the synagogue district. In this year the Breisach district synagogue, supported by the Sulzburg provincial syngagoue, includes the communities of Breisach, Eichstetten, Ihringen, Emmendingen with Lower Emmendingen. (Lewin, *Geschichte der badischen Juden* [History of the Baden Jews]). According to the Altdorf mohel book, it was written "Socher" [dealer] for the child Wolf ben Chaim H. Bensbach in Altdorf, 14 Nissan 5588 (Father teacher in Breisach according to the mohel book); according to the Altdorf birth entry: Benhamin, child of the unmarried Gitel Guggenheim (daughter of Meier Guggenheim) and Teacher Bensbach, born 3/20/1828 in Altdorf.

	communities of Karlsruhe, Mannheim, Heidelberg, Breisach and Pforzheim in regard to the good standing of their public schools.[515] The Israeli school board of Altbreisach sent a "Most obedient report to the Chief Council of the Israelites in Karlsruhe, the review and also the internal and external nature of the Israeli religious and elementary schools in that very place in general," dated 7/5/1829 in Breisach.[516] The Israeli school in Breisach owes much to its first teacher, Heinrich Halle, appointed July 10, 1828.[517]
1828	Community accountant Emanuel Weil
1830-1835	Teacher Moses Richter from Buchen, died 25 Adar, 1835, in Breisach[518] (Mosche ben Menachem halevi)
1822-1887	Cantor Joseph Guggenheimer, born Ihringen 1802, died Breisach 6 June 1887[519]
from 1828 on	Teacher Heinrich Halle[520]
1852-1864	Litanist and Teacher Isak Billigheimer[521]
until 1860	Samuel Blotzheimer, glazier, appointed synagogue warden in August 1860 (died before 1911)
until 1876	Teacher Mager
ca. 1868-1919	Cantor Paul Weinberg, mohel, teacher, kosher butcher,[522] born in Danzig? 1847, died in Breisach 7/2/1919 after an over 50-year career.
1886-1890	Cantor and Teacher Dottenheimer. He left Breisach around 1890
ca. 1890	Teacher Bergmann,[523] born around 1845
from 1897 on	Teacher Zimmern in Breisach[524]
1900-1925	Elkan Strauss, teacher at secondary, primary, and religious school;[525] born in

[515] Adolf Levin, *Geschichte der badischen Juden* [History of the Baden Jews] (1909), p. 217

[516] GLA 235/20711, Haselier II, p. 348

[517] Appointment decision of the senior administrator of the Israelite, Karlsruhe July 10, 1828 (GLA 235/20711)

[518] Richter was still a teacher in 1828 in Schmieheim and as a cantor for Gideon Moos from Tiengen. Around this time, the litanist Daniel (=Haunel) Reinauer from Breisach held office in Kippenheim and Altdorf

[519] General Archives, Jerusalem owns documents about his lengthy employment as cantor and kosher butcher (*shochet*). Guggenheimer was married three times

[520] He came from Wangen am Untersee, married Keile Bickart from Gailingen. The marriage engendered some sons and a daughter Bertha, married Greilsamer in Breisach. The scholarly family Halle came from the famous "Rema." As a retired official, he acted as a spy for a short time in Alsace using the pseudonym "Mortara." (Haselier, Geschichte der Stadt Breisach am Rhein). Jakob Isak, son of Henoch, born Schmini Azeret already in Breisach in 1828. A son of Heinrich Halle lived in Riegel am Kaiserstuhl.

In his *Festschrift* for the 100-year anniversary of the synagogue, District Rabbi Dr. Chone in Wangen am Untersee captures details about Teacher Henoch (Heinrich), son of Josef Halle from Eschelbach. He inlaid a report written in Hebrew in 1827 in the corner stone of that synagogue.

[521] He was married first to Karoline Steinhard from Döttigheim on 6/19/1828, who bore him 13 children between 1829 and 1847. In Schmieheim he entered his second marriage, to Henriette Schnurmann (born 7/20/1823 in Schmieheim and died 10/14/1891 in Freiburg), who gave him another four children: Johanna, born still in Schmieheim on 12/20/1851 (married Schey in Kassel); Rosa Billigheimer, born 12/20/1853 in Altbreisach, died 12/3/1921 (married to Emil Petzold, Catholic).

Elise, born 6/25/1857 in Altbreisach, died in 1912 in Breslau, married Salo Lewy, bank official, Breslau; Toderus Billigheimer, born—according to the Altbreisach wimple—on 8 Schvat 1859. Isak Billigheimer, born 3/17/1801, came in 1852 from Schmieheim and died in Breisach on 8/6/1864.

[522] He practiced his last circumcision on a later-born little son of Salomon Kleefeld, who then died as a result of the operation. The last barmitzvah boy he instructed was Ludwig Breisacher in 1917. His wife Mathilde Werner, born 2/3/1846, died in Breisach 1/19/1923, bore 5 children.

[523] He was still living in 1925 in Karlsruhe as a retired old man.

[524] Wedding with Berta, daughter of David Kleefeld from Breisach (Zimmern family from Walldürn)

	1860 in Michelfeld, died in Breisach in 1931
until 1922	Aron Blum, synagogue sexton (s'l'shamash)
around 1920	after Weinberg's death, the position of cantor remained unoccupied for a short time in Breisach.[526]
1920-1923	Cantor Leo Halpern, teacher and kosher butcher, moved with family in 1923 to Upper Silesia[527]
1923	Litanist and bass singer Bronkurst, 6 months in office
1923-1938	Michael Eisemann, teacher, cantor, litanist, preacher, and kosher butcher,[528] born in Bad Orb in 1894; suicide in Freiburg hospital in January 1939 after hardships in the Dachau concentration camp
1923-1929	Jakob Rosenberg,[529] community scribe, born Breisach 1875, died 8/5/1929
1923-1938	Hermann Greilsamer,[530] community sexton (s'l'shamash), died New York City, tailor
1929-1931	Ferdinand Geismar, community scribe, born 1862, unmarried died 1939 in Gailingen
1931-1940	Julius Rosenberger, community scribe and representative-deputy,[531] born 10/11/1900 in Breisasch. Deported from Gurs to the east; son of Nathan R.

Auschwitz
Foundation Auschwitz, Brussels

Appendix 8: Index of the Breisach Heads of the Congregation (Parnassim)

before 1700   In French Breisach before 1698, the army supplier Alexander Doterle (Wurmser) could become a parnus; he held office after 1700 in Colmar. In "Ville Neuf de Brisach," at the founding of the community in 1692, there was a trio of representatives: Wolf Bloch, Isak Netter, and Meyer Raby. They last one was likely responsible for religious questions, although he was not officially recognized as a rabbi.

---

[525] Strauss, named "Kappsuell" by his students, married Berta, daughter of Jakob Mock, Breisach

[526] When no cantor was available in Breisach, Teacher Strauss took over some functions at the barmitzvah of Sig. Greilsamer in Feb. 1920. Mohel Dreyfuss carried out circumcisions, leather trade, Freiburg, later Mohel Daube, his successor, and Eisemann in Basel.

[527] During his time in office in Breisach, a son was born whose godfather was representative Isak Levi. The hiring contract was dismissed before its termination and the family moved back to Upper Silesia. Leo Halpern was living in Columbus, Ohio, in 1978

[528] Cantor Eisemann came to Breisach from Buchen during the weeks of festivals in summer 1923 with his wife Klara (Keile) born Marx (born Boedigheim, died New Jersey 24 Oct. 1973) and sons Ludwig and Ralph. He again led a synagogue choir. A little son Heinz, born in Breisach, died a yearling in 1926. The role of godfather was held by Victor Kleefeld, parnus in 1925. He gave his first sermon at the burial of Hermann Wurmser in July 1926 and worked from then on as a preacher and orator, instead of Rabbi Zimels from Freiburg. His son Ludwig settled in Israel, son Rolf in Cliff, N.J., USA

[529] Jakob Rosenberg married Bertha Blum

[530] H. Greilsamer married Julchen Geismar

[531] Julius R. managed community matters during the absence of Parnus H. Baehr in the last years. During his forced stay at the Gurs Camp, he had a religious wedding in 1941 with Emmy Geismar from Breisach. (Both died in the East.)

1700-1726	Josel (Joseph) Guenzburger,[532] parnus in the Austrian Alt-Breisach and margravial uplands, army supplier and horse handler, born around 1655, died in Breisach in 1726.
1726-1727	Wolf Mock (nominated by the magistrate)[533]
1727-1750	David Guenzburger,[534] oldest son of Josel
until 1746	Vice parnus Hirz Mock[535]
until 1752	Isak Levi was nominated by the magistarate for the representative office that previously vacant for a short time, but he was not elected.
1752 until after 1761	Lehmann Guenzburger, son of the abovementioned wealthy Josel, was a successor of his deposed brother[536]
1754	Community deputy on 11/18/1754: Philipp Guenzburger (Hebrew signature Lipmann Breisach), Jacob Greilsamer, Isaac Levi and Leopold Mogg (Mock)
1770-1803	Wolf Mock, born around 1739, died in Breisach in 8/8/1818[537]
1804-1820	Gedeon Jakob Uffenheimer, born around 1738 in Hohenems, died and buried in Breisach 1824[538]
1820-1823	Salomon Geismar, 1823 named as representative,[539] born 1756, died on 5/22/1839 in Breisach, son of Seligmann
1823-1824	Seligmann Geismar, parnus,[540] born Breisach 1793, died Colmar 4/23/1862, son of Jakob G.[541]
Feb. 1825	Salomon Geismar, place eldest
1827	"Parnus Geismar," nominated as witness[542]
1827-1837	Seligmann Geismar[543]
1829	Salomon Geismar[544]
1836	Emanuel Weil, born 1770, born Breisach[545]
1840	Lipmann Guenzburger, born Breisach in 1803 (Elieser Dov ben David), died

---

[532] Through his influence a resettling of Jews in the margravial uplands (Sulzburg, Emmendingen, Ihringen, Eichstetten, and Müllheim)

[533] Complaints by Breisach Jewry against the parnus Wolf Mock, nominated by the magistrate

[534] On request, David Guenzburger was appointed as successor to his father Josel. He was an imperial army supplier and court Jew to the Imperial General Field Marshall Count von Hohenzollern in Freiburg, 1739 protection also in Sulzburg, baptized in 1752 in Freiburg, also parnus for the margravial uplands, born around 1697, died in Guenzburg.

[535] On 12/7/1746, Hirtz (Naftali) Mock, an inhabitant of Breisach for 40 years, wants to resign from his position as vice parnus.

[536] Lehmann G. signs as parnus the 1755 contract with the Breisach St. Stephan's Church concerning the establishment of a cemetary and the synagogue. Lehmann appears still in 1761 as a Jewish representative.

[537] Wolf Mock, named in documents from 1772, 11 Feb. 1775, 1782, 1787, 1803.

[538] Trader Uffenheimer was active already in the community since the beginning of the 80s.
In 1776 he paid 60 ff. as a "foreign Jew"

[539] Salomon's (Zalles) wife was Klara Levi Burgheimer

[540] Seligmann G., parnus, November 1823, his wife was named Sara (Zerle) Lanzenberg. Seligmann as parnus and witness, death entry Gottschall, S. d. Marx Guenzburger, 1/16/1824

[541] Jakob Geismar, surely born in Ihringen, married Suessel Schwob from Lower Sept (Seppois le-Bas), Alsace

[542] Parnus Geismar, Witness in the entry of the *Standesbuch* August 1827

[543] Witness at the wedding of Salomon David Geismar – Maria Guenzburger 2/19/1828 and witness in the death entry of Aron Mock, 1837

[544] Parnus Salomon Geismar, witness at the wedding of Meyer Guenzburger – Hanna Greilsamer 3/18/1829

[545] married to Sara Blum, daughter of Lukas Joseph Blum

	Breisach 1879[546]
1872-1880	Viktor Kleefeld[547]
until 1895	Gustav Bergheimer,[548] married Fratele Geismar
ca. 1899-1907	Gideon Uffenheimer, son of Leopold, born 1835, died Breisach Feb. 1907[549]
1907-1914	Isak Levi, born Breisach Oct. 1859, died Breisach 4/4/1828[550] (successor of Gid. Uffenheimer), 27 years a representative and on city council
1914-1923	Viktor Kleefeld, born 1868, died 1929.[551]
1923-1940	Herman Baehr, born Breisach 1873, died in Gurs Camp, France[552]

Appendix 9: List of the Names of Breisach Jews from the 17th and 18th Centuries

1) **List of those Jews in Breisach who request of Your Royal Highness, the Lord Margrave of Baden-Durlach a year's escort (GLA 196/238):**

Marx Gintzburger	Marx Geissmer
Marx Wormbser	Joseph Gintzburger
Coschel Levi	Lehmann Gintzburger
Isaac Nether	Paulli Riesser
Alexander Isaac	Nathan Metz
Lazerus Metz	Meyer Nether
Simon Gintzburger	Paulus Metz
Mosi Lepooll	Vasi Bloch
	Joseph Salomon

Emmendingen, the 27th of July 1698

2) **Jewish protected relatives of old Breisach, January 1761**

Lehmann Guenzburger, Parnus	David Lehmann
Jacob Greilsamer	Moyses Geismar
Wolf Mock	Daniel Wurmbser
Lazarus Wurmbser	Alexander Simon
Siskind Levi	Marx Guenzburger[553]
Joseph Limburger	Isak David
Alexander Wurmser	Lazarus Greilsamer

---

[546] Lipmann G., married to Hindel Geismar from Ihringen (1806-1883), daugher of Sal. Geismar and Treine Mock
[547] Victor Kleefeld, son of Abraham Kleefeld and Bräunle Bloch. (A Viktor Kleefeld, son of Jakob, born 7/26/1828 – 10/4/1914 (cousin?), married to Jeanette Guenzburger 10/6/1932, died in Breisach on 9/30/1902
[548] Grandfather of Max Bergheimer, born around 1902 in Baltimore
[549] Wife Gertrud Hirschel
[550] I. Levy, horse trader, married to Klara Maier from Müllheim, born 1866? died Fargo, N. Dak. 1944
[551] Cattle and horse dealer (first wife Frieda Blum, second wife Hedwig Schwab)
[552] Baehr, parnus 1924 (according to "Führer"), wife Fanny Frank, born Rimpar, Bavaria, died New York 1974
[553] Marum b. Joseph Guenzburger

	Jacob Geismar
Deserving poor:	Salomon Wurmser
Simon David	Lazarus Mez
Joseph Levi	Joseph Simon[554]
Leopold Levi	Marx Kahn, a poor schoolmaster
	Meyer Weil
	Joseph Hirsch, a poor schoolmaster

3) Signatures 1772[555]

Lazarus Wormser	(Elieser Loeb W., died ca. 1791; born ca. 1705)
Sender Wormser	(Daughter Ester, b. ca. 1774; and Roselie, b. ca. 1775)
Marx Guenzburger	(Called Gumpel; son of Josef Guenzburger)
Marx David Guenzburger	(Marum G., married 1745; sons Marcus, born 1779, and Gideon, b. 1782)
Elias Wormser	(Son of Lazarus, died ca. 1794, and brother-in-law of Suesskind Levi)
Suesskind Levi[556]	(Seligmann Levi Burgheimer, born ca. 1720, married to Merle Wurmser, oldest daughter Feye, married around 1774 to Daniel Isak Weil of Eichstetten; 1774 held the right to protection in 1774 in Breisach)
Daniel Wurmser	(born ca. 1710; died 3/13/1787)
Abraham Neder	(Daughters Paula, b. 1773, and Maria, b. 1775)
Koppel Mayer	
Nathan Geismar	(b. 1734 daughters Johanna, b. 1776, and Merle, b. 1778)
Marx Halbrunn[557]	(Son Daniel, b. 1777, and son Nathan, b. 1779)
Lazarus Kann-Greilsamer	(paid burial money in 1744 for a little boy who was buried in Emmendingen)
Allich Sander the Young	(- Alexander)
Isak Wormser	(Son Simon, b. 1774, and daughter Esther, b. 1776)
Aron Levi	(Daughter Lea (Loh?), b. 1777)
Alexander Simon (Siskind)	(b. ca. 1702, first protection 1736)
Lebolt Levy	
Josef Levy	
Wolf Mock	(already appointed parnus in 1772)

---

[554] A Joseph Simon was a butcher according to a 1773 entry

[555] Signatures of various Breisach Jews in an entry of Hirzel Boneff, engaged at that time to the daughter of the recently deceased Marx Kahn and based for 10 years in Breisach, in order to have the right to protection. Hirzel Boneff supposedly got no protection right in 1772 in Breisach. In the 1784 census of Alsace, a Hirz Boneff appears in Oberdorf (Alsace), married to Bessel Katz (= Kahn), with son Abraham and daugthers Esther and Madeline. (There are explanatory notes each time in parentheses.)

[556] Sueskind Levi married around 1752

[557] Heilbrunner

4) Consignation of Jewish protected relatives to Alt-Breysach on 11 Feb. 1775

The Wealthy:

Wolf Mock, currently parnus
Lazarus Wormbser
Suesskind Levi
Alexander Wormser
Baer Mock
Josua Uffenheimer's son, whose industry will, however, continue functioning, is absent
Elias Wormser
Marx David Guenzburger

The Deserving Poor:

Joseph Levi and son
Leopold Levi
Lazarus Grailsamer
Alexander Wormser the Younger
Marx Guenzburger
Marx David
Nathan Geismar
Abraham Netter
Joseph Hirsch
Daniel Wormser
Mayer Schwab (is to receive nothing)
Joseph Limburger
Hirsch Isaac*
Zottig Rheinnauer   0
Josua Levi
Simon Grumbach   0
Wolf Levi   0

Schoolteachers:
Koppel Meyer
Alexander Simon and son
Samuel Metz
Marx Heilbronner
Salomon Geismar
Isaak Wormser

The signs * and 0 are shown by the names in the original. 0 indicates that the person had no money or that nothing is to be expected from him.

Pro Nota:
Abraham Marx Wertheimer, who had worked three years earlier as an accountant for the

penitentiary and workhouse factory that pertained to the estates of the Altbreysach realm, and who, however, had not yet received protection in that realm, undertook most obediently, and excelled, to contribute a half year ago to all the complaints against the Jewry. We therefore find Wertheimer guilty of propagating the greatest interest in particular to pursue the present consignation.

1) Consignation of Jewish protected relatives to Alt-Breysach for 1778

The Wealthy:

Wolf Mock
Lazarus Wormser
Siskind Levi
Elias Wormser
Marx David Guenzburger the Younger
Alexander Wormser
Daniel Weyll
Hertz Mock
Josua Uffenheimer's son

The Deserving Poor:

Joseph Levi and son
Leopold Levi
Simon Levi
Lazarus Greilsamer
Alexander Wormser the Young
Marx Guenzburger
Abraham Marx Wertheimer, all Jewish scriveners
Marx David
Joseph Hirsch, who was let go from his office by high governmental decree of 9/24/1777
and instructed to find his bread elsewhere; also indicted to be unworthy and unfavorable as a schoolteacher in reports from the Chief Rabbi Isaac Kaan, in the most humble of conceptions.

Samuel Metz
Simon Grumbach
Nathan Geismar
Herzel Levi
Zodek Rheinauer
Hirsch Isaac
Hirsch Joseph
Abraham Neder
Salomon Geismar
Wolf Levi

Schoolteachers:

Isaac Wormser
Simon Levi the Young
Koppel Meyer
Alexander Simon and son

Nothing to receive:
Marx Heybrun
Daniel Wormser
Mayer Schwob, the petitioner
Götz Jacob Uffenheimer, who should be free after his service

Appendix 10: List of the Names from the Early 19th Century (from Central Archives, Jerusalem)

1) **Signatures October 2, 1801:**
   Raising of funds

Wolf Mock	Judas Levi
Ge. Jacob Uffenheimer	David Geismar
Marx Gintzburger	Abraham bar Dovid
Salomon Geismar	Herz Mock, Pheisel K"z
Isaias Levy	Herz Lewy
Alexander Ries	Moyses Geismar
Moyses Kahn	Marx Geismar
Daniel Weil	Salomon Wormser
Aron Mock	Hirsch Isaac
Alexander Levi	Simon Krumbach
Aron Levi	Nathan Geismar
Lukas Joseph	Meier ben Eli (?)
Raffel Greilsamer	

2) **Signatures November 18, 1801:**

   Wolf Mock
   Ge. Jacob Uffenheimer
   Joseph Marx
   Marx Gintzburger
   Salomon Geismar
   David Gintzburger
   Isaias Levy
   Alexander Ries
   Moyses Kahn
   Daniel Weil
   Aron Mock

Alexander Lefi
Aron Levi
Lucas Joseph
Philip Mock
Raffel Greilsamer
Judas Levi
Dafit Geismar
Herz Mock
Jacob Geismar
Herz Lewy
Moyses Geismar
Marx Geismar
Salomon Wormser
Hirsch Isaak
Isac Levit
Simon Krumbach
Nathan Geismar
Rafal Levi
Isaac Guentzburger

Hebrew signatures:

Lipchok (?) Scholem
Todres bar? Jischi
Mordechai bar Jacob
Schimon Segal
Daub? bar Elchonon
. . . . Segal
Abraham bar Dovid
Pheisel K,z
Hirsch bar Jauseph
Meier bar

3) **The Jews in Breisach in 1809** (Table from Gedeon Jakob Uffenheimer, Karlsruhe; 8/2/1809)

Nr.	married men / age	married women / age	widowed /age	sons / age	daughters / age	male servants /age	female servants /age	total male	total female	total all
1	Gedeon Jakob Uffenheimer, 69	Esther, 47		Jonathan, 41 Marx, 37				3	1	4
2	Wolf Mock, 71	Merle, 61				Moses, 16 Abraham, 14		3	1	4
3	Josef Marx, 57	Boehla, 61		Feiber Jakob, 16	Lea, 19			2	2	4
4	Salomon Geismar, 54	Klehr, 44		Seligmann, 12 Suesskind, 10, David, 6	Lea, 19 Feye, 18 Sara, 6 Zerra, 4	David, 23		5	5	10
5	David Hirsch, 24	Elle, 21		Marx, 3 Mordche, 1	Boehle, 4		Rebekka, 22	3	3	6
6	Marx Guenzburger, 70	Hendele, 63				Loeb, 32	Sara, 24	2	2	4
7	Philipp Mock'sche Kinder,			Emanuel, 9	Hendele, 17 Schenele, 3 Sara, 10 Elle, 3			1	4	5
8	David Guenzburger, 55	Reichel, 47		Herz Loeb, 17 Hirschel, 16 Lippmann,	Madel, 13 Rosina, 11 Heffa, 4			4	4	8

				10						
9	Israel Weil, 32	Zier, 23		Abraham, 3			Jendel, 19	2	2	4
10	Hirsch Isack Opfinger, 69	Hanna, 65		Jakob, 24	Keile, 19 Sara, 17			2	3	5
11	Salomon Wurmser, 37	Zerra, 35			Blimle, 6 Sara, 3			1	3	4
12	Moses Jakob, 43	Elle, 41		Josel, 9 Jakob, 7	Grenele, 12			3	2	5
13			Sara, 85					0	1	1
14	Aron Mock, 46				Hindel, 18	Jonas, 28	Malka, 17	2	2	4
15	Herz Mock, 22	Miriam, 20		Jakob, 1				2	1	3
16	Jakob Geismar, 44	Sisel, 41		Seligmann, 16 David, 12 Wolf, 9 Sander, 2	Sara, 14 Jendel, 7	Koschel, 26	Janna, 22	6	4	10
17	Josajas Levi, 67	Feyele, 65						1	1	2
18	Alexander Levi, 57	Kelle, 59		Jescheyes, 25	Rabeka, 18			2	2	4
19	Lehmann Wurmser, 43	Boehla, 37		Jakob, 15 Abraham, 9 Todres, 2 Sender, ¼	Zerra, 12 Reichel, 7 Sara, 5	Simon, 30	Merle, 30	6	5	11
20	Herz Mock, 52	Mindel, 51		Josef, 18	Resela, 26			2	2	4
21	Mathias Reinauer, 67	Reichele, 42		Isak Loeb, 24 Neder Lehmann, 14 Haunel, 3	Sara, 10			4	2	6
22	Loeb Model'sche Kinder			Toder (Alex), 22 Abraham, 15				2	0	2
23	Alexander Riss,	Zipperla, 37		Abraham, 9	Zirle, 7		Cheye, 26	4	3	7

Nr.	Name			Söhne	Töchter					
34				Jakob, 4 Isack, 2			Gittle	4	3	7
24	Abraham Uffenheimer, 32	Fratel, 25		Jakob, 5 Loeb, 1	Zirle, 4	Salomon, 24		1	2	3
25	Isack Wurmser, 67	Sara, 69			Marian, 24			3	4	7
26	Jakob Levi, 45	Elle, 38		Getsch Loeb, 6 Isak Hirsch, 1	Gittel, 14 Frummet, 12 Esther, 10					
27	Alexander Wurmser, 76	Boehle, 71						1	1	2
28	Isack Samuel, 46	Hindel, 31						1	1	2
29	Judas Levi, 47	Boehle, 37		Jische (Isajas), 16 Samuel, 12 Hirschele, 4 Loeb, 1	Jedele, 10 Gresle, 2		Mindel, 15	5	4	9
30	Raphael Levi, 43	Reichel, 35		Baruch, 15	Hanne, 5 Bune, 3		Mindel, 14	2	4	6
31	Natan Wurmser, 38	Sara, 27		Moses, 4 Wolf, 2	Esther, 6			3	2	5
32	Aron Levi, 72	Reichel, 55		Mayer, 25 Isak, 9	Feyele, 25			3	2	5
33			Merle 67					0	1	1
34	Natan Levi, 34	Hindele, 41			Zipperle, 6 Feyele, 3			1	3	4
35			Klehr, 54				Resele, 26	0	2	2
36	David Geismar, 25	Rabeka, 21			Sara, 1		Gitel, 24	1	3	4
37	Natan Braunschweig, 41	Dienel, 40			Schoenele, 10 Brendele,	Herzel, 18		2	3	5

140

No.	Head of Household	Spouse		Sons		Daughters					
38	Marx Geismar, 35	Reiss, 31		Zallel, 9 / Salomon, 7	8	Elle, 5		3		2	5
39	Heinrich Geismar	Gitel, 31		Alexander, 2		Elle, 5		2		2	4
40	Alexander Guenzburger, 57	Brendel, 41		Marx, 25 / Meier, 21 / Goetsch, 11 / Josef, 4		Boehle, 15 / Beyerle, 1		5		3	8
41	Samuel Metz, 67	Lea, 46				Elle, 30		1		2	3
42			Simon Levi, 75					1		0	
43	Emanuel Weil, 40	Sara, 28		Leime, 4 / Isack, 2				3		1	4
44	Marx Heilbrunner, 72	Reiss, 57		Jeschile, 33 / Natan, 31			Jachefet	3		2	5
45	Josef Hirsch, 71	Reitz, 51		Moses, 31 / Isack, 29 / Elias, 17				4		1	5
46	Marx Geismar, the Elder, 59	Rechal, 51						1		1	2
47	Simon Wormser, 36	Schoenle, 29		Loeb, 4 / Salomon, 2				3		1	4
48	Natan Grumbach, 35	Feye, 22		Seligmann, 5		Jachetle, 3 / Besele, 1	Breinle, 15	2		4	6
49	Philipp Greilsamer, 41	Blimle, 34		Jakob, 9 / Jesche, 4		Hanna, 7 / Lea, 2		3		3	6
50	David Geismar, the Elder, 35	Esther, 31		Zalle, 10 / Salomon, 8 / Samuel, 3		Lea, 1		4		2	6
51			Natan Geismar, 75			Merle, 28		1		1	2

No.	Head	Wife	Other	Sons	Daughters	Extra			
52	Alexander Salomon, 37	Sara, 35		Jakob, 3	Elle, 12 Hindele, 9 Scheinele, 6 Keile, 4		2	5	7
53	Herzel Levi, 68	Brendel, 56		Elias, 33 Salomon, 23			3	1	4
54	Elias Heilbrunner, 41	Gitel, 36		Liebermann, 6 David, 4	Rebekka, 2	Blimle, 9	3	3	6
55	Heinrich Isak, 35	Meriam, 25		Jakob, 3	Hanna, 1	Brendel, 24	2	3	5
56	Marx Weyl, 41	Gittele, 29			Bessele, 5 Reichel, 2		1	3	4
57	Moses Dreyfuss, 48	Rosina, 41		Mayer, 16 Getsch, 13	Zipperle, 14 Gittele, 11		3	3	6
58	Moses Geismar, 39	Zerla, 43		Isak, 10	Resele, 6		2	2	4
59			Feyele, 51	Philipp, 9			1	1	2
60	Isack Levit, 49			Salomon, 11 Lippmann, 1	Hina, 7 Feyel, 4	Mariam, 30 Blimle, 16	3	4	7
61			Merle, 76				0	1	1
62	Alexander Wurmser, the Young, 55	Reichele, 43			Frumet, 21 Zerra, 10 Esther, 5		1	4	5
63	Isak Joseph, 53	Malka, 55		Hirsch, 21 David, 16 Natan, 14			4	1	5
64			Boehl	Seligmann,	Lea, 17		2	2	4

No.	Head	Wife	Widow/Other	Sons	Daughters			
			e, 49	23; Hirschele, 15				
65			Behrel, 53	Simon, 23	Schenele, 23; Hindele, 21; Hanna, 15	1	4	5
66			Meriam, 66	Herzberle, 20		1	1	2
67			Zirla, 32	Jakob, 8; Herzele, 7; Berle, 4		3	1	4
68			Gitel, 80			0	1	1
69	Isak Weil, 32	Golis, 30				1	1	2
70	Moses Levi, 28	Jidele, 28				1	1	2
71	Rafael Greilsamer, 48	Bessele, 37		Jakob, 15; Herzele, 7; Jesche, 4	Hanna, 9	4	2	6
72	Isak Guenzbuerger, 55	Guettele, 47			Reichel, 19; Beile, 17	1	3	4
73	Moses Kahn, 51	Minkele, 46		Marx, 24; David, 17; Jische, 13; Koschel, 11	Fege, 19; Hindele, 6; Rechel, 5	6	4	10
74			Elle, 53	Marx, 30; Jakob, 27; Lazarus, 25; Moses, 24; Josef, 20; Elias, 13	Besele, 28; Sara, 27; Jendele, 19	6	4	10
75			Boehle, 57			0	1	1

No.	Head, age	Wife, age	Children		Daughter			
76	Daniel Weil, 50	Feyele, 50	Abraham, 20 / Lieber, 16	Joset, 17 / Meriam, 10		3	3	6
77		Meriam, 65	Samuel, 35	Elle, 27		1	2	3
78	Marx Bloch, 44	Reichel, 33	Natan, 1 / Josef, 5		Madele, 14	3	2	5
79		Fratel, 45	Siskind Loeb, 25 / Juda Loeb, 18	Boehle, 20		2	2	4
80	Jakob Mockh, 31	Saar, 22				1	1	2
81	Hirschel Levi, 37	Jendel, 24		Josef, 22	Madele, 16	2	2	4
82		Dienele, 58	Abraham, 16 / Jakob, 15	Beyerle, 12		2	2	4
83			Philipp Kan, 27			1	0	1
84			Jonathan Abr. Uffenheimer, 28 / Loeb Uffenheimer, 26			2	0	2
85	Moses Wurmser, 52	Zerla, 47	Rafael, 14	Kelle, 20		2	2	4
86	Isack Loeb, 36	Elle, 30	Heyum, 17 / Elias, 12 (both singers)			3	1	4
						198	188	386

144

4) The community made a list around 1830 of the members[558] who were single at that time with Hebrew names that were used in the call to the Torah:

Israelis
1. Seligmann Grumbach (b. 1803)
2. Liebermann Heilbronn   (b. 1804)
3. David Heilbronn   (b. 1805)
4. Jechiel Heilbronn   (b. 1775)
5. Nate Blum
6. Koppel Ohlesheim   (b. 1803)
7. Salme Geismar
8. Todres Wurmser
9. Berle
10. Lipmann Guenzburger
11. Eisik bar Mausche
12. Schulem bar Todres
13. Joel Nieheim
14. Horav Siskind Leib
15. Mordechai Berkheimer   (b. 1808)
16. Getsch Dreifuss   (b. 1821)
17. Leib Uffenheim   (b. 1809)
18. Zallel bar Chaim Geismar
19. Jauseph Bloch
20. Nathan Bloch
21. Mosche Wurmser   (b. 1804, son of Nathan)
22. Wolf Wurmser   (b. 1807, son of Nathan)
23. Eisik Ris   (b. 1807, son of Alexander)
24. Jikef Mock
25. Leime Weil   (b. 1805, son of Menle)
26. Jeisle Weil   (b. 1807, son of Menle)
27. Haunel Reinauer
28. Meier Guenzburger
29. Getsch Guenzburger
30. Jeisle Guenzburger
31. Seligmann Blum   (d. 6/8/1846)
32. Feisel Heilbrunn
33. Scholaum Wurmser
34. R(eb) J(om) T(ov) Uffenthal
35. J(om) T(ov) Uffenheim   (d. 5/18/1840)
36. Maharam Uffenheim (b. 1773, d. 1840, son of E. Goetz)
37. Ascher Heilbrunn
38. Nathan Weishaupt
39. Rephoel bar Sender Neter
40. Eli(ohu) Weishaupt

---

[558] "For the local unmarried people, as such should be aule letorah."

41. Jeisle Weishaupt
42. Seligmann b. D. (bar David) Geismar
43. Mendel Uffenheim   (b. 1812, son of Abraham)
44. Jekel Grumbach   (b. 1813)
45. Nathan Guenzburger
46. Abraham bar Chaim
47. Jekele Wolf
48. Abraham Wertheim
49. Salme Levit   (son of Isak Levit)
50. Mosche Wertheim
51. Sender Schwab
52. Nathan Geismar

Kohanim (Jewish priests)

1. Jokel Greilsamer
2. Jokel b. Feisel Greilsamer
3. Herzel Greilsamer
4. Jische Greilsamer (Isai)
5. Izik bar Meier hakohen   (b. 1798, son of Mos. Meier Kahn)
6. Wolf bar Rephuel hakohen
7. Senter Greilsamer

Leviim

Menke Wolf	(b. 1809, son of Mose Levi Gradheimer)
Getsch Leib	(Gottschall, b. 1802, son of Jakob Rosenberg)
Izik Hirsch	
H(oraw) Leib Breisacher	(Arie Jehudo Loeb, b. 1808, d. Eichstetten 1867)
Jakob Breisacher	
Schmuel bar Eli(ohu)	(Samuel, b. 1815, son of Elias Blozheimer)

Appendix 11: Index of Family Names Assumed by the Jews of Breisach, with their Ages, following the IX. Constitution Edict of January 13, 1809

(Manuscripts from the former Breisach Jewish Community Archive, before 1936)

1. Moses **Baer**, widower = M. Eichstetter, widow Zierl, 32 years
Children: Jacob 9, Hirz 6, Baer 4

2. Joseph Marx = J.M. **Bergheimer**, 56 years
Wife: Pauline, 46 years
Children: Pfeifer Jakob, 17. Lea 18 (from the wife's first marriage)

3. David Hirsch Marx = D.H. **Bergheimer**, 24 years

Wife: Eva, 23 years
Children: Beile 4 ½ , Maria 2, Marx ½

4. Marx **Bloch** = M.B., 44 years
Wife: Rachel, 34 years
Children: Joseph 4, Nathan ¼

5. Lukas Josef widower = (Bela née Geissmar) – Bela **Blum**, 48 years
Children: Seligmann 23, Hirsch 14, Lea 17
                (in custody of a steward with Jakob and Salomon Geissmar)

6. Isak Joseph = I.J. **Blum** (absent for 12 years), 56 years
Wife: Malche, 55 years
Children: Hirsch 22, David 16, Nathan 13

7. Josef Hirsch, widower = (Guettele née Guenzburger) = J. Blum widow, 76 years

8. Nathan **Braunschweig** = N.B., 42 years
Wife: Dina, 38 years
Children: Schoena 10, Brendele 8

9. Nathan **Braunschweig** = N.B., 42 years [repeated twice in German *Juden in Breisach*]
Wife: Dina, 38 years
Children: Schoena 10, Brendele 8

10. Nathan **Braunschweig** = N.B., 42 years
Wife: Dina, 38 years
Children: Schoena 10, Brendele 8

11. Isais Levi = I.L. **Breisacher**, 67 years
Wife: Voegele, 65 years

12. Judas Levi = J. L. **Breisacher**, 46 years
Wife: Bela, 37 years
Children: Isaias 16, Samuel 12, Hirsch 3, Judit 10, Kroesel 2, Leopold ¼

13. Raphael Levi = R. L. **Breisacher**, 44 years
Wife: Rachel, 38 years
Children: Borach 15, Johanna 6, Buna 3

14. Aaron Levi = A.L. **Breisacher**, 70 years
Wife: Rachel, 52 years
Children: Mayer 23, Isaak 9, Veya 25

15. Nathan Levi = N.L. **Breisacher**, 70 years
Wife: Haendel, 38 years

Children: Zipperle 6, Veyele 3

16. Simon Levi, widower = S.L. **Brumberg**, widower 74 years

17. Simon Levi, widower = S.L. **Brumberg**, widower 74 years

18. Alexander Levi = A. **Burgheimer**, 57 years
Wife: Kaula, 49 years
Children: Isaias 25, Rebekka 17

19. Seligmann Levi, widower = S. **Burgheimer**, Widow, 76 years
(Maria Anna née Wurmser)

20. Moses **Dreyfuss** = M.D., 44 years
Wife: Roesele, 43 years
Children: Mayer 16, Gottschall 12, Sybilla 15, Guetele 10

21. Wolf Levi, widower = Maria Anna **Floerschheimer**, 68 years
Child: Herz Baer, 20 years

22. Jakob Baer, widower = Fradel **Floerscheim**, 45 years
Children: Boehle 20, Judas Loew 18, Susskind Loew 25
                 (The children are from the first marriage of the widow with Jakob Alex. Loew)

23. Isak Loew = I.L. **Freund**, 38 years, cantor
Wife: Ella, 30 years

24. Jacob **Geismar** = J.G., 45 years
Wife: Suesel, 42 years
Children: Israel = Seligmann 16, Sara 14, David 12, Wolf 10, Jendel 7, Alexander 1 ½

25. Salomon **Geismar** = S.G., 53 years
Wife: Klara, 43 years
Children: Lea 18, Feya 16, Seligmann 12, Suesskind 10, David 8, Sara 6, Zera 4

26. Marx **Geismar** = M.G., 38 years
Wife: Roesele, 26 years
Children: Zallel 10, Salomon 7, Elle 5

27. David **Geismar** = D.G., 40 years
Wife: Ester, 30 years

28. Nathan **Geismar** = n:G. widower, 75 years
Daughter (?): Maria Anna (Moehrle), 32 years

29. Moses **Geismar** = M.G., 39 years

Wife: Zierla, 42 years
Children: Isak 10, Roesele 6

30. Marx **Geismar** = M.G., 58 years
Wife: Rachel, 52 years

31. Heinrich **Geismar** = H.G., 33 years
Wife: Guetele, 24 years
Children: Ella 11, Alexander 1 ½

32. David **Geismar** = D.G., 25 years
Wife: Rebekka, 20 years
Children: Sara, 4 weeks (born 4/18/1809)

33. Jakob Isaak **Geismar** = J.I. G. (died 1807)
Wife: Beyla, 60 years

34. Moses Levi = M. **Gradheimer**, 34 years
Wife: Judith, 27 years

35. Philipp **Greilsamer** = P.G., 42 years
Wife: Bluemle, 36 years
Children: Jakob 8, Johanna 8, Isai 4, Lea 2

36. Raphael **Greilsamer** = R.G., 47 years
Wife: Baessle, 36 years
Children: Jakob 14, Anna 9, Herzel 6, Joseph 4, Wolf ¾

37. Nathan **Grumbach** = N.G., 32 years
Wife: Veya, 23 years
Children: Seligmann 6, Jachet 3, Baessle 1

38. Simon **Grumbach**, widower = Maria Anna G., 52 years
Children: Samuel 32, Helene 25, Breunle 17

39. Marx **Guenzburger** = M.G., 70 years
Wife: Helena, 69 years

40. David **Guenzburger** = D.G., 53 years
Wife: Rachel, 48 years
Children: Herz Loew 17, Hirsch 14, Lippmann 6, Magdalena 12, Roesle 10, Eva 4

41. Isaak **Guenzburger** = J.G., 54 years
Wife: Guetele, 44 years
Children: Rachel 18, Bela 16

42. Alexander **Guenzburger** = A.G., 51 years
Wife: Braendel, 40 years
Children: Marx 42, Johanna 22, Mayer 20, Gottschall 10, Josef 3 ½, Beyerle ½, Beila 16

43. Elias **Heilbroner** = E.h., 41 years
Wife: Guetele, 36 years
Children: Lieberman 5, David 3 1/2 , Rebekka 1 ½

44. Marx **Heilbroner** Wwe. = Veyla H., 42 years (lives on charity)
Wife: Roesele, 43 years
Children: Philipp 9

45. Marx **Heilbruner** = M.H., 72 years
Wife: Bess, 56 years
Children: Daniel 34, Nathan 32, Eva 22

46. Moses **Kahn** = M.K., 54 years
Wife: Muendel, 48 years
Children: Marx 24, Voegele 18, David 17, Isai 13, Isak 10, Koschel 8, Haendel 6, Rachel 4

47. David Levi, widower = Dina **Kleefeld**, 48 years
Children: Abraham 17, Jakob 16, Beyla 13

48. Isaak **Levit** = I.L., 44 years
Wife: Rachel, 28 years
Children: Salomon 10, Huehna 6, Vegola 3, Lippmann 1

49. Samuel **Metz** = S. M., 65 years
Wife: Lea, 50 years
Children: Ella 26, Roesele 23

50. Wolf **Mock** = W.M., 70 years
Wife: Maria Anna (Moehrle), 54 years

51. Philipp **Mock** children (under care of the grandfather):
Hindel (Helena) 15, Sara 11, Schoenel 10, Emanuel 7, Ella 2 ½

52. Aaron **Mock**, widower = A.M. 43 years
Child: Hindel-Helena 18

53. Herz **Mock** = H.M., 54 years
Wife: Muendel, 48 years
Children: Roesle 22, Josef 17

54. Jakob **Mock** = J.M., 34 years
Wife: Sara, 21 years

55. Herz Aron **Mock** = H.A.M., 23 years
Wife: Maria Anna, 21 years
Child: Jakob ½

56. Isak Loew Neder children = **Neder**:
Children: Roesle 25, Morle (Maria Anna) 23, (both are servants)

57. Loew Model children = **Neuburg**:
Alexander Moses 22, Abraham 15 (both under care of Salomon Geismar and Lehmann Wurmser)

58. Jakob Samuel = J.S. **Neumark**, 45 years
Wife: Ester, 32 years

59. Alexander Salomon = A.S. **Nieheim**, 37 years
Wife: Sara, 33 years
Children: Ella 13, Helene 8, Schoena 7, Veyele 4 1/2 , Jakob 2

60. Moses Jacob = M.J. **Ohlesheimer**, 42 years
Wife: Ella, 44 years
Children: Kroenle 11, Joseph 9, Jakob 7

61. Hirsch Isak = H.I. **Opfinger**, 68 years
Wife: Johanna, 66 years
Children: Jakob 24, Scholastica 19, Sara 17

62. Heinrich Isak = H.I. **Opfinger**, 34 years
Wife: Maria Anna, 24 years
Children: Jakob 2, Johanna ¼

63. Herzel Levi = H. **Plotzheim**, 69 years
Wife: Braeuna, 58 years
Children: Elias 32, Salomon 23

64. Isak Loew, widower = Berle **Reichhover**, 52 years
(wants to take the name of her son living in France)
Children: Guetele 26, Kroenle 24, Simon 22, Helena 20, Malcha 16

65. Mathias **Rheinauer** = M.R., 70 years
Wife: Rachel, 45 years
Children: Daniel 13 and both stepkids Lehmann and Sara Neder, both 13

66. Alexander **Riess** = A.R., 33 years
Wife: Sibilla, 32 years
Children: Abraham 9, Zierl 7, Jakob 4, Isak 2

67. Jakob Levi = J. **Rosenberg**, 46 years
Wife: Helene,38 years
Children: Guetele 14, Frommel 11, Ester 9, Gottschall 7, Isak ½

68. Nathan Levi = N. **Rosenberg**, 61 years
Wife: Rebekka, 50 years
Children: Gottschall 25, Joseph 20, Helene 16

69. Abraham **Rotenburger** = A.R. widower (Maerle), 55 years

70. Hirschel Levi = H. **Schwabich**, 42 years
Wife: Jendel, 25 years

71. Gideon Jakob **Uffenheimer** = G.J.U., 69 years
Wife: Ester, 45 years
Children: Jonatan 39, Marx 36

72. Abraham **Uffenheimer** = A.U., 32 years
Wife: Fradel, 27 years
Children: Jakob 5, Zierl 3, Loew 6 weeks

73. Israel **Weil** = I.W., 30 years
Wife: Zierle, 23 years
Child: Abraham 11

74. Isack **Weil** = I.W., 32 years
Wife: Galoth, 34 years

75. Emanuel **Weil** = E.W., 38 years
Wife: Sara, 28 years
Children: Lehmann 3 ½, Isack 1

76. Marx **Weil** = M.W., 41 years
Wife: Guetele, 30 years
Children: Baessle 4 ½ , Rachel 2

77. Daniel **Weil** = D.W., 65 years
Wife: Veyele, 52 years
Children: Abraham 19, Bluemle 17, Lazarus 15, Tuset 12, Maria Anna 10

78. Hirsch Joseph = H.J. **Weishaupt**, 70 years
Wife: Reiz, 50 years
Children: Moses 32, Isack 29, Elias 17

79. Abraham Marx widower = Ella **Wertheimer**, 55 years
Children: Marx 36, Jakob 30, Baessle 27, Lazarus 26, Moses 24, Joseph 20, Sara 20, Jentele

18, Jonathan 13

80. Moses **Wurmser** = M.W., 52 years, Rabbi
Wife: Sara, 42 years
Children: Raphael 14

81. Salomon **Wurmser** = S.W., 40 years
Wife: Zierle (Sara), 34 years
Children: Bluemle 5, Ranle 3

82. Isack **Wurmser** = I.W. (living separated from his second wife), 66 years
Wife: Sara, 65 years
Children: Salomon (trade servant) 38, Maria Anna 23

83. Alexander **Wurmser** = A.W., 77 years
Wife: Bella, 71 years

84. Isack Guenzburger, widower = I. **Wurmser** widower Klara, 56 years

85. Alexander **Wurmser** the younger = A.W.., 55 years
Wife: Rachel, 40 years
Children: Frommet 20, Maendel 16, Sara 10, Ester 6

86. Nathan **Wurmser** = N.W., 39 years
Wife: Sara, 26 years
Children: Ester 6 ½ , Moses 4 ½ , Wolf ½

87. Simon **Wurmser** = S.W., 36 years
Wife: Schoenela, 26 years
Children: Loew 4, Salomon 1½

88. Lehmann **Wurmser** = L.W., 48 years
Wife: Beyla, 34 years
Children: Jakob 14, Zierle 12, Abraham 9, Rachel 7, Sara 5, Alexander 2½

Appendix 12: Israeli Students List
(Manuscripts from the former Breisach Jewish Community Archive, before 1936)

1) **School list 1788**
   (6- to 16-year-old children in Breisach)

	Years	Parents
Levi Abraham	8	Abraham Jona Uffenheimer
Samuel	14	Simon
Elisabeth	9	Simon
Rosa	11	Simon Levi

Name	Age	Parents
Henoch	13	Isak Hirsch
Johanna	12	Nathan Geismar
Marianna	10	"
Isak	11	Daniel Weil
Rebekka	9	"
Marx	14	Salomon Geismar
Henoch	12	"
Marx	9	Markus David Guenzburger
Gedeon	6	"
Sara	6	Lukas Josef
Esther	14	Wolff Levi
Abraham	14	Isak Juda
Nehemias	9	"
Julia	14	Samuel Metz
Sara	10	"
Jakob	6	Marx Geismar
Paula	15	Abraham Netter
Maria	13	"
Eliakim	12	Naftali Mock
Sara	14	"
Rahel	16	"
Marx	15	Gedeon Jakob Uffenheimer
Abraham	11	"
Loh (Lea?)	9	Aron Levi
Marx	8	Abraham Marx Wertheimer
Elisabeth	12	"
Simon Isak	14	Isak Wormser
Esther	12	"
Esther	14	Alexander Wormser
Rosalie	13	"
Daniel	11	Markus Heilbrunner
Nathan	9	"
Moises	10	Naftali Josef
Isak	7	"

2) List of Israeli schoolage children, who paid tuition from 1 November 1825 to 15 April 1827

No.	Schoolchild	Age	Parents	Amt of money flor. kreuz.		Notes
Boys						
1	Isaak Geismar	10	HL: S. Geismar	3	-	Itzig b. 6/27/1816 S.d.Parnus Reb.

154

						Selig. Geism.
2	Raphael Ries	13	Alexander Ries	3	-	-
3	Raphael Grumbach	11	Nathan	3	-	10/26/1815
4	Joseph Weishaupt	14	Widow Weishaupt	3	-	7/14/1812
5	Marx Weil	11	Heinrich Weil	3	-	from Freiburg
6	Abraham Weil	9	ditto	3	-	1817
7	Jakob Wolf Opfinger	13	Heinrich	3	-	11/20/1813
8	Samuel Weil	11	Marx	3	-	3/22/1816
9	Abraham Wertheimer	12	Lazarus	3	-	6/10/1814
10	Alexander Schwab	11	Leopold	3	-	6/27/1815
11	Veist Schwab	10	ditto	3	-	9/6/1816
12	Samuel Levy	12	Elias	3	-	4/13/1815
13	Salomon Levy	8	ditto	3	-	8/16/1818
14	Loeb Nieheim	10	Alexander	3	-	8/1/1816
15	Wolf Breisacher	7	Baruch	3	-	2/7/1820
16	Gottschalk Rosenberg	8	Joseph	3	-	9/26/1818
17	Wolf Levy	9	Hirz Baer	3	-	9/23/1818
18	Moses Mock	7	Hirz	3	-	Tischri 1819
19	Aron Weil	7	Emanuel	3	-	1/1/1820
20	Raphael	8	Joseph	3	-	1/9/1819
21	Aron Bergheimer	8	David Hirsch	3	-	1/30/1818
22	Abraham Geismar	13	Heinrich (Chaim)	3	-	12/17/1813
23	Isaak Geismar	10	ditto	3	-	7/29/1816
24	Nathan Geismar	12	David and Esther	3	-	5/19/1815
25	Loeb Model	9	David Moses	3	-	(Dotter Mosche) 5/2/18
26	Lippmann Guenzburger	9	Hirz Loeb	3	-	11/10/1817
27	Suesskind Geismar	8	David Heinrich	3	-	Father from Ihringen 4/7/1819
28	Salomon Loeb Wurmser	9	Nathan	3	-	9/3/1817
29	Alexander Greilsamer	12	Philipp	3	-	2/8/1815
Girls						
30	Sophie Geismar	8	Seligmann	2	-	1818
31	Sara Grumbach	9	Nathan	2	-	2/26/1818
32	Kendel Schwab	7	Leopold	2	-	1819
33	Hannchen Breisacher	8	Baruch	2	-	6/7/1818
34	Sara Mock	10	Hirz	2	-	4/18/1817, daughter of Hirz

						Aron M. and Maria
35	Babet Mock (Katherina)	12	ditto	2	-	"
36	Malin Weil	10	Emanuel	2	-	4/5/1817
37	Lina Burgheimer	10	Joseph	2	-	Haya Math. 5/29/1816
38	Bayerle Bergheimer	7	David Hirz	2	-	4/1/1820
39	Mina Bergheimer	10	ditto	2	-	7/25/1815
40	Teich Guenzburger	11	Hirz Loeb	2	-	9/1/1815
41	Malin Geismar	11	David Heinrich	2	-	4/20/1816
42	Zipora Dreyfuss	11	Mayer Dreyfuss	2	-	7/10/1817
43	Malin Levy	9	Salomon	2	-	
44	Buna Uffenheimer	9	Abraham	2	-	5/22/1817
45	Mina Mock	10	Joseph	2	-	2/7/1817
46	Rebecka Schwab	10	Hirsch	2	-	5/6/1817
47	Regina Weishaupt	11	Isaak Weishaupt	2	-	2/10/1816 (Rachel)
48	Guetel Blum	10	Hirsch	2	-	9/7/1816
49	Malin Blum	8	ditto	2	-	11/16/1818
50	Hindel Wertheimer	10	Marx	2	-	2/2/1816
51	Rana Wertheimer	8	Marx	2	-	1818
52	Veie Bloch	11	Marx	2	-	10/28/1815
53	Guetel Blum	9	Hirsch S.	2	-	Hirsch BL. Senior
54	Sara Mock	11	Aron and Dina	2	-	10/13/1815
55	Malin Weil	13	Aron Mock	2	-	Stepfather
56	Malin Heibron	11	Elias	2	-	7/9/1815

3) Elementary and religious school of the Israeli Altbreisach, May 1830[559]

	born
Samuel Weil	1815
Marx Weil von Freiburg	1815
Isaak S. Geismar	1816
Raphael Grumbach	1815
Philipp Schwab	1815
Leopold Model	1818
Aaron Weil	1817
Aaron Bergheimer	1817
Salomon Loevy	1818
Isaac H. Geismar	1816
Leo Guenzburger	1817

---

[559] Note: According to the documents of "school witnesses" (in possession in 1938 by Ludwig Dreyfuss), produced by Sigmar Breisacher.

Moses Mock	1819
Amalie Loey	1816
Julie Blum	1818
Babet Woog	
Hanna Breisacher	1817

signed H. Halle, teacher

4) Elementary and religious school of the Israeli Altbreisach, 1832[560]

	born		born
Theodor Grumbacher	1825	Marx Kahn	1824
Jakob Guensburger	1826	Abraham Netter	1824
Isak Mock	1826	David Wurmser	1822
Model Breisacher	1825	Leopold Geismar	1823
Philip Geismar	1826	Lazarus Burgheimer	1824
Berle Baer	· 1826	Lazarus Jakobsohn	1821
Isaak Rosenberger	1826	Leopold Heinrich	
Hirschel Geismar	1826	Johanna Breisacher	1823
Simon Jakobsohn	1825	Fanni Geismar	1823
Fanie Judas	1825	Rosina Uffenheimer	1822
Amalia Geismar	1824	Schanett Schwab	1823
Sophie Weil	1825	Fannie Bergheimer	1822
Minett Dreifuss	1825	Helene Rosenberger	1823
Luise Blum	1825	Maria Judas	1827
Isak Schnerb	1825	Pauline Kleefeld	1827
Josef Halle	1826	Fanie Grumbach	1827
Lipman Mock	1824	Maier Mock	1827
Wolf Guensburger	1824	Lehman Kahn	1827
Josef Blum	1825	Beer Baer	1827
Isaak Levi	1823	Koschel Dreifuss	1826
Raphael Mock	1823	Philipp Geismar	1826
Seligman Meir		Hirschel Geismar	1826
Alexander Mock	1823	Mina Wertheimer	1826
Raphael Breisacher	1824	Sara Blum	1826
Jakob Burgheimer	1821	Mina Netter	1826
Maier Mock	1822	Jette Wurmser	
Babett Reichshofer	1824	Minette Dreifuss	1824
Julie Geismar	1824	Mina Kahn	1826
Karoline Blum	1823	Theodor Grumbach	1825
Sara Model	1823	Berla Baer	1826
Helene Bergheimer	1824	Seligman Maier	1826
Isak Schwab		Model Breisacher	1825
Isak Mock	1825		

---

[560] Note: According to the documents of "school witnesses" (in possession in 1938 by Ludwig Dreyfuss), produced by Sigmar Breisacher.

Wolf Guenzburger	1824
Raphael Breisacher	1824
Isak Rosenberger	1826
Maier Mock	1822
Jakob Burgheimer	1821
Fanie Judas	1825
Sophie Weil	1825
Julie Geismar	1825
Amalie Geismar	1824
Helene Bergheimer	1824
Sara Model	1823
Leopold Breisacher	1828
Abraham Wertheimer	1820
Moses Levi	1828
Jakob Judas	1829

Appendix 13: Emigrants List
(cf. G. Haselier, *Geschichte der Stadt Breisach am Rhein*, Vol. 2 Breisach 1971, p. 672 f)

1) List of Israeli Emigrants without Family 1846-1859

Name	Position or Profession	Status per Information from Relatives
Berkheimer, Alexander	Baker	Works as baker, good
Baer, Samuel	Baker	Works in the schnapps business
Baer, Moses	Stonelayer	Works as stonelayer, good
Breisacher, Leopold	Butcher	Works as butcher, good
Breisacher, Alexander	Butcher	Works at restaurant, good
Breisacher, Salomon	Baker	Works at baking, good
Guggenheimer, Jakob	Baker	Works at baking, good
Guggenheimer, Samuel	Ironworker	Does ironwork, good
Guggenheimer, Marx	Carpenter	Works as carpenter
Gaismar, Simon	Stonelayer	Works as stonelayer
Gaismar, Hirsch		Has business, good
Gaismar, Lazarus	Ironworker	Does ironwork
Guenzburger, Jakob	Cobbler	
Guenzburger, Nathan		Unknown
Guenzburger, Jakob		Died
Guenzburger, Moritz	Cobbler	Died
Guenzburger, Herrmann		Keeps an inn
Lazarus, Lazarus	Tailor	Has profession, good
Levi, Simon	Tailor	Works as tailor
Levi, Leopold (boy)		
Netter, Samuel	Cobbler	Unknown
Rosenberger, Josef		Unknown
Rosenberger, Goetz		Has business, good

Rosenberger, Elias		Has business, good
Rosenberger, Nathan	Cobbler	Died
Rosenberger, Marx	Tailor	Died
Wertheimer, Heinrich		Unknown
Berkheimer, Susanne		Unknown
Baer, Jakob	Widow	Unknown
Baer, Ernestine	Maidservant	Unknown
Gaismar, Susanna	Maidservant	Unknown
Brumbach, Babette	Seamstress	Works as seamstress, good
Heilbrunner, Magdalena	Maidservant	Unknown
Levi, Babette		Unknown
Mock, Karolina		Unknown
Netter, Rosa		
Rosenberger, Babette		Died
Rosenberger, Helena	Maidservant	Unknown
Rosenberger, Fanny		
Rosenberger, Rosa		Unknown
Weisshaupt	Maidservant	Maidservant
Wurmser, Sara		

2) List of Israel Families Who Emigrated 1846-1859

Name	Profession	Family members	Status per information from Relatives
Heilbrunner, David	Cobbler	2	was wealthy earlier; now those relations are bad
Mock, Herz	Businessman	11	is a caregiver, good
Mock, Benjamin	Businessman	5	has a business, good
Weil, Lehmann	Businessman	3	unknown
Wurmser, Marx	Butcher	2	works as butcher, good
Weishaupt, Josef	Clothier	6	has a business, good

Appendix 14: The Testament of Rabbi Raphael Ris (1811)
A Contemporary Document of the History of the Surbtal and Altbreisach Jews.
(Raphael Ris's son Reb Alexander Ris and daughter Jachet, married to Levi Burgheimer, based on Breisach families)

[561]"One of the most beautiful documents from the old Surbtal communities is the testament of Rabbi Raphael Ris, who died in 1813. It is preserved for us in a document that accompanies the inventory of his assets. We have already reported on the personality of this highly revered and all-around beloved rabbi, and also on numerous ancestors (see IW Nr. 5 from 21 Jan. 1958, and also the notebook "Aus einem alten Endinger Gemeindebuch" [From an old Endinger community book], Zurich 1952). At that time the wish was expressed that the testament be made accessible to a wider audience. We give below the German translation of the testament, which was written in classical Hebrew. The translation transmits to us a vivid picture of the deep piety

---

[561] Florence Guggenheim-Gruenberg, Isr. Wochenblatt Nr. 30-32 (24 July / 7 August 1959)

that animated the scribe.

The main concern of the venerable rabbi before his passing is, given the "new-fashioned" trends of the time, to exhort his sons and grandchildren to be loyal to the old traditions and a righteous G"d-fearing life path. Interspersed throughout his statements are many biblical and Talmudic citations, quoted often only with their initial part; the scribe could presuppose that his offspring have an inner familiarity with the texts. (To help today's reader better understand, we have provided sources of the quotes in parentheses). In regard to the spiritual well-being of his descendants in the testament, and then provision for the welfare of the faithful wife, to whom Rabbi Ris left his whole estate and all its contents.

Only the Torah scrolls and the large library are reserved for the sons alone and will be divided among them according to their level of scholarship: The oldest son, Rabbi Abraham, who would later succeed his father in his office, holds the Kabbalistic and Halachic works; Rabbi Sender from Breisach his father's handwritten notes on the Talmud, and the Bible commentary is given to the more worldly educated son Reb Aisisk. Finally, Raphael Ris peacefully requests his sons and grandchildren to honor his memory through study of the writings he left, at least during the year of mourning.

The true, modest piety that speaks to us from each line of the testament leaves shining on us in an endearing splendor the Jewish ghetto of the late 18th century.

The text:
I shall not die, but I shall live, and recount the deeds of the Lord (Psalm 118:17). To G"d—may he be praised—I beseech that he may give us and the whole community of Israel a long life, a life of good, blessings, peace, and piety. It is the true word; R. Jochanan cherished proclaiming: The end of men, etc. who occupy themselves with the Torah and are raised with a good name, etc. Talmud, Berachoth 17a: When R. Jochanan finished the book of Job, he used to say the following: The end of man is to die, and the end of a beast is to be slaughtered, and all are doomed to die. Happy he who was brought up in the Torah and whose labor was in the Torah and who has given pleasure to his Creator and who grew up with a good name and departed the world with a good name; and of him the scripture says: A good name is better than precious oil, and the day of death than the day of one's birth. (Kohelet 7, 1).

Each man is obligated to keep his house in order so that he knows what to do over the years and days, otherwise, G"d forbid, chaos reigns. In Sohar, at the end of the Behukausat passage, it is written in the Bible verse "A son honors his father, and a slave his master" (Malachi 1:6). It is worth this only during the lifetime of the father, and the son, free after this death: with nothing. He is obligated to honor him even more after his death. Because if the son chooses the wrong paths, he shames the father and makes him a disgrace; if he goes down the right paths and does good deeds, then he definitely honors his father. He honors him in each world before men, and he honors him in that world before the Holy Spirit—may he be praised—and the Holy Spirit –may he be praised—takes pity on his and places him in the seat of glory, so he is truly "etc." And how many times will such things and wonderful stories be mentioned, deeds and honoring of father. As the wise king said: "Be wise, my son, and bring joy to my heart" (Proverbs 27:11). And he says: "Discipline your children, and they will give you peace; they will bring you the delights you desire" (Proverbs 29:17).

And now, my dear children, although I already know well that absolutely nothing false nor crooked lies within you-our sages said: "We move only those who are eager" (Sifre, Nasso,

5).

And how it also is in this lineage; as we hear, in many places in the community sects, as they are called in the latest fashion, as one hears, they go—because of our many sins—on crooked, deceitful and ironic paths—only in their eyes are they wise—and despise many things. They turn darkness to light and light to darkness, they raze the fence that our Holy Father built , and there are even those who desecrate the Sabbath. Indeed, my sons and grandchildren, do not go down those paths with them; do not take their advice and do not be rebellious with them, because "the scepter of the wicked will not remain over the land allotted to the righteous" (Psalm 125:3).

Nor should you enter into business with them, when it is possible, because their end is ruin, and if they appear to have riches, evil will find them. This calls to them. As the wise king said: "Give me neither poverty nor riches, but give me only my daily bread; otherwise, I may have too much and disown you and say "Who is the Lord?" or that I may become poor and steal and so dishonor the name of my G"d" (Proverbs 30:8 [and 30:9]). Riches keeps its owner in calamity (Koheleth 5:12). But why do I go on so long about something that each reasonable man who believes in G"d—may he be praised—knows.

Known to all who have associated with me that I am obliged, my sons—may they prosper—to convey and communicate to my learned students. Maybe they will also recommend to the Lord of compassion, because they know that I have given my soul to the Halachic discussion, according to my strength, with much trouble and with all my heart.
"Listen to the instruction of your father."

And you, my sons and grandchildren, listen to the instruction of your father and do not forsake your mother's teaching" (Proverbs 1:8), because she is the guiding principle and the enclosure that our wise ones—their memory be blessed—have made. May G"d also strike down even a small thing from that, even if it be nothing, because it is written: "Do not turn aside from any of the words that I command you today" (V. Book Mos. 28:11[Deuteronomy 28:14]). Come to an understanding with me and make an effort with all your strength to obtain earnings for your weak and feeble father, who truly needs compassion, namely the many compassions of heaven. You know well that I, through the grace of G"d, have done well by you from your youth on, in that I let you go to school and saw to your other needs, as a father should help his children when possible. And all of this I did with great exertion and great trouble, through the grace of our father in heaven, which he demonstrated to me.

He also helped you, through to today. I have asked of you neither big nor small things, but now I ask of you the following: Beware G"d's path to right and righteousness, and all your paths should be to honor G"d's. Be careful of anger, jealousy and hate, and of the sight of women. Conduct your business loyally. The word is true (Makkot 23b), that Habakkuk came and based the 613 precepts all on one principle, namely that "The righteous man will live by his faith" (Habakkuk 2:4).

But this has already been clearly elaborated, especially in the "Shenei" (Shenei Luhot HaBerit[*Two Tablets of the Covenant*]), that almost everything is embodied in the word "faith" (*emunah*). I do not need to elaborate further, because I know well that with G"d's help you all know the Musar books. Let your hands be strong through the characteristics of the fathers, which are enumerated there. And teach your children in this way, and your children their children in every time, then G"d will glorify us in the midst of those of our people who remain righteous.

Distribution of goods:

This is my last will this year and beyond:

Because I do not have such a large estate, everything should go to your pious mother—may she live—except for the books. This belong to my sons alone, my daughters have no share of them. They should be divided in three parts for my three sons—G"d protect them—equally, with this exception: Because I have given my son, the Rabbi Abraham—may his light shine—only a small endowment, he should be the first to take from the three following books mentioned: Pardess gadol and Pardess rimonim (Compendium of the older Kabbalahs by R. Moses Cordovero, 1522-1570, author's note), Ginnat egos (kabbalistic book of R. Josef C. Abraham Gikatilia, 13th c., author's note), and the book of R. Meir Gabbaj. (Kabbalist, 15th-16th c., author's note); notwithstanding that, I have already given him important books, he is to inherit the abovementioned books from now on, for the reasons given. After this, they should divide all the books, and except for the two holy Torah scrolls with the little cover, the silver hand, however, also belongs to the small Torah scroll, three equal shares for my three sons—G"d protect them.

And I also order that some of my possessions, this year and beyond, shall be given to charity: Between death and funeral of the name Raphael ben Abraham, in shillings—the two names together yield 613—and thereafter, between death and funeral, let worthy men say devout psalms and also receive 613 shillings according to the reckoning above, and likewise 613 shillings at the funeral, after the value of my name is figured, which all comes to 18 kronenthaler, and a small remainder is 39 shillings, which corresponds to the number of penalizing hits (Malkut).

Should my wife refuse to cooperate and impede the division of books among my sons—may they live—then she should be given what is hers according to our marriage contract; there it is designated that her blessed father gave her a dowry of one thousand thaler, which is 125 louis d'or, and the increase amounts to 500 thaler, totaling 1500 thaler; because I never inherited anything later from her father, as she knows.

Now at this time there are in my possession—with G"d's help, may he be praised—four credits, for which we have established a distribution: one in the amount of 1000 thaler, which is 125 louis d'or, one of 50 louis d'or, and two each of 25 louis d'or, which, as we saw from the above distribution, run a total of 225 louis d'or, excluding the household goods in silver, furniture and traveling goods, which are worth at least 100 louis d'or. All this should be given my wife, as explained above.

And as you will see from the aforementioned documentation, my son-in-law Elia owes me 50 louis d'or. In this matter I command my wife to allow my son-in-law to make payments in installments over 10 years, so that he should pay her 5 louis d'or each year, without interest, so that this debt is not a burden to him.

I will end where I began: be cautious and have a healthy fear of illegitimate money, because the souls of men lust after that (Talmud Chagigah 11), and at times they grant themselves the indulgence, with the words "what's already done," and it takes great resolve to protect oneself from it. You know well, when illegitimate money is mixed with other money, it ruins the good money. Therefore going into business with faith offers a great protection, from Jews as well as non-Jews. Then the name of G"d will be made holy through your hands and the blessing will rest upon your territories. And so I request this too of your children and children's children.

Further, I request of my sons—their rock and savior protect them—that those writings that I wrote with the new Talmud expositions and that can be found in their possession, written down in the four notebooks and everything that I have written on any piece of paper—also the small things, like those in the four notebooks, and thus G"d willing, I will make a book from them—these writings should be given to my son Rabbi Sender—may his light shine.

And of the remaining manuscripts, some of which are under greater and smaller dispute (Chilukim), the greatest part should be given to my son Rabbi Abraham—may his light shine—and some should be given to my son Rabbi Sender—may his light shine. And if he wants to copy what his brother has in his hands, he must be given access. And if my son Reb Aisik—may he love—wants to copy from those abovementioned manuscripts, or from what is written in the remaining manuscripts, he must be permitted.

And you, my sons—may your rock and your savior protect you—should study, at least in the first year, a Talmud novella or a Bible commentary through my writings each week, and you will then choose Good; because this is not possible without insight. But align yourselves exactly with my words, because all were learned with great effort, and many of them with students who are mostly great scholars. It will certainly bring me joy in the eternal light if the Talmud novellas say of that which I have brought something new, "and my lips[562] speak in the grave of a scholar, if in this world one of the words belonging to him is passed on." And also after the first year, when it is possible for you or your learned sons—it is toward them that I have turned with my new interpretations—may this be instead of their lips. And this merit will bring about G"d's teaching in your mouth, in the mouths of your descendants, and in the mouth of the descendant of your descendant will be eternal.

Everything above I have written down today, and if G"d's grace—may he be praised—will encompass me and extend my days and years, then I will still be able to change what G"d gives to me.
These are the words of the author, today, Tuesday, the 24th Kislew 5572, 10 December 1811. Everything mentioned above should be taken with all strength and might, and after a fee I come to the signature.
Raphael ben Abraham, residing here in Lengnau and Endingen, G"d preserve them, Amen.

Summary of all the aforementioned as follows:
1. The 50 louis d'or owed by my son-in-law Elia—may he live—and my daughter Sissel—may she live, I have now given as a gift to my daughter—G"d keep her—and no G"d-fearing (Jew) and no officer (non-Jew) can demand something of them because of this 50 louis d'or.

And my son-in-law Elia must add the sum of the above louis d'or and its appreciation for his wife, my daughter, to their ketubah.

2. My son Rabbi Abraham should be given Shenei Luhot HaBerit (foundational religious, kabbalistic work of R. Jeschaja Horowitz 1555-1625, author's note) before the division, in addition to the books above.

3. From my clothing, not one thread may be sold. They should only be given to my sons, daughters, and grandchildren, and these should be given as presents to those who want them.

---

[562] "And my lips will speak, etc." (Talmud Yebamoth 97a: "The lips . . . of a scholar)

Naturally, if they themselves want to take them, that is fine with me, even the robe.

4. For the whole year a light should burn, as is needed.

5. My son Reb Aisik should be given "Kli jakar" (Commentary to the Pentateuch by R. Schlomo Efraim Luntenschutz, died 1619, author's note), in addition to the Chumoschim with the Mendelssohn commentary and also some books that I have already given him.
And my son Reb Sender should be given all written trade documents about the Talmud novellas; he should give them to his sons.

Raphael, Rabbi"

The Ancestors of Rabbi Raphael Ris[563]

Rabbi Raphael B. Abraham Ris, born 1728, probably came as a rabbi to the Surbtal communities Endingen and Lengnau from the large Alsatian community Hagenthal around the end of 1787, where he had been a representative of a Talmud high school. In the Surbtal he served as high overseer and very beloved rabbi until his death 25 May 1813. He was married to Mirjam, born 1734, daughter of community cashier Goetschel Levy from Hagentahl, who survived him. She had three sons and seven daughters.

The eldest son was Rabbi Abraham Ris, who held office 19 years in Mühringen in the Schwarzwald, and since 1812 in Surbtal functioned as head teacher and aid to his father, whom he later succeeded. Offspring of Rabbi Abraham Ris, who died in Lengnau in 1834, are not only the Family Ris, Schwab, Braunschweig, i.a., but also the many children and grandchildren of Markus G. Dreifuss, whose mother was a daughter of Abraham. The offspring of the second son of Raphael, Isaak, are not known to me (he lived intermittently in Endingen). Those of the youngest son, Sender (Alexander), grew up in Alt-Breisach. The oldest daughter of Raphael was Beile, wife of Isaak Blum in Straßburg; the second oldest Pessel, wife of Judel Bloch in Sennheim. Then came the daughter Rechel, married to the learned Rabbi Samuel Ullmann from Fürth; later in Lackenbach in Hungary, the *Stammutter* (original mother) of a line of rabbis, doctors, and business people.
The fourth daughter, Jachet, who died young, was the wife of Todres Levy[564] in Alt-Breisach and her daughter was married to Nathan Grumbach himself. Raphael's fifth daughter, Zere, was living in 1813 in Basel, widow of Joseph Pikart, while the sixth daughter, Sissel, wife of the well-known Rabbi Elia (Reb Elje), engendered a great number of offspring. Only the youngest daughter, Gitel, could take on supervision of her old parents, because she, as the wife of Jakob Emanuel Guggenheim (Hitziges), continued to live in Lengnau.

---

[563] from Fl. Guggenheim, Israelitisches Wochenblatt, Zurich, Jan. 1758 (Nr. 3)
[564] Levi-Burgheimer from 1809 on

Appendix 15: Early Breisach Israeli Registrar Records (1784-1820)
(Manuscripts from the former Jewish Community Archive of Breisach, before 1936)

1) Birth Register 1784-173

Month	Day	House	Name of Children	Name of Father	Name of Mother
1784 July	23	409	Fratel	Lehmann Josef	Beile
Aug.	27	395	Josef	Todres Levi	Jachet
Sept.	27	433	Klaerla	Danel Weil	Feyllen
Oct.	23	373	Breyna	David Guenzburger	Reichel
Nov.	27	399	Alexander Loew	Jacob Alexander	Tilla
Nov.	28	397 ½	Roessel	Hirtz Mock	Hina
Dec.	14	399	Marix	Isak Guenzburger	Guettel
3 boys 4 girls					
1785 Jan.	13	432	Marix	Alexander Guenzburger	Brendel
Feb.	23	404	Kroenele	Isak Loew Reichshofer	Berel
Mar.	14	394	Jentel	Salomon Geismar	Klaerla
Mar.	26	396	Nesanel	Goetz Uffenheimer	Zir
Apr.	28	412	Marix	Mayer Kahen	Muenkel
May	25	398	Merla	Alexander Wormser	Reichel
Jun.	18	401	Esther	Samuel Metz	Jentel

Month	Day	House	Name of Child	Name of Father	Name of Mother
Jun.	23	397	Treyna	Aron Mock	Marian
Aug.	14	411	David Hirsch	Josef Marix	Beyla
Sept.	24	392	Josef	Aron Levi	Reichel
Oct.	22	422	Jacob	Hirsch Isak	Hana
Nov.	26	395	Moyses	Abraham Marix	Ella
7 boys 5 girls					
1786 Jan.	30	441	Bella	Simon Levi	Foeglen
Mar.	4	410	Blimel	Marix Heilbrunner	Sesel
May	11	433	Abraham	Salomon Geismar	Sara
Aug.	29	490	Keula	Meyer Kahan	(Esther)

Month	Day	House	Name of Child	Name of Father	Name of Mother
					Muenkel
Sept.	16	489	Feisel	David Kahan	Esther
Sept.	22	485	Salomon	Hirzel Levi	Breinel
Oct.	4	487	Marian	Isak Wormser	Sara
Oct.	24	407	Simon	Isak Loew	Berel
Nov.	10	468	Seligmann	Lehmann Josef	Beille
5 boys, 4 girls					
Month	**Day**	**House**	**Name of Child**	**Name of Father**	**Name of Mother**
1787 Jan.	19	451	Chana	Alexander Guenzburger	Brendel
Jan.	27	449	Esther	Daniel Weil	Feilen
Mar.	23	483	Feyllen	Alexander Levi	Jachet
May	19	467	Ella	Josef Marix	Beilla
May	21	413	Sara	David Guenzburger	Rachel
June	4	470	Beyerla		Huendele
Aug.	29	478	Rebeka	Salomon Geismar	Klara
Sept.	8	476	Hirz	Aron Mock	Marjana
Sept.	16	484	Dotter	Loew Marx Model	Muendel
Oct.	11	483	Jentel	Abr.Marx Wertheimer	Ella
Oct.	23	474	Rachel	Isak Guenzburger	Guettel
Dec.	13	482	Mayer	Aron Levi	Reichel
3 boys, 9 girls					
1788 Jan.	23	484	Eva	Adam Wormser	Rachel
Feb.	3	468	Naftali	Isak Josef	Ester
Apr.	28	437	Rachel	Isak Hirsch	Joanna
May	18	490	Ubigail	Moyses Kahan	Eva
Sept.	25	470	Ester	Isak Juda	Judith
Nov.	13	437	Kaulia	Simon Levi	Regina
Dec.	9	413	Natan	David Guenzburger	Rachel
2 boys, 5 girls					
Month	**Day**	**House**	**Name of Child**	**Name of Father**	**Name of Mother**
1789 April	24	488	Kaulia	Naftali Josef	Regina
May	12	474	Sara	Jakob Alex. Loew	Rachel
May	17	433	Uriel	Alexander	Rosa

Month	Day	House	Name of Child	Name of Father	Name of Mother
				Guenzburger	
May	21	452	Josef	Natan Levi	Rebekka
May	23	469	Naftali	Wolf (Wangen) Levi	M. Anna
June	2	449	Abraham	Daniel Weil	Feia
June	4	465	?Josef	?Abraham Wertheimer	
Sept.	12	478	Libuscha	Salomon Geismar	Caecilie
5 boys, 3 girls					
1790					
Jan.	10	490	Sara	Moses Kahan	Eva
Jan.	10	476	Judith	Aron Mock	Maria
July	16	474	Josef	Isak Guenzburger	Ubigail
July	22	470	Ester	Isak Juda	Judith
Aug.	22	452	Sara	Isak Hirsch	Johanna
Sept.	27	468	Maria	Isak Josef	Ester
Oct.	22	478	Ubigail	Salomon Geismar	Caecilie
1 boys, 6 girls					
Month	**Day**	**House**	**Name of Child**	**Name of Father**	**Name of Mother**
1791					
Aug.	12	483	Rebekka	Alexander Levi	Keile
Dec.	12	474	Paula	Isak Guenzburger	Ubigail
1792					
Feb.	4	470	Sara	Isak Juda	Judith
Feb.	8	477	David Kaan	Moyses Baer	Eva Marx
Apr.	28	462	Abraham Levi	David Levi	Demut
Mar.	3	488	Naftali	David Guenzburger	Rachel
May	16	446	Rosa	Daniel Weil	Ubigail
June	6	491	Barbara	Lucas Josef	Paula
June	?	?	Elias Josef	Naftali Josef	?
Aug.	25	417	Marxus	Moisses Dreyfuss	
Dec.	17	482	Josef	Judas Levi	Judith
Dec.	31		Rachel	Salomon Geismar	Keile
5 boys, 5 girls					
1793					
Jan.	25	475	Josef	Naftali Mock	Susanna

Feb.	11	469	Judith	Philipp Mock	Kaulia
Feb.	20	448	Paula	Alexander Guenzburger	Rosa
Mar.	23	463	Seligmann	Jakob Geismar	Susanna
Apr.	11	445	Judit Lewin	Natan Levi	Rebekka
May	5		Baruch Levi	Raphael Levi	Rachel
June	?	48?	Lazarus	Alexander	Kaulia (?)
4 boys, 3 girls					

2) Birth Register for Boys 1792-1805[565]

Date		Name of the Child and the Father
25 Aug.	1792	Maier Dreyfuss
5 May	1793	Baruch Levi Breisacher
24 Feb.	1794	Abrah. Loeb Marx (Model)
6 Jan.	1795	Josef Hirsch, Isak Marx Guenzburger
29 Jan.	1795	Jakob Raphael Greilsamer
11 Feb.	1795	Naftali Hirsch, Lukas Josef
16 Apr.	1795	Jakob Lehmann Wurmser
22 July	1795	Judas Loeb Gimmel Levit
26 Dec.	1795	Natan Isak Josef
7 Jan.	1798	Jakob D. Lazarus
28 July	1798	Isak Moses Kahn
Oct.	1798	Goetsch (Theodor) Alexander Guenzburger
7 Oct.	1798	Naftali David Guenzburger
16 Dec.	1798	Bezalel Todres Geismar
4 May	1799	Sueskind, Salomon Geismar
21 Dec.	1799	Jakob Philipp Greilsamer
15 July	1800	Manuel, Philipp Mock
19 Nov.	1800	Moses Kahn, Moses Kahn (Koschel)
2 Dec.	1800	Salomon Dottres Geismar
5 Jan.	1801	Jakob Moses Baer
21 Dec.	1801	David Salomon Geismar
8 Feb.	1802	Götsch Loeb Jakob Levi
6 July	1802	Herz Raphael Greilsamer
17 Mar.	1802	Salomon Marx Geismar
2 Jan.	1803	Jakob Moses Olesheimer
8 Dec.	1803	Seligmann, Natan Bollweiler
7 . . .	1803	Liebmann Guenzburger, David Guenzburger
5 Jun.	1804	Jakob Abraham Uffenheimer
27 Nov.	1804	Moses Natan Wurmser

---

[565] From the mohel book of Wolf Wangen Levi, mohel in Breisach; circumstances mostly take place in surrounding areas, where the Breisach Jews were evacuated.

6 Apr.	1805	Isai, Rafael Greilsamer
23 May	1805	Josef Marx Bloch
21 Jun.	1805	Abraham Israel Weil

3) Reconstructed Birth Register 1800-1810[566]

Child	1800-1802	Information about the Parents
Gottschalk Levi		Jacob Levy (Rosenberg)
Salomon Marx Geismar		Marx Geismar and Rosina
(Brother of Ella)	= 10 Feb. 1800	
	= 21 Schwat	
David Geismar		Salomon Geismar (Bezalel) and Klaer.
(Brother of Sara and Zera)	12/20/1801	according to Levi mohel book
Brendel Braunschweig		Nathan Braunschweig
(in April 1815, 13 ½ yrs old)		
Schöna Nieheim		Alexander N.
		(= Al. Salomon)
Hana Greilsamer		Philip Greilsamer
Roesle Geismar		Salomon Marx Geismar
Hirz Greilsamer		Raphael Greilsamer
(Naftali, b. 7/6/1802		

Child	1803	Information about the Parents
Jacob Olesheimer		Moses Olesheimer
Hirzel Baer		Lazarus Greilsamer, stepfather
Hana Bloch		Moses Wurmser
		Rabbi, stepfather, 1815

Child	1803	Information about the Parents
Hendel Kahn		Widow Minkla Kahn
Sara Geismar		Salomon Geismar and Klaer
(sister of David and Zera)		
Zirle Ries		Alexander Ries
Genofeva Levid		Isaac Levid
(sister of Fayette)		
Reichel Wurmser		Lehmann Wurmser
(sister of Sara and Alex)		
Ziperle Levi		Nathan Levi
(sister of Fayette)		

Child	1804	Information about the Parents
Hanna Levy		Raphael Levy (Breisacher)
B. Sara Wurmser		Salomon Wurmser
Lipmann Guenzburger		David Guenzburger
Seligmann Grumbach		Natan Grumbach
(Jehoschua)		
Ella Geismar		Heinrich Geismar and Gitel

---

[566] Approximate birth year calculated from a list of Breisach Israeli schoolage children, which was sent to the Breisach district office on 4/23/1815, signed by Parnus Gedeon Jacob Uffenheimer

Schwab
(sister of Alexander)

Child	1805	Information about the Parents
Jacob Uffenheimer		Abraham Uffenheimer and Fratel Auerbach
Baer Baer (Dov ben Dov m'Breisach)		Lazarus Greilsamer, stepfather
Jesaias Greilsamer	4.6.1805	Raphael Greilsamer and Bessel
Lipmann Heilbronner		Elias Heilbronner
Moses Wurmser		Nathan Wurmser
Joseph Bloch		Marx Bloch
Loeb Wurmser		Marx Wertheimer, stepfather
Lehmann Weil	Nov. 1805	Emanuel Weil and Sara Blum
Fayette Nieheim		Alexander (= Al. Salomon)
Heva Guenzburger		David Guenzburger
Esther Wurmser		Alexander Wurmser
Reichel Kahn		Widow Minkla Kahn
Bela Bergheimer		David Hirsch Marx Bergheimer
Sara Weidenbach		Cantor Weidenbach
Sara Wurmser (sister of Reichel and Alex)		Lehmann Wurmser
Hirschel Levy (Zwiben Juda Halevi Breisacher)	18. Tamus 1805	Judas Lehmann Levy
David Heilbronner	2 Cheshvan 1805	Elias Heilbronner
Child	**1806**	**Information about the Parents**
Buna Levy		Raphael Levy Breisacher and Reichel
Rana Wurmser (sister of B. Sara)		Salomon Wurmser
Joseph Guenzburger		Alexander Guenzburger
Daniel Rheinauer		Mathias Rheinauer
Jachet Grumbach		Natan Grumbuch
Zera Geismar (sister of Sara and David)		Salomon Geismar and Klaer
Fayette Levid (sister of Genofeva)		Isaac Levid
Child	**1807**	**Information about the Parents**
Zirle Uffenheimer		Abraham Uffenheimer and Fratel Auerbach
Jacob Nieheim		Alexander Nieheim (= Alex. Salomon)
Salomon Geismar		David Geismar, Sr.
Lea Greilsamer		Philipp Greilsamer
Jacob Opfinger		Heinrich Opfinger
Raphael Neder		Alexander Neder
Louis Weidenbach		Cantor Weidenbach

Alexander Wurmser (brother of Reichel and Sara)		Lehmann Wurmser
Alexander Geismar (brother of Ella)	4. Aw 1807	Heinrich Geismar and Gitta Schwob
Fayette Levi (sister of Ziperle		Nathan Levy
Child	**1808**	**Information about the Parents**
Jacob Mock		Hirz Aron Mock
Wolf Greilsamer		Raphael Greilsamer
Wolf Wurmser		Nathan Wurmser
Marx Bergheimer		David Hirsch Marx Bergheimer
Salomon Wurmser		Marx Wertheimer, stepfather
Isaak Ries	11. Adar II. 1807	Alexander Ries
Ella Geismar (sister of Marx)		Salomon Geismar
Bessel Grumbach		Nathan Grumbach
Kresel Levy		Judas Lehmann Levy
Child	**1809**	**Information about the Parents**
Loeb Uffenheimer		Abraham Uffenheimer and Fratel
Isaac Hirsch Levi		Jacob Levy
Nathan Bloch		Marx Bloch
Alexander Geismar		Jacob Geismar
Sara Geismar		David Heinrich Geismar and
	4/18/1809	Rebekka born Geismar
Rebekka Heilbroner		Elias Heilbroner
Child	**1810**	**Information about the Parents**
Zipora Uffenheimer[567]		Abraham Uffenheimer and Fratel Auerbach

4) Birth Register 1811-1820[568]

Name	Date	Parents
Daniel Heilbronner[569]	11/9/1811	Elias Heilbronner and Guetel
Joseph Weishaupt	7/14/1812	Moses Weishaupt
Seligmann Geismar	8/18/1812	David Geismar and Rebeka née Geismar
Emanuel Uffenheimer	10/2/1812	Emanuel Uffenheimer and Fragel Auerbach
Jakob Grumbach	4/9/1813	Nathan Grumbach and Faie
Nathan Guenzburger	6/20/1813	Herz Loeb Guenzburger
Jakob Wolf Opfinger	11/20/1813	Heinrich Opfinger (Johann = Elchanan)
Abraham Geismar	12/17/1813	Heinrich Geismar (= Chaim)

---

[567] Born in the just finished home (according to oral tradition)
[568] A remnant still existing in 1938 in the Breisach Israelit. Community Archive.
[569] Information from marriage entry of 1/11/1844 in Emmendigen, bride Jeanette Weil, born 11/27/1822 in Emmendingen, daughter of Daniel Weil, Emmendingen, and Sara Dreyfuss from Altdorf.

Raphael Ries	1813	Hochl. Alexander Ries and Zirle Uffenheimer
Jachet Levi Burgheimer	1813	Joseph Levi Burgheimer (= Jische and Sara G.)
Malin Weil	ca. 1813	Aron Mock, stepfather
Rosine Weil	12/20/1813	Emanuel Weil ad Sara Blum
Abraham Wertheimer	6/18/1814	Lazarus Wertheimer
Jerachmiel Opfinger	2/25/1814	Jakob Opfinger
Natann Heilbronner	3/21/1814	Natan Heilbronner[570]
Judith Wertheimer	1/4/1814	Marx Wertheimer
Sara Wertheimer	1/4/1814	Marx Wertheimer
Eva Heilbronner	3/1/1814	Elias Heilbronner
Koehla Rachel Wurmser	6/11/1814	Nathan Wurmser
Rachel Breisacher	6/25/1814	Judas Levi-Breisacher
Rachel Uffenheimer	10/25/1814	Abraham Uffenheimer
Magdalena Geismar	11/19/1814	Seligmann Geismar
Alexander Cohen Greilsamer	2/8/1815	Philipp Greilsamer and Blimle Wurmser
Samuel Levi	4/13/1815	Elias Levi and Esther (Blozheimer née Weil)
Marx Weil	4/13/1815	Heinrich Weil von Freiburg
Natan Geismar	5/19/1815	David Geismar the Elder
Alexander Schwab	6/27/1815	Leopold Schwab and Helena (Mock)
Semaias (Schimmi) Opfinger	7/10/1815	Heinrich Opfinger and Maria (Geismar)
Raphael Grumbach	10/26/1815	Natan Grumbach and Faie Levi Burgheimer
Teich Guenzburger (Daichel Guenz)	9/1/1815	Hirz Loeb Guenzburger (Hirz Loewe G. and Joha. Sch.)
Veie Bloch (Faie)	10/28/1815	Marx. and Rachel Bloch
Sara Mock	10/13/1815	Aron Mock and Dina
Magdalena Heilbronner (Malin Heilbronner)	7/9/1815	Elias Heilbronner and Guettel
Michaelin Levi[571]	3/28/1815	Moses Levi and Judith
Maria Bergheimer	7/25/1815	David Hirsch Bergheimer and Helena (Weil from Altdorf)
Katharina Mock[572]	10/31/1815	Hirz Aron Mock
Helena Wertheimer (Hindel W.)	2/2/1816	Marx Wertheimer and Schoenle,[573] schoolmaster
Rachel Weishaupt (= Regina)	2/10/1816	Isak Weishaupt and Judith
Samuel Weil	3/22/1816	Marx Weil and Guettah

[570] Natan Heilbronner married around 1813 and died before the birth of his son Natann

[571] Malin named on the 1829 list as sister of Menke Wolf Levi, who was liable to enlist in the military. Their mother is Judith, born Mayer, born in Müllheim.

[572] In the table of those who owe school dues 11/1/1825-4/15/1827, Babet Mock as 12 years old is listed. Sister of Sara Mock, 10 years old, children of Hirz Mock.

[573] Schoenle Wertheimer born Israel of Altdorf or Schmieheim, born 1785, daughter of Keile born Levi, who moved to Breisach as a widow, and around 1793 married the widower Alexander (Toder) Levi Burgheimer.

Mathilda Geismar (Malin)	4/20/1816	David Geismar, Jr. and Rebekka (= D. Heinr. G.) born Geismar
Judas Hirsch Metz (out of wedlock)	5/26/1816	Rosalia Metz
Zeby Hirsch Wertheimer	5/27/1816	Lazarus Wertheimer and Sara
Haya Mathilda	5/29/1816	Joseph Levi Burgheimer and Sara
Gella Weidenbach	6/2/1816	Leon Weidenbach (cantor) and Reitzle
Isak Geismar	6/27/1816	Seligmann Geismar and Zerr (Sara) (= H'loebel. S. Geismar, parnus)
Isak H. Geismar (brother of Abraham Geismar)	7/29/1816	Heinrich Geismar and Guettel (Schwab)
Judas Loewe (Julius Loeb) Nieheim	8/1/1816	Alexander Nieheim and Sara (Mock)
David Wurmser	8/6/1816	Nathan Wurmser and Sara
Uri Schraga Feisel (known as Philipp = Feist Schwab)	9/6/1816	Leopold Schwab and Helena Mock
Guettela Blum	9/7/1816	Naftali Hirsch Lukas Blum and Kendel
Zeby Hirsch Opfinger	1/12/1817	Jakob Opfinger and Sara
Huena Mock[574]	1/7/1817	Joseph Mock and Schoena born Mock
Breinel Levi (Blozheimer)	2/12/1817	Elias Levi and Esther (born Weil from Emmendingen)
Isak Seligmann	3/10/1817	Simon Seligmann from Merzbach bei Bamberg and Zirla
Zipor Dreyfuss (out of wedlock)	3/10/1817	Maier Dr. and fiancee Vogel Kahn
Mathilde (Malin) Weil	4/5/1817	Emanuel Weil and Sara Blum
Sara Mock	4/18/1817	Hirz Aron Mock and Maria
Haya Rebekka Levi Schwab	5/6/1817	Naftali Hirsch Levi Schwab and Johanna Jendel Geismars
Bunna Uffenheimer	5/22/1817	Abraham Uffenheimer and Fratel Auerbacher
End of this table: signed by Moses Wurmser, Rabbi		
Mina Bergheimer (sister of Beierle)	1817[575]	David Hirz Bergheimer
Lina Burgheimer	1817	Joseph Burgheimer
Abraham Weil (brother of Marx from Freiburg)	1817	Heinrich Weil
Salomon Wurmser	9/3/1817	Nathan Wurmser, Breisach, and Sara Bloch from Sulzburg
Liebmann Guenzburger	11/10/1817	Herz Loewe Guenzburger and Johanna Schwab

[574] Huena Henriette Mock, born Altbreisach 2/7/1817, daughter of Joseph Mock and Jeanette born Mock (daughter of Philipp), married to Samuel Kahn on 12/11/1839 in Sulzburg; Kahn was born on 9/20/1817 in Sulzburg, son of Joseph Kahn (born 1777 in Sulzburg) and Rosina Dreifuss; Hina died on 12/24/1890 in Sulzburg.
[575] Year of birth calculated from details about age from school-age children

Aron Bergheimer	1/30/1818[576]	David Hirsch Marx Bergheimer and Helena Weil
Sara Grumbach	2/26/1818[123]	Nathan Grumbach and Faie Levi Burgheimer
Loew Model[577]	born in the night of 1/2 May 1818[123]	Alexander Loew Model, Breisach, and Sara Weil from Kippenheim
Hanna Breisacher	6/7/1818	Baruch Levi Breisacher and Magdalena Guenzburger
Itta Hirsch Blum (Julie in 1832 school list)	7/15/1818[123]	Isak Joseph Blum and Sara Lehmann
Salomon Levy (Blozheimer)	8/16/1818	Elias Levy
Wolf Levy	9/23/1818	Herberle Levy
Gottschall Rosenberg	9/26/1818	Joseph Levi Rosenberg
Madlen Blum	11/16/1818	Hirsch Lucas Blum and Kindel Geismar
Magdalena Blum	10/27/1818	
Sophie Geismar	1818[125]	Seligmann Geismar
Rana Wertheimer	1818[578]	Marx Wertheimer
Raphael Burgheimer	1/9/1819[579]	Joseph Burgheimer and Sara Geismar
Suesskind Geismar	4/7/1819	David Heinrich Geismar and Rebekka born Geismar
Moses Mock[127]		Hirz Mock
Kendel Schwab[580]		Leopold Schwab
Bayerle Bergheimer (sister of Mina)	4/1/1820	David Hirz Bergheimer
Aron Weil	1/1/1820[126]	Emanuel Weil and Sara Blum
Wolf Breisacher	2/7/1820[126]	Baruch Levi Breisacher and Magdalena Guenzburger

5) Standesbuch of the Israelis of Alt-Breisach[581] (1812-1817)

Births 1812-1814:

Josef ben Moses Weishaupt   14 Jul. 1812
Seligmann David Geismar   18 Aug. 1812
Emanuel, Abr. Uffenheimer   2 Oct. 1812

---

[576] According to the *Standesbuch*
[577] Jehudo Loew ben Toder Mosche: according to wimple (Father David Moses in school list)
[578] According to the school list
[579] According to the *Standesbuch*
[580] According to the school list
[581] From the Jewish community archives of Breisach (1936), partially with details of the parents and godparents

Jakob, Natan Grumbach   9 Apr. 1813
Natan, Herz Loeb Guenzburger   20 Jun. 1813
Jakob Wolf, Johann Opfinger   20 Nov 1813
Abr. Chaim Geismar   17 Dec. 1813
Judit, Marx Wertheimer   4 Jan. 1814
Sara, Marx Wertheimer (twin) 4 Jan. 1814
Jerachmiel, Jakob Opfinger   25 Febr. 1814
Eva Elias Heilbronner   1 Mar. 1814
Natan, Natan Heilbronner   21 Mar. 1814
Koehla Rachel, Natan Wurmser   11 Jun. 1814
Abrah, Lazarus Wertheimer   18 Jun. 1814
Rachel Judas Breisacher   25 Jun. 1814
Rachel Abr. Uffenheimer   25 Oct. 1814
Magdalena Seligmann Geismar   19 Nov. 1814

Married 1814:
Protected Jew Leopold Schwab   20 April 1814
by Hirsingen in Alsace with the bachelorette
Helena Mock from here.[582]

Deaths 1814
Natan Heilbronner   3 Feb.
Jerachmiel, Jakob Opfinger   1 Mar.
Josef, Philipp Kahn   3 Mar.
Abr. Isac Gerson, *Judenbott*   7 Apr.
Eva, Elias Heilbronner   6 May
Isak Freund, cantor   15 May
Simon Levi   10 Jun.
Maria Simcha Wittib   22 Jun.
Samuel Simcha (single)   23 Jun.
Alexander, Lehmann Wurmser   16 Aug.
Helena, Hirz Aaron Mock   25 Aug.
Jachad, Josef Levi-Burgheimer   30 Aug.
Rafael (out of wedlock)   9 Sep.

Births 1815
8   Feb.   Alexander, Philipp Cohen Greilsamer and Blimle Wurmser
28   Mar.   Michaelin Levi, Moses Levi and Judit
13   Apr.   Samuel Levi, Elias Levi and Ester
19   May   Natan, David (Toder) Geismar the Elder and Ester
27   Jun.   Alexander, Leopold Schwab and Helena Mock
9   Jul.   Magdalena, Elias Heilbronner and Guettel
1   Sep.   Daichel, Hirz Loewe Guenzburger and Johanna Schwab
10   Sep.   Semaias (Schimmi),[583] Heinrich Opfinger and Maria Geismar

---

[582] Helena, named Hindel, died 1852 in Breisach

25	Sep.	Maria, David Hirsch Marx Bergheimer and Helena
13	Oct.	Sara, Aron Mock and Dina
26	Oct.	Raphael, Natan Grumbach and Faya Levi-Burgheimeer
28	Oct.	Faia, Marx Bloch and Rachel
31	Oct.	Katharina, Hirz Aron Mock and Maria

Births 1816

2	Feb.	Helena, Marx Wertheimer, Schoolmaster, and Shoenla
10	Feb.	Rachel, Isak Weishaupt and Judith
22	Mar.	Samuel, Marx Weil and Guettcha
20	Apr.	Mathilde, David Geismar, Jr., and Rebekka G.
26	May	Judas Hirsch (out of wedlock), Rosalia Metz
27	May	Zeby Hirsch, Lazarus Wertheimer and Sara
29	May	Haya Mathilde, Josef Levi-Burgheimer and Sara
2	Jun.	Gella, Leon Weidenbach, Cantor, and Reitzle
27	Jun.	Isak, Seligmann Geismar and Zerrle (Sara)
29	Jul.	Isak, Heinrich Geismar and Guettel
1	Aug.	Judas Loewe, Alexander Nieheimer and Sara
6	Aug.	David, Nathan Wurmser and Sara
6	Sept.	Uri Schraga Feisel, commonly known as Philipp, Leopold Schwab and Helena
7	Sept.	Guettela, Naftali Hirsch Lukas Blum and Kendel

Births 1817

12	Jan.	Zwy Hirsch,[584] Jakob Opfinger and Sara
7	Feb.	Huena Mock, Josef Mock and Schoena[585]
12	Feb.	Breinel, Elias Levi and Ester[586]
10	Mar.	Isak, Simon Seligmann from Merzbach near Bamberg and Zerla
10	Mar.	Zipor (unmarried), Maier Dreyfuss and fiancee Vogel Kahn
5	Apr.	Mathilde, Emanuel Weil and Sara Blum
18	Apr.	Sara, Hirz Aron Mock and Maria
6	May	Buna, Abraham Uffenheimer and Fratel

The 1814-1817 lists are undersigned by Moses Wurmser, Rabbi. He was born in Bollweiler as the son of David Wurmser and held office in Altbreisach until about 1819. He died in Müllheim in 1826 and was buried in Sulzburg.

6) Circumcision dates from the mohel book of Baruch Weil[587]

[583] Simon ben Elchanan Opfinger, died in 1820 in Breisach
According to a note in the Berthold Rosenthal Archive, NYC, Hirsch Joseph Weishaupt died in Breisach in 1815
[584] Hirsch Opfinger died on 11/20/1819 in Breisach
[585] Schoena Mock was born a Mock
[586] Esther Levi-Blozheimer born Weil came from Emmendingen
[587] Baruch Weil, Mohel in Altdorf (Baden) 1783-1833
A transcript of the mohel book was drawn up by history teacher Berthold Rosenthal and lies in that collection bequeathed to the Leo-Baeck Institute, New York (1959).

Boy and Father's Name	Date	Year	Notes
Feisle Arye ben David	?	5552	
Elieser ben Todres	Parsche Korach	5553	
Jakob ben David	12 Tewes	5554	Together with mohel from Emmendingen
Liwer ben Jechiel marked in Eichstetten	23 Adar II	5554	
Baruch ben Rafael	12 Siwan	5554[588]	With the mohel in Eichstetten
Model ben Lema	21 Tewes	5556	marked in Emmendingen
Elia ben ?	Parsche Trumo	5556	with the other mohel from Altdorf
Schmuel ben Lema	2 Day Pesach	5556	
Simon ben David	20 Siwan	5561	
Elieser Tuf? ben David[589]	19 Aw	5562	
Marum ben Rab. David Zwi[590]	15 Schwat	5567	
Mordechai ben David Hersch[591]	4 Cheshvan	5569	Mohel was also godfather
Aron ben Rabb. David Hersch[592]	1 Adar I	5578	

7) Circumcision dates from the mohel book of Wolf Wangen Levi[593]

Boy and Father's Name	Date
Maier Dreyfuss	8 / 25 / 1792
Baruch Levi Breisacher	5 / 5 / 1793
Abrah Loeb Marx (Model)	2 / 24 / 1794
Josef Hirsch, Isak Marx Guenzburger	1 / 6 / 1795
Jakob Rafael Greilsamer	1 / 29 / 1795
Naftali Hirsch, Lukas Josef	2 / 11 / 1795
Jakob Lemann Wurmser	4 / 16 / 1795
Judas Loeb Gimmel Levit	7 / 22 / 1795
Natan, Isak Josef	12 / 26 / 1795
Jakob, D. Lazarus	1 / 7 / 1798

---

[588] Wolf Wangen Levi was present
[589] Guenzburger
[590] Bergheimer
[591] Bergheimer
[592] Aron Bergheimer
[593] Wolf L., first living in Wangen, married Miriam (Marie Anna), daughter of Rabbi Isaak Kahn and Schönle Weil, and died on 6 Tamus 1805 in Breisach. According to lore, he was a "coin porter" likely meaning cashier of Princess Maria Theresia from Austria. The leather-bound mohel book still existed in 1938 in the possession of descendant Hermann Levi in Breisach and today should be considered missing.

Isak Moses Kahn	7 / 28 / 1798
Goetsch, (Theodor) Alexander Guenzburger[594]	10 / 1798
Naftali, David Guenzburger	10 / 7 / 1798
Bezalel Todres Geismar	12 / 16 / 1798
Sueskind, Salomon Geismar	5 / 4 / 1799
Jakob Philipp Greilsamer	12 / 21 / 1799
Manuel, Philipp Mock	7 / 15 / 1800
Moses Kahn, Moses Kahn (Koschel)[595]	11 / 19 / 1800
Salomon Dottres Geismar[596]	12 / 2 / 1800
Jakob Moses Baer	1 / 5 / 1801
David Sal. Geismar	12 / 21 / 1801
Goetsch Loeb, Jakob Levi[597]	2 / 8 / 1802
Herz, Rafael Greilsamer	7 / 6 / 1802
Salomon, Marx Geisamer	3 / 17 / 1802
Jakob Moses Olesheimer	1 / 2 / 1803
Seligmann, Natan Bollweiler	12 / 8 / 1803
Liebmann Guenzburger, David G.	… / 7 / 1803
Jakob Abraham Uffenheimer	6 / 5 / 1804
Moses, Natan Wurmser	11 / 27 / 1804
Isai, Rafael Greilsamer	4 / 6 / 1805
Josef Marx Bloch	5 / 23 / 1805
Abr. Israel Weil	6 / 21 / 1805

8) Death Register of the Breisach Jewish Community 1784-1788

Year and Month	House No.	Name	Name of the Parents	Age	Illness / Cause of Death
1784					
9 June	399	Naftali Jakob	Jak. Alex, and Tilla	1 10/12	rigidification of the abdomen
11 July	396	Rechlen Uffenheimer	Goetz U. and Zir	1 ¾	typhus
22 July	401	Emanuel Metz	Samuel and Jentel	1 7/12	red hairiness
2 men, 1 woman					
1785					
20 Feb.	433 ½	Elias Weil	Daniel W. and Feilen	3	typhus

[594] Alexander G., married Brendel Bloch
[595] Moses Kahn, Moses Kahn (Koschel); father's Hebrew name was Meir
[596] Called Salomon David Geismar
[597] Later Rosenberg

17 April	386	Isac Levi		28	short-winded stabbing
2 men					
1786					
16 Oct.	487	Hindele Wormser	Isak W. and Sara	3	at the doctor
13 Dec.	474	Tilla Alexander		34 8/12	at the doctor
1787					
20 Jan.	488	Blimel Heilbrunner	Marx H. and Sesel (Resel)	10/12	articular gaut
1 Mar.	470	Daniel Wormser		76	cachexia
7 Sept.	437	Bella Levi	Simon Levi and Regina	1 8/10	smallpox
8 Sept.	484	Model Loew Model	Loew Model and Muendel	6	big lump
7 Oct.	470	Baeurrla	Mother: Huendele	4/10	articular gaut
11 Dec.	489	Abraham Kahn		23	
3 men, 3 women					
1788					
4 July	477	Esther Uffenheimer		40	lump in the chest and typhus
12 Nov.	476	Judith Mockin		50	common
2 women					

[i]sl. may mean "Segan Leviyah" (Levitical excellence, i.e., a Levite); jzv. may mean "May his Rock and Redeemer preserve him."

[ii]"*Kozin*"

CPSIA information can be obtained
at www.ICGtesting.com
Printed in the USA
LVHW060259060721
691962LV00009B/256